China Hat & Cap Producers Directory

Just The facts101

Textbook Key Facts

by Cram101

Texbook NOT Included

Table of Contents

Index: Answers

Just The Facts101

Exam Prep for

China Hat & Cap Producers Directory

Just The Facts101 Exam Prep is your link from the textbook and lecture to your exams.

Just The Facts101 Exam Preps are unauthorized and comprehensive reviews of your textbooks.

Just The Facts101 Exam Prep

eAIN 449583

Foundations of Business

A business, also known as an enterprise, agency or a firm, is an entity involved in the provision of goods and/or services to consumers. Businesses are prevalent in capitalist economies, where most of them are privately owned and provide goods and services to customers in exchange for other goods, services, or money.

:: Accounting software ::

__________ is any item or verifiable record that is generally accepted as payment for goods and services and repayment of debts, such as taxes, in a particular country or socio-economic context. The main functions of __________ are distinguished as: a medium of exchange, a unit of account, a store of value and sometimes, a standard of deferred payment. Any item or verifiable record that fulfils these functions can be considered as __________ .

Exam Probability: **High**

1. *Answer choices:*

(see index for correct answer)

- a. Money
- b. Cheqbook
- c. Chrysler Comprehensive Compensation System
- d. 2Clix Software

Guidance: level 1

:: Packaging ::

In work place, _________ or job _________ means good ranking with the hypothesized conception of requirements of a role. There are two types of job _________ s: contextual and task. Task _________ is related to cognitive ability while contextual _________ is dependent upon personality. Task _________ are behavioral roles that are recognized in job descriptions and by remuneration systems, they are directly related to organizational _________, whereas, contextual _________ are value based and additional behavioral roles that are not recognized in job descriptions and covered by compensation; they are extra roles that are indirectly related to organizational _________. Citizenship _________ like contextual _________ means a set of individual activity/contribution that supports the organizational culture.

Exam Probability: **Low**

2. *Answer choices:*

(see index for correct answer)

- a. Packaging gas
- b. Thermoforming
- c. Obi
- d. Performance

Guidance: level 1

:: Supply chain management terms ::

In business and finance, _________ is a system of organizations, people, activities, information, and resources involved inmoving a product or service from supplier to customer. _________ activities involve the transformation of natural resources, raw materials, and components into a finished product that is delivered to the end customer. In sophisticated _________ systems, used products may re-enter the _________ at any point where residual value is recyclable. _________ s link value chains.

Exam Probability: **Medium**

3. *Answer choices:*

(see index for correct answer)

- a. Consumable
- b. Last mile
- c. Supply chain
- d. Capital spare

Guidance: level 1

:: Television commercials ::

_________ is a phenomenon whereby something new and somehow valuable is formed. The created item may be intangible or a physical object .

Exam Probability: **High**

4. *Answer choices:*

(see index for correct answer)

- a. Creativity
- b. The Program Exchange
- c. Pipes
- d. Lamp

Guidance: level 1

:: ::

A _________ is an organization, usually a group of people or a company, authorized to act as a single entity and recognized as such in law. Early incorporated entities were established by charter . Most jurisdictions now allow the creation of new _________ s through registration.

Exam Probability: **Low**

5. *Answer choices:*

(see index for correct answer)

- a. corporate values
- b. open system
- c. Corporation
- d. Character

Guidance: level 1

:: Systems theory ::

A _________ is a set of policies, processes and procedures used by an organization to ensure that it can fulfill the tasks required to achieve its objectives. These objectives cover many aspects of the organization`s operations . For instance, an environmental _________ enables organizations to improve their environmental performance and an occupational health and safety _________ enables an organization to control its occupational health and safety risks, etc.

Exam Probability: **Medium**

6. *Answer choices:*

(see index for correct answer)

- a. Management system
- b. co-design
- c. Viable System Model
- d. process system

Guidance: level 1

:: Treaties ::

An __________ is a relationship among people, groups, or states that have joined together for mutual benefit or to achieve some common purpose, whether or not explicit agreement has been worked out among them. Members of an __________ are called allies. __________s form in many settings, including political __________s, military __________s, and business __________s. When the term is used in the context of war or armed struggle, such associations may also be called allied powers, especially when discussing World War I or World War II.

Exam Probability: **Low**

7. *Answer choices:*

(see index for correct answer)

- a. Investor state dispute settlement
- b. Multilateral treaty
- c. Alliance
- d. Subsidiary alliance

Guidance: level 1

:: Survey methodology ::

An __________ is a conversation where questions are asked and answers are given. In common parlance, the word " __________ " refers to a one-on-one conversation between an __________ er and an __________ ee. The __________ er asks questions to which the __________ ee responds, usually so information may be transferred from __________ ee to __________ er . Sometimes, information can be transferred in both directions. It is a communication, unlike a speech, which produces a one-way flow of information.

Exam Probability: **Low**

8. *Answer choices:*

(see index for correct answer)

- a. Census
- b. Interview
- c. Public opinion
- d. Data editing

Guidance: level 1

:: Classification systems ::

__________ is the practice of comparing business processes and performance metrics to industry bests and best practices from other companies. Dimensions typically measured are quality, time and cost.

Exam Probability: **High**

9. *Answer choices:*

(see index for correct answer)

- a. Viridiplantae
- b. International Classification of Diseases for Oncology
- c. Benchmarking
- d. House numbering

Guidance: level 1

:: Consumer theory ::

_________ is the quantity of a good that consumers are willing and able to purchase at various prices during a given period of time.

Exam Probability: **Medium**

10. *Answer choices:*

(see index for correct answer)

- a. Business contract hire
- b. Bliss point
- c. Demand
- d. Lexicographic preferences

Guidance: level 1

:: Project management ::

In political science, an __________ is a means by which a petition signed by a certain minimum number of registered voters can force a government to choose to either enact a law or hold a public vote in parliament in what is called indirect __________, or under direct __________, the proposition is immediately put to a plebiscite or referendum, in what is called a Popular initiated Referendum or citizen-initiated referendum).

Exam Probability: **Medium**

11. *Answer choices:*

(see index for correct answer)

- a. Research program
- b. Responsibility assignment matrix
- c. Association for Project Management
- d. ISO 10006

Guidance: level 1

:: Income ::

_________ is a ratio between the net profit and cost of investment resulting from an investment of some resources. A high ROI means the investment`s gains favorably to its cost. As a performance measure, ROI is used to evaluate the efficiency of an investment or to compare the efficiencies of several different investments. In purely economic terms, it is one way of relating profits to capital invested. _________ is a performance measure used by businesses to identify the efficiency of an investment or number of different investments.

Exam Probability: **Low**

12. *Answer choices:*

(see index for correct answer)

- a. Return on investment
- b. Return of investment
- c. Independent income
- d. Real estate investing

Guidance: level 1

:: Infographics ::

A _________ is a symbolic representation of information according to visualization technique. _________ s have been used since ancient times, but became more prevalent during the Enlightenment. Sometimes, the technique uses a three-dimensional visualization which is then projected onto a two-dimensional surface. The word graph is sometimes used as a synonym for _________ .

Exam Probability: **Low**

13. *Answer choices:*

(see index for correct answer)

- a. National Fire Protection Association
- b. Wigmore chart
- c. Diagram
- d. Walam Olum

Guidance: level 1

:: Legal terms ::

An _________ is an action which is inaccurate or incorrect. In some usages, an _________ is synonymous with a mistake. In statistics, " _________ " refers to the difference between the value which has been computed and the correct value. An _________ could result in failure or in a deviation from the intended performance or behaviour.

Exam Probability: **High**

14. *Answer choices:*

(see index for correct answer)

- a. Dispositive motion
- b. Judicial opinion

- c. Misconduct
- d. Error

Guidance: level 1

:: Service industries ::

__________ are the economic services provided by the finance industry, which encompasses a broad range of businesses that manage money, including credit unions, banks, credit-card companies, insurance companies, accountancy companies, consumer-finance companies, stock brokerages, investment funds, individual managers and some government-sponsored enterprises. __________ companies are present in all economically developed geographic locations and tend to cluster in local, national, regional and international financial centers such as London, New York City, and Tokyo.

Exam Probability: **Medium**

15. *Answer choices:*

(see index for correct answer)

- a. Maid service
- b. Independent Financial Adviser
- c. Financial services
- d. Financial services in Japan

Guidance: level 1

:: Management ::

__________ is the process of thinking about the activities required to achieve a desired goal. It is the first and foremost activity to achieve desired results. It involves the creation and maintenance of a plan, such as psychological aspects that require conceptual skills. There are even a couple of tests to measure someone's capability of __________ well. As such, __________ is a fundamental property of intelligent behavior. An important further meaning, often just called " __________ " is the legal context of permitted building developments.

Exam Probability: **High**

16. *Answer choices:*

(see index for correct answer)

- a. Performance management
- b. Statistical process control
- c. Kata
- d. Planning

Guidance: level 1

:: Costs ::

In microeconomic theory, the __________, or alternative cost, of making a particular choice is the value of the most valuable choice out of those that were not taken. In other words, opportunity that will require sacrifices.

Exam Probability: **Medium**

17. *Answer choices:*

(see index for correct answer)

- a. Implicit cost
- b. Opportunity cost
- c. labor cost
- d. Direct labor cost

Guidance: level 1

:: ::

__________ is the production of products for use or sale using labour and machines, tools, chemical and biological processing, or formulation. The term may refer to a range of human activity, from handicraft to high tech, but is most commonly applied to industrial design, in which raw materials are transformed into finished goods on a large scale. Such finished goods may be sold to other manufacturers for the production of other, more complex products, such as aircraft, household appliances, furniture, sports equipment or automobiles, or sold to wholesalers, who in turn sell them to retailers, who then sell them to end users and consumers.

Exam Probability: **High**

18. *Answer choices:*

(see index for correct answer)

- a. imperative
- b. empathy
- c. Manufacturing
- d. process perspective

Guidance: level 1

:: Statistical terminology ::

_________ is the magnitude or dimensions of a thing. _________ can be measured as length, width, height, diameter, perimeter, area, volume, or mass.

Exam Probability: **Low**

19. *Answer choices:*

(see index for correct answer)

- a. Size
- b. Formation matrix
- c. Random variate
- d. Testimator

Guidance: level 1

:: ::

Some scenarios associate "this kind of planning" with learning "life skills".Schedules are necessary, or at least useful, in situations where individuals need to know what time they must be at a specific location to receive a specific service, and where people need to accomplish a set of goals within a set time period.

Exam Probability: **Low**

20. *Answer choices:*

(see index for correct answer)

- a. Scheduling
- b. similarity-attraction theory
- c. hierarchical perspective
- d. Character

Guidance: level 1

:: ::

__________ is the means to see, hear, or become aware of something or someone through our fundamental senses. The term __________ derives from the Latin word perceptio, and is the organization, identification, and interpretation of sensory information in order to represent and understand the presented information, or the environment.

Exam Probability: **Low**

21. *Answer choices:*

(see index for correct answer)

- a. levels of analysis
- b. open system
- c. interpersonal communication
- d. Perception

Guidance: level 1

:: Statistical terminology ::

_________ is the ability to avoid wasting materials, energy, efforts, money, and time in doing something or in producing a desired result. In a more general sense, it is the ability to do things well, successfully, and without waste. In more mathematical or scientific terms, it is a measure of the extent to which input is well used for an intended task or function . It often specifically comprises the capability of a specific application of effort to produce a specific outcome with a minimum amount or quantity of waste, expense, or unnecessary effort. _________ refers to very different inputs and outputs in different fields and industries.

Exam Probability: **Medium**

22. *Answer choices:*

(see index for correct answer)

- a. Concentration parameter
- b. Fisher consistency

- c. Statistical error
- d. Efficiency

Guidance: level 1

:: Credit cards ::

The _________ Company, also known as Amex, is an American multinational financial services corporation headquartered in Three World Financial Center in New York City. The company was founded in 1850 and is one of the 30 components of the Dow Jones Industrial Average. The company is best known for its charge card, credit card, and traveler`s cheque businesses.

Exam Probability: **High**

23. *Answer choices:*

(see index for correct answer)

- a. American Express
- b. Access
- c. Netbanx
- d. Visa Inc.

Guidance: level 1

:: International trade ::

_________ or globalisation is the process of interaction and integration among people, companies, and governments worldwide. As a complex and multifaceted phenomenon, _________ is considered by some as a form of capitalist expansion which entails the integration of local and national economies into a global, unregulated market economy. _________ has grown due to advances in transportation and communication technology. With the increased global interactions comes the growth of international trade, ideas, and culture. _________ is primarily an economic process of interaction and integration that`s associated with social and cultural aspects. However, conflicts and diplomacy are also large parts of the history of _________, and modern _________.

Exam Probability: **Low**

24. *Answer choices:*

(see index for correct answer)

- a. Asian Clearing Union
- b. New Zealand Meat Producers Board
- c. End-use certificate
- d. Directive on services in the internal market

Guidance: level 1

:: Critical thinking ::

An _________ is a set of statements usually constructed to describe a set of facts which clarifies the causes, context, and consequences of those facts. This description of the facts et cetera may establish rules or laws, and may clarify the existing rules or laws in relation to any objects, or phenomena examined. The components of an _________ can be implicit, and interwoven with one another.

Exam Probability: **Low**

25. *Answer choices:*

(see index for correct answer)

- a. Scientific temper
- b. Intellectual responsibility
- c. Critical-Creative Thinking and Behavioral Research Laboratory
- d. Explanation

Guidance: level 1

:: Management ::

_________ is the identification, evaluation, and prioritization of risks followed by coordinated and economical application of resources to minimize, monitor, and control the probability or impact of unfortunate events or to maximize the realization of opportunities.

Exam Probability: **Medium**

26. *Answer choices:*

(see index for correct answer)

- a. Certified Energy Manager
- b. Tacit knowledge
- c. Risk management
- d. Technology scouting

Guidance: level 1

:: Stochastic processes ::

_________ is a system of rules that are created and enforced through social or governmental institutions to regulate behavior. It has been defined both as "the Science of Justice" and "the Art of Justice". _________ is a system that regulates and ensures that individuals or a community adhere to the will of the state. State-enforced _________ s can be made by a collective legislature or by a single legislator, resulting in statutes, by the executive through decrees and regulations, or established by judges through precedent, normally in common _________ jurisdictions. Private individuals can create legally binding contracts, including arbitration agreements that may elect to accept alternative arbitration to the normal court process. The formation of _________ s themselves may be influenced by a constitution, written or tacit, and the rights encoded therein. The _________ shapes politics, economics, history and society in various ways and serves as a mediator of relations between people.

Exam Probability: **Medium**

27. *Answer choices:*

(see index for correct answer)

- a. Law
- b. Mean value analysis
- c. Convergence of random variables
- d. Heston model

Guidance: level 1

:: Quality management ::

__________ ensures that an organization, product or service is consistent. It has four main components: quality planning, quality assurance, quality control and quality improvement. __________ is focused not only on product and service quality, but also on the means to achieve it. __________, therefore, uses quality assurance and control of processes as well as products to achieve more consistent quality.What a customer wants and is willing to pay for it determines quality. It is written or unwritten commitment to a known or unknown consumer in the market . Thus, quality can be defined as fitness for intended use or, in other words, how well the product performs its intended function

Exam Probability: **High**

28. *Answer choices:*

(see index for correct answer)

- a. QC Reporting
- b. Quality management system
- c. Regulatory translation

- d. Bureau Veritas

Guidance: level 1

:: Human resource management ::

_________ are the people who make up the workforce of an organization, business sector, or economy. "Human capital" is sometimes used synonymously with " _________ ", although human capital typically refers to a narrower effect . Likewise, other terms sometimes used include manpower, talent, labor, personnel, or simply people.

Exam Probability: **High**

29. *Answer choices:*

(see index for correct answer)

- a. The Giving of Orders
- b. Human resources
- c. Job enrichment
- d. CEO succession

Guidance: level 1

:: Stock market ::

A __________, securities exchange or bourse, is a facility where stock brokers and traders can buy and sell securities, such as shares of stock and bonds and other financial instruments. __________s may also provide for facilities the issue and redemption of such securities and instruments and capital events including the payment of income and dividends. Securities traded on a __________ include stock issued by listed companies, unit trusts, derivatives, pooled investment products and bonds. __________s often function as "continuous auction" markets with buyers and sellers consummating transactions via open outcry at a central location such as the floor of the exchange or by using an electronic trading platform.

Exam Probability: **Low**

30. *Answer choices:*

(see index for correct answer)

- a. Alternative display facility
- b. All or none
- c. Selling climax
- d. Stock exchange

Guidance: level 1

:: Casting (manufacturing) ::

A __________ is a regularity in the world, man-made design, or abstract ideas. As such, the elements of a __________ repeat in a predictable manner. A geometric __________ is a kind of __________ formed of geometric shapes and typically repeated like a wallpaper design.

Exam Probability: **Medium**

31. *Answer choices:*

(see index for correct answer)

- a. Pattern
- b. Investment casting
- c. Sand casting
- d. Permeability

Guidance: level 1

:: International trade ::

In finance, an _________ is the rate at which one currency will be exchanged for another. It is also regarded as the value of one country's currency in relation to another currency. For example, an interbank _________ of 114 Japanese yen to the United States dollar means that ¥114 will be exchanged for each US$1 or that US$1 will be exchanged for each ¥114. In this case it is said that the price of a dollar in relation to yen is ¥114, or equivalently that the price of a yen in relation to dollars is $1/114.

Exam Probability: **Low**

32. *Answer choices:*

(see index for correct answer)

- a. Bilateral trade

- b. Gravity model of trade
- c. Trade Act
- d. Trans-Atlantic trade

Guidance: level 1

:: Marketing ::

A _________ is the quantity of payment or compensation given by one party to another in return for one unit of goods or services.. A _________ is influenced by both production costs and demand for the product. A _________ may be determined by a monopolist or may be imposed on the firm by market conditions.

Exam Probability: **High**

33. *Answer choices:*

(see index for correct answer)

- a. MARC USA
- b. Book of business
- c. Electronic money
- d. European Information Technology Observatory

Guidance: level 1

:: Customs duties ::

A __________ is a tax on imports or exports between sovereign states. It is a form of regulation of foreign trade and a policy that taxes foreign products to encourage or safeguard domestic industry. __________s are the simplest and oldest instrument of trade policy. Traditionally, states have used them as a source of income. Now, they are among the most widely used instruments of protection, along with import and export quotas.

Exam Probability: **High**

34. *Answer choices:*

(see index for correct answer)

- a. Canadian import duties
- b. Duty-free shop
- c. Tariff
- d. Wines in bond

Guidance: level 1

:: Stock market ::

__________ is a form of corporate equity ownership, a type of security. The terms voting share and ordinary share are also used frequently in other parts of the world; " __________ " being primarily used in the United States. They are known as Equity shares or Ordinary shares in the UK and other Commonwealth realms. This type of share gives the stockholder the right to share in the profits of the company, and to vote on matters of corporate policy and the composition of the members of the board of directors.

Exam Probability: **Medium**

35. *Answer choices:*

(see index for correct answer)

- a. Box spread
- b. Alternative display facility
- c. Barbell strategy
- d. Fill or kill

Guidance: level 1

:: National accounts ::

__________ is a monetary measure of the market value of all the final goods and services produced in a period of time, often annually. GDP per capita does not, however, reflect differences in the cost of living and the inflation rates of the countries; therefore using a basis of GDP per capita at purchasing power parity is arguably more useful when comparing differences in living standards between nations.

Exam Probability: **Medium**

36. *Answer choices:*

(see index for correct answer)

- a. National Income
- b. Gross domestic product
- c. capital formation

Guidance: level 1

:: Telecommunication theory ::

In reliability theory and reliability engineering, the term __________ has the following meanings.

Exam Probability: **Medium**

37. *Answer choices:*

(see index for correct answer)

- a. Availability
- b. Anisochronous
- c. Blind equalization
- d. Bias distortion

Guidance: level 1

:: Electronic feedback ::

_________ occurs when outputs of a system are routed back as inputs as part of a chain of cause-and-effect that forms a circuit or loop. The system can then be said to feed back into itself. The notion of cause-and-effect has to be handled carefully when applied to _________ systems.

Exam Probability: **Medium**

38. *Answer choices:*

(see index for correct answer)

- a. feedback loop
- b. Positive feedback

Guidance: level 1

:: Industrial design ::

In physics and mathematics, the __________ of a mathematical space is informally defined as the minimum number of coordinates needed to specify any point within it. Thus a line has a __________ of one because only one coordinate is needed to specify a point on it for example, the point at 5 on a number line. A surface such as a plane or the surface of a cylinder or sphere has a __________ of two because two coordinates are needed to specify a point on it for example, both a latitude and longitude are required to locate a point on the surface of a sphere. The inside of a cube, a cylinder or a sphere is three- __________ al because three coordinates are needed to locate a point within these spaces.

Exam Probability: **High**

39. *Answer choices:*

(see index for correct answer)

- a. Dimension
- b. Flip
- c. Industrial design
- d. Bauhaus

Guidance: level 1

:: ::

__________ is a marketing communication that employs an openly sponsored, non-personal message to promote or sell a product, service or idea. Sponsors of __________ are typically businesses wishing to promote their products or services. __________ is differentiated from public relations in that an advertiser pays for and has control over the message. It differs from personal selling in that the message is non-personal, i.e., not directed to a particular individual. __________ is communicated through various mass media, including traditional media such as newspapers, magazines, television, radio, outdoor __________ or direct mail; and new media such as search results, blogs, social media, websites or text messages. The actual presentation of the message in a medium is referred to as an advertisement, or "ad" or advert for short.

Exam Probability: **Medium**

40. *Answer choices:*

(see index for correct answer)

- a. co-culture
- b. Sarbanes-Oxley act of 2002
- c. levels of analysis
- d. cultural

Guidance: level 1

:: Product management ::

A _________ , trade mark, or trade-mark is a recognizable sign, design, or expression which identifies products or services of a particular source from those of others, although _________ s used to identify services are usually called service marks. The _________ owner can be an individual, business organization, or any legal entity. A _________ may be located on a package, a label, a voucher, or on the product itself. For the sake of corporate identity, _________ s are often displayed on company buildings. It is legally recognized as a type of intellectual property.

Exam Probability: **High**

41. *Answer choices:*

(see index for correct answer)

- a. Product information management
- b. Trademark
- c. Product cost management
- d. Swing tag

Guidance: level 1

:: Management ::

A _________ is an idea of the future or desired result that a person or a group of people envisions, plans and commits to achieve. People endeavor to reach _________ s within a finite time by setting deadlines.

Exam Probability: **Medium**

42. *Answer choices:*

(see index for correct answer)

- a. Goal
- b. Line manager
- c. Business economics
- d. Management fad

Guidance: level 1

:: Information science ::

A __________ is a written, drawn, presented, or memorialized representation of thought. a __________ is a form, or written piece that trains a line of thought or as in history, a significant event. The word originates from the Latin __________ um, which denotes a "teaching" or "lesson": the verb doceo denotes "to teach". In the past, the word was usually used to denote a written proof useful as evidence of a truth or fact. In the computer age, " __________ " usually denotes a primarily textual computer file, including its structure and format, e.g. fonts, colors, and images. Contemporarily, " __________ " is not defined by its transmission medium, e.g., paper, given the existence of electronic __________ s. " __________ ation" is distinct because it has more denotations than " __________ ". __________ s are also distinguished from "realia", which are three-dimensional objects that would otherwise satisfy the definition of " __________ " because they memorialize or represent thought; __________ s are considered more as 2 dimensional representations. While __________ s are able to have large varieties of customization, all __________ s are able to be shared freely, and have the right to do so, creativity can be represented by __________ s, also. History, events, examples, opinion, etc. all can be expressed in __________ s.

Exam Probability: **Medium**

43. *Answer choices:*

(see index for correct answer)

- a. Agricultural Information Management Standards
- b. Education informatics
- c. American Documentation Institute
- d. Document

Guidance: level 1

:: Human resource management ::

_________ is the corporate management term for the act of reorganizing the legal, ownership, operational, or other structures of a company for the purpose of making it more profitable, or better organized for its present needs. Other reasons for _________ include a change of ownership or ownership structure, demerger, or a response to a crisis or major change in the business such as bankruptcy, repositioning, or buyout. _________ may also be described as corporate _________, debt _________ and financial _________.

Exam Probability: **Medium**

44. *Answer choices:*

(see index for correct answer)

- a. Mergers and acquisitions

- b. Restructuring
- c. Selection ratio
- d. TPI-theory

Guidance: level 1

:: Strategic alliances ::

A __________ is an agreement between two or more parties to pursue a set of agreed upon objectives needed while remaining independent organizations. A __________ will usually fall short of a legal partnership entity, agency, or corporate affiliate relationship. Typically, two companies form a __________ when each possesses one or more business assets or have expertise that will help the other by enhancing their businesses. __________s can develop in outsourcing relationships where the parties desire to achieve long-term win-win benefits and innovation based on mutually desired outcomes.

Exam Probability: **Low**

45. *Answer choices:*

(see index for correct answer)

- a. Strategic alliance
- b. International joint venture
- c. Defensive termination
- d. Management contract

Guidance: level 1

:: Commercial item transport and distribution ::

A __________ is a commitment or expectation to perform some action in general or if certain circumstances arise. A __________ may arise from a system of ethics or morality, especially in an honor culture. Many duties are created by law, sometimes including a codified punishment or liability for non-performance. Performing one`s __________ may require some sacrifice of self-interest.

Exam Probability: **Low**

46. *Answer choices:*

(see index for correct answer)

- a. Currency adjustment factor
- b. Air cargo
- c. Cargo airline
- d. Backhaul

Guidance: level 1

:: Information science ::

__________ is the resolution of uncertainty; it is that which answers the question of "what an entity is" and thus defines both its essence and nature of its characteristics. __________ relates to both data and knowledge, as data is meaningful __________ representing values attributed to parameters, and knowledge signifies understanding of a concept. __________ is uncoupled from an observer, which is an entity that can access __________ and thus discern what it specifies; __________ exists beyond an event horizon for example. In the case of knowledge, the __________ itself requires a cognitive observer to be obtained.

Exam Probability: **High**

47. *Answer choices:*

(see index for correct answer)

- a. ArchiMate
- b. Information
- c. Integrated Operations in the High North
- d. Informing science

Guidance: level 1

:: ::

Culture is the social behavior and norms found in human societies. Culture is considered a central concept in anthropology, encompassing the range of phenomena that are transmitted through social learning in human societies. _________ universals are found in all human societies; these include expressive forms like art, music, dance, ritual, religion, and technologies like tool usage, cooking, shelter, and clothing. The concept of material culture covers the physical expressions of culture, such as technology, architecture and art, whereas the immaterial aspects of culture such as principles of social organization , mythology, philosophy, literature , and science comprise the intangible _________ heritage of a society.

Exam Probability: **Medium**

48. *Answer choices:*

(see index for correct answer)

- a. Cultural
- b. surface-level diversity
- c. open system
- d. Sarbanes-Oxley act of 2002

Guidance: level 1

:: Semiconductor companies ::

_________ Corporation is a Japanese multinational conglomerate corporation headquartered in Konan, Minato, Tokyo. Its diversified business includes consumer and professional electronics, gaming, entertainment and financial services. The company owns the largest music entertainment business in the world, the largest video game console business and one of the largest video game publishing businesses, and is one of the leading manufacturers of electronic products for the consumer and professional markets, and a leading player in the film and television entertainment industry. _________ was ranked 97th on the 2018 Fortune Global 500 list.

Exam Probability: **High**

49. *Answer choices:*

(see index for correct answer)

- a. General Instrument
- b. Qulsar
- c. Silicon Systems
- d. Sony

Guidance: level 1

:: Business terms ::

A __________ is a short statement of why an organization exists, what its overall goal is, identifying the goal of its operations: what kind of product or service it provides, its primary customers or market, and its geographical region of operation. It may include a short statement of such fundamental matters as the organization`s values or philosophies, a business`s main competitive advantages, or a desired future state—the "vision".

Exam Probability: **High**

50. *Answer choices:*

(see index for correct answer)

- a. front office
- b. Strategic partner
- c. churn rate
- d. customer base

Guidance: level 1

:: Organizational structure ::

An __________ defines how activities such as task allocation, coordination, and supervision are directed toward the achievement of organizational aims.

Exam Probability: **High**

51. *Answer choices:*

(see index for correct answer)

- a. The Starfish and the Spider
- b. Automated Bureaucracy
- c. Blessed Unrest
- d. Organizational structure

Guidance: level 1

:: Mereology ::

__________ , in the abstract, is what belongs to or with something, whether as an attribute or as a component of said thing. In the context of this article, it is one or more components , whether physical or incorporeal, of a person`s estate; or so belonging to, as in being owned by, a person or jointly a group of people or a legal entity like a corporation or even a society. Depending on the nature of the __________ , an owner of __________ has the right to consume, alter, share, redefine, rent, mortgage, pawn, sell, exchange, transfer, give away or destroy it, or to exclude others from doing these things, as well as to perhaps abandon it; whereas regardless of the nature of the __________ , the owner thereof has the right to properly use it , or at the very least exclusively keep it.

Exam Probability: **Low**

52. *Answer choices:*

(see index for correct answer)

- a. Gunk

- b. Mereology
- c. Simple
- d. Mereological essentialism

Guidance: level 1

:: Marketing analytics ::

__________ is a long-term, forward-looking approach to planning with the fundamental goal of achieving a sustainable competitive advantage. Strategic planning involves an analysis of the company`s strategic initial situation prior to the formulation, evaluation and selection of market-oriented competitive position that contributes to the company`s goals and marketing objectives.

Exam Probability: **High**

53. *Answer choices:*

(see index for correct answer)

- a. Sumall
- b. Marketing strategy
- c. Marketing resource management
- d. marketing dashboard

Guidance: level 1

:: International trade ::

_________ involves the transfer of goods or services from one person or entity to another, often in exchange for money. A system or network that allows _________ is called a market.

Exam Probability: **Medium**

54. *Answer choices:*

(see index for correct answer)

- a. Trade
- b. Monopolistic advantage theory
- c. Arab Chamber of Commerce
- d. Agreement on Technical Barriers to Trade

Guidance: level 1

:: Project management ::

Contemporary business and science treat as a _________ any undertaking, carried out individually or collaboratively and possibly involving research or design, that is carefully planned to achieve a particular aim.

Exam Probability: **Low**

55. *Answer choices:*

(see index for correct answer)

- a. Enterprise project management
- b. The International Association of Project and Program Management
- c. Alexander Laufer
- d. P3M3

Guidance: level 1

:: Management ::

__________ is the practice of initiating, planning, executing, controlling, and closing the work of a team to achieve specific goals and meet specific success criteria at the specified time.

Exam Probability: **Low**

56. *Answer choices:*

(see index for correct answer)

- a. Management fad
- b. Just in time
- c. Project management
- d. Quality, cost, delivery

Guidance: level 1

:: Television commercials ::

_________ is a characteristic that distinguishes physical entities that have biological processes, such as signaling and self-sustaining processes, from those that do not, either because such functions have ceased , or because they never had such functions and are classified as inanimate. Various forms of _________ exist, such as plants, animals, fungi, protists, archaea, and bacteria. The criteria can at times be ambiguous and may or may not define viruses, viroids, or potential synthetic _________ as "living". Biology is the science concerned with the study of _________ .

Exam Probability: **High**

57. *Answer choices:*

(see index for correct answer)

- a. Swimblack
- b. Blipvert
- c. Life
- d. Frozen Peas

Guidance: level 1

:: Stock market ::

__________ is a form of stock which may have any combination of features not possessed by common stock including properties of both an equity and a debt instrument, and is generally considered a hybrid instrument. __________s are senior to common stock, but subordinate to bonds in terms of claim and may have priority over common stock in the payment of dividends and upon liquidation. Terms of the __________ are described in the issuing company`s articles of association or articles of incorporation.

Exam Probability: **Low**

58. *Answer choices:*

(see index for correct answer)

- a. Shadow stock
- b. Immediate or cancel
- c. Wealth management
- d. Somalia Stock Exchange

Guidance: level 1

:: Monopoly (economics) ::

A __________ is a form of intellectual property that gives its owner the legal right to exclude others from making, using, selling, and importing an invention for a limited period of years, in exchange for publishing an enabling public disclosure of the invention. In most countries __________ rights fall under civil law and the __________ holder needs to sue someone infringing the __________ in order to enforce his or her rights. In some industries __________ s are an essential form of competitive advantage; in others they are irrelevant.

Exam Probability: **High**

59. *Answer choices:*

(see index for correct answer)

- a. Natural monopoly
- b. Economies of scope
- c. Monopsony
- d. Ramsey problem

Guidance: level 1

Management

Management is the administration of an organization, whether it is a business, a not-for-profit organization, or government body. Management includes the activities of setting the strategy of an organization and coordinating the efforts of its employees (or of volunteers) to accomplish its objectives through the application of available resources, such as financial, natural, technological, and human resources.

:: ::

In logic and philosophy, an __________ is a series of statements , called the premises or premisses , intended to determine the degree of truth of another statement, the conclusion. The logical form of an __________ in a natural language can be represented in a symbolic formal language, and independently of natural language formally defined " __________ s" can be made in math and computer science.

Exam Probability: **Low**

1. *Answer choices:*

(see index for correct answer)

- a. Argument
- b. functional perspective
- c. hierarchical
- d. Sarbanes-Oxley act of 2002

Guidance: level 1

:: Workplace ::

__________ is asystematic determination of a subject`s merit, worth and significance, using criteria governed by a set of standards. It can assist an organization, program, design, project or any other intervention or initiative to assess any aim, realisable concept/proposal, or any alternative, to help in decision-making; or to ascertain the degree of achievement or value in regard to the aim and objectives and results of any such action that has been completed. The primary purpose of __________ , in addition to gaining insight into prior or existing initiatives, is to enable reflection and assist in the identification of future change.

Exam Probability: **Low**

2. *Answer choices:*

(see index for correct answer)

- a. Workplace democracy
- b. Queen bee syndrome
- c. Evaluation
- d. Discrimination based on hair texture

Guidance: level 1

:: ::

_________ is a kind of action that occur as two or more objects have an effect upon one another. The idea of a two-way effect is essential in the concept of _________ , as opposed to a one-way causal effect. A closely related term is interconnectivity, which deals with the _________ s of _________ s within systems: combinations of many simple _________ s can lead to surprising emergent phenomena. _________ has different tailored meanings in various sciences. Changes can also involve _________ .

Exam Probability: **Low**

3. *Answer choices:*

(see index for correct answer)

- a. information systems assessment
- b. Sarbanes-Oxley act of 2002
- c. hierarchical
- d. levels of analysis

Guidance: level 1

:: Project management ::

A _________ is a type of bar chart that illustrates a project schedule, named after its inventor, Henry Gantt , who designed such a chart around the years 1910–1915. Modern _________ s also show the dependency relationships between activities and current schedule status.

Exam Probability: **High**

4. *Answer choices:*

(see index for correct answer)

- a. Trend analysis
- b. Float
- c. Identifying and Managing Project Risk
- d. Gantt chart

Guidance: level 1

:: Business terms ::

A __________ is a short statement of why an organization exists, what its overall goal is, identifying the goal of its operations: what kind of product or service it provides, its primary customers or market, and its geographical region of operation. It may include a short statement of such fundamental matters as the organization`s values or philosophies, a business`s main competitive advantages, or a desired future state—the "vision".

Exam Probability: **High**

5. *Answer choices:*

(see index for correct answer)

- a. churn rate
- b. strategic plan
- c. Mission statement
- d. noncommercial

Guidance: level 1

:: Production and manufacturing ::

Automatic __________ in continuous production processes is a combination of control engineering and chemical engineering disciplines that uses industrial control systems to achieve a production level of consistency, economy and safety which could not be achieved purely by human manual control. It is implemented widely in industries such as oil refining, pulp and paper manufacturing, chemical processing and power generating plants.

Exam Probability: **Low**

6. *Answer choices:*

(see index for correct answer)

- a. Advanced product quality planning
- b. Licensed production
- c. Total productive maintenance
- d. Process control

Guidance: level 1

:: Systems thinking ::

In business management, a _________ is a company that facilitates the learning of its members and continuously transforms itself. The concept was coined through the work and research of Peter Senge and his colleagues.

Exam Probability: **Low**

7. *Answer choices:*

(see index for correct answer)

- a. Interdependence
- b. Tt30
- c. Ted Coombs
- d. Bioterrorism

Guidance: level 1

:: Problem solving ::

A _________ is a unit or formation established to work on a single defined task or activity. Originally introduced by the United States Navy, the term has now caught on for general usage and is a standard part of NATO terminology. Many non-military organizations now create " _________ s" or task groups for temporary activities that might have once been performed by ad hoc committees.

Exam Probability: **High**

8. *Answer choices:*

(see index for correct answer)

- a. Task force
- b. Cognitive acceleration
- c. Proof by exhaustion
- d. Creativity techniques

Guidance: level 1

:: Elementary mathematics ::

_________ is a numerical measurement of how far apart objects are. In physics or everyday usage, _________ may refer to a physical length or an estimation based on other criteria . In most cases, " _________ from A to B" is interchangeable with " _________ from B to A". In mathematics, a _________ function or metric is a generalization of the concept of physical _________ . A metric is a function that behaves according to a specific set of rules, and is a way of describing what it means for elements of some space to be "close to" or "far away from" each other.

Exam Probability: **High**

9. *Answer choices:*

(see index for correct answer)

- a. Pre-algebra
- b. Constant function
- c. Square root

- d. Distance

Guidance: level 1

:: Export and import control ::

" ________ " means the Government Service which is responsible for the administration of ________ law and the collection of duties and taxes and which also has the responsibility for the application of other laws and regulations relating to the importation, exportation, movement or storage of goods.

Exam Probability: **Low**

10. *Answer choices:*

(see index for correct answer)

- a. VNIIS Exemption Letter
- b. Customs
- c. Customs valuation
- d. Export of cryptography

Guidance: level 1

:: ::

Business is the activity of making one`s living or making money by producing or buying and selling products . Simply put, it is "any activity or enterprise entered into for profit. It does not mean it is a company, a corporation, partnership, or have any such formal organization, but it can range from a street peddler to General Motors."

Exam Probability: **Medium**

11. *Answer choices:*

(see index for correct answer)

- a. open system
- b. interpersonal communication
- c. Sarbanes-Oxley act of 2002
- d. Firm

Guidance: level 1

:: Employee relations ::

_________ ownership, or employee share ownership, is an ownership interest in a company held by the company`s workforce. The ownership interest may be facilitated by the company as part of employees` remuneration or incentive compensation for work performed, or the company itself may be employee owned.

Exam Probability: **Medium**

12. *Answer choices:*

(see index for correct answer)

- a. Employee stock
- b. Employee surveys
- c. Industry Federation of the State of Rio de Janeiro
- d. Employee motivation

Guidance: level 1

:: Cash flow ::

_________ s are narrowly interconnected with the concepts of value, interest rate and liquidity.A _________ that shall happen on a future day tN can be transformed into a _________ of the same value in t0.

Exam Probability: **Low**

13. *Answer choices:*

(see index for correct answer)

- a. Operating cash flow
- b. Propequity
- c. Cash flow
- d. Discounted payback period

Guidance: level 1

:: Supply chain management terms ::

In business and finance, _________ is a system of organizations, people, activities, information, and resources involved inmoving a product or service from supplier to customer. _________ activities involve the transformation of natural resources, raw materials, and components into a finished product that is delivered to the end customer. In sophisticated _________ systems, used products may re-enter the _________ at any point where residual value is recyclable. _________s link value chains.

Exam Probability: **Low**

14. *Answer choices:*

(see index for correct answer)

- a. Capital spare
- b. Price look-up code
- c. Stockout
- d. Supply chain

Guidance: level 1

:: ::

_________ or accountancy is the measurement, processing, and communication of financial information about economic entities such as businesses and corporations. The modern field was established by the Italian mathematician Luca Pacioli in 1494. _________ , which has been called the "language of business", measures the results of an organization`s economic activities and conveys this information to a variety of users, including investors, creditors, management, and regulators. Practitioners of _________ are known as accountants. The terms " _________ " and "financial reporting" are often used as synonyms.

Exam Probability: **Medium**

15. *Answer choices:*

(see index for correct answer)

- a. functional perspective
- b. Accounting
- c. corporate values
- d. hierarchical perspective

Guidance: level 1

:: Decision theory ::

Within economics the concept of _________ is used to model worth or value, but its usage has evolved significantly over time. The term was introduced initially as a measure of pleasure or satisfaction within the theory of utilitarianism by moral philosophers such as Jeremy Bentham and John Stuart Mill. But the term has been adapted and reapplied within neoclassical economics, which dominates modern economic theory, as a _________ function that represents a consumer`s preference ordering over a choice set. As such, it is devoid of its original interpretation as a measurement of the pleasure or satisfaction obtained by the consumer from that choice.

Exam Probability: **High**

16. *Answer choices:*

(see index for correct answer)

- a. Ambiguity aversion
- b. Expected value of sample information
- c. Price of stability
- d. Outcome primacy

Guidance: level 1

:: Leadership ::

_________ Theory, or the _________ Model, is a model created by Paul Hersey and Ken Blanchard, developed while working on Management of Organizational Behavior. The theory was first introduced in 1969 as "life cycle theory of leadership". During the mid-1970s, life cycle theory of leadership was renamed " _________ Theory."

Exam Probability: **Low**

17. *Answer choices:*

(see index for correct answer)

- a. Situational leadership
- b. Sex differences in leadership
- c. Consideration and Initiating Structure
- d. servant leader

Guidance: level 1

:: Game theory ::

To _________ is to make a deal between different parties where each party gives up part of their demand. In arguments, _________ is a concept of finding agreement through communication, through a mutual acceptance of terms—often involving variations from an original goal or desires.

Exam Probability: **High**

18. *Answer choices:*

(see index for correct answer)

- a. La Relance
- b. Compromise
- c. Superrationality

- d. Subgame

Guidance: level 1

:: Organizational theory ::

Decentralisation is the process by which the activities of an organization, particularly those regarding planning and decision making, are distributed or delegated away from a central, authoritative location or group. Concepts of _________ have been applied to group dynamics and management science in private businesses and organizations, political science, law and public administration, economics, money and technology.

Exam Probability: **High**

19. *Answer choices:*

(see index for correct answer)

- a. Smart city
- b. Organisational semiotics
- c. Mary Parker Follett
- d. Catfish effect

Guidance: level 1

:: Management ::

_________ is the practice of initiating, planning, executing, controlling, and closing the work of a team to achieve specific goals and meet specific success criteria at the specified time.

Exam Probability: **Medium**

20. *Answer choices:*

(see index for correct answer)

- a. Product Development and Systems Engineering Consortium
- b. Supplier relationship management
- c. Mushroom management
- d. Power to the edge

Guidance: level 1

:: Project management ::

A _________ is a professional in the field of project management. _________ s have the responsibility of the planning, procurement and execution of a project, in any undertaking that has a defined scope, defined start and a defined finish; regardless of industry. _________ s are first point of contact for any issues or discrepancies arising from within the heads of various departments in an organization before the problem escalates to higher authorities. Project management is the responsibility of a _________ . This individual seldom participates directly in the activities that produce the end result, but rather strives to maintain the progress, mutual interaction and tasks of various parties in such a way that reduces the risk of overall failure, maximizes benefits, and minimizes costs.

Exam Probability: **Low**

21. *Answer choices:*

(see index for correct answer)

- a. Resource
- b. Collaborative project management
- c. Project manager
- d. Effort management

Guidance: level 1

:: ::

_________ is the amount of time someone works beyond normal working hours. The term is also used for the pay received for this time. Normal hours may be determined in several ways.

Exam Probability: **High**

22. *Answer choices:*

(see index for correct answer)

- a. Sarbanes-Oxley act of 2002
- b. Overtime
- c. process perspective
- d. hierarchical perspective

Guidance: level 1

:: Planning ::

__________ is a high level plan to achieve one or more goals under conditions of uncertainty. In the sense of the "art of the general," which included several subsets of skills including tactics, siegecraft, logistics etc., the term came into use in the 6th century C.E. in East Roman terminology, and was translated into Western vernacular languages only in the 18th century. From then until the 20th century, the word " __________ " came to denote "a comprehensive way to try to pursue political ends, including the threat or actual use of force, in a dialectic of wills" in a military conflict, in which both adversaries interact.

Exam Probability: **Low**

23. *Answer choices:*

(see index for correct answer)

- a. Plano Trienal
- b. Implementation intention
- c. Reproductive life plan
- d. Default effect

Guidance: level 1

:: ::

_________ is the process of two or more people or organizations working together to complete a task or achieve a goal. _________ is similar to cooperation. Most _________ requires leadership, although the form of leadership can be social within a decentralized and egalitarian group. Teams that work collaboratively often access greater resources, recognition and rewards when facing competition for finite resources.

Exam Probability: **High**

24. *Answer choices:*

(see index for correct answer)

- a. Sarbanes-Oxley act of 2002
- b. levels of analysis
- c. Collaboration
- d. similarity-attraction theory

Guidance: level 1

:: Employment ::

The _________ is an individual's metaphorical "journey" through learning, work and other aspects of life. There are a number of ways to define _________ and the term is used in a variety of ways.

Exam Probability: **High**

25. *Answer choices:*

(see index for correct answer)

- a. Participatory ergonomics
- b. Birch index
- c. Job shadow
- d. Extra role performance

Guidance: level 1

:: ::

_________ , in its broadest context, includes both the attainment of that which is just and the philosophical discussion of that which is just. The concept of _________ is based on numerous fields, and many differing viewpoints and perspectives including the concepts of moral correctness based on ethics, rationality, law, religion, equity and fairness. Often, the general discussion of _________ is divided into the realm of social _________ as found in philosophy, theology and religion, and, procedural _________ as found in the study and application of the law.

Exam Probability: **Low**

26. *Answer choices:*

(see index for correct answer)

- a. cultural
- b. functional perspective

- c. personal values
- d. Justice

Guidance: level 1

:: Discrimination ::

In social psychology, a __________ is an over-generalized belief about a particular category of people. __________ s are generalized because one assumes that the __________ is true for each individual person in the category. While such generalizations may be useful when making quick decisions, they may be erroneous when applied to particular individuals. __________ s encourage prejudice and may arise for a number of reasons.

Exam Probability: **High**

27. *Answer choices:*

(see index for correct answer)

- a. Stereotype
- b. Anti-Americanism
- c. Elitism

Guidance: level 1

:: Organizational theory ::

_________ refers to both a body of non-elective government officials and an administrative policy-making group. Historically, a _________ was a government administration managed by departments staffed with non-elected officials. Today, _________ is the administrative system governing any large institution, whether publicly owned or privately owned. The public administration in many countries is an example of a _________, but so is the centralized hierarchical structure of a business firm.

Exam Probability: **High**

28. *Answer choices:*

(see index for correct answer)

- a. Solid line reporting
- b. Bureaucracy
- c. Resource dependence theory
- d. Battlefield promotion

Guidance: level 1

:: Operations research ::

_________ is a method to achieve the best outcome in a mathematical model whose requirements are represented by linear relationships. _________ is a special case of mathematical programming .

Exam Probability: **Medium**

29. *Answer choices:*

(see index for correct answer)

- a. Goal programming
- b. Participatory modeling
- c. Linear programming
- d. Differential evolution

Guidance: level 1

:: Management ::

__________ is the identification, evaluation, and prioritization of risks followed by coordinated and economical application of resources to minimize, monitor, and control the probability or impact of unfortunate events or to maximize the realization of opportunities.

Exam Probability: **High**

30. *Answer choices:*

(see index for correct answer)

- a. Radical transparency
- b. Risk management
- c. Business process interoperability
- d. Management styles

Guidance: level 1

:: Marketing ::

_________ is based on a marketing concept which can be adopted by an organization as a strategy for business expansion. Where implemented, a franchisor licenses its know-how, procedures, intellectual property, use of its business model, brand, and rights to sell its branded products and services to a franchisee. In return the franchisee pays certain fees and agrees to comply with certain obligations, typically set out in a Franchise Agreement.

Exam Probability: **Medium**

31. *Answer choices:*

(see index for correct answer)

- a. Market intelligence
- b. Mobile marketing
- c. Digital native
- d. Licensing International Expo

Guidance: level 1

:: Human resource management ::

__________ means increasing the scope of a job through extending the range of its job duties and responsibilities generally within the same level and periphery. __________ involves combining various activities at the same level in the organization and adding them to the existing job. It is also called the horizontal expansion of job activities. This contradicts the principles of specialisation and the division of labour whereby work is divided into small units, each of which is performed repetitively by an individual worker and the responsibilities are always clear. Some motivational theories suggest that the boredom and alienation caused by the division of labour can actually cause efficiency to fall. Thus, __________ seeks to motivate workers through reversing the process of specialisation. A typical approach might be to replace assembly lines with modular work; instead of an employee repeating the same step on each product, they perform several tasks on a single item. In order for employees to be provided with __________ they will need to be retrained in new fields to understand how each field works.

Exam Probability: **Medium**

32. *Answer choices:*

(see index for correct answer)

- a. Talascend
- b. Job enlargement
- c. Expense management
- d. Job design

Guidance: level 1

:: Autonomy ::

In developmental psychology and moral, political, and bioethical philosophy, _________ is the capacity to make an informed, uncoerced decision. Autonomous organizations or institutions are independent or self-governing. _________ can also be defined from a human resources perspective, where it denotes a level of discretion granted to an employee in his or her work. In such cases, _________ is known to generally increase job satisfaction. _________ is a term that is also widely used in the field of medicine — personal _________ is greatly recognized and valued in health care.

Exam Probability: **Low**

33. *Answer choices:*

(see index for correct answer)

- a. National personal autonomy
- b. Autonomy
- c. Rhex
- d. Anti-individualism

Guidance: level 1

:: Management ::

__________ is the process of thinking about the activities required to achieve a desired goal. It is the first and foremost activity to achieve desired results. It involves the creation and maintenance of a plan, such as psychological aspects that require conceptual skills. There are even a couple of tests to measure someone's capability of __________ well. As such, __________ is a fundamental property of intelligent behavior. An important further meaning, often just called " __________ " is the legal context of permitted building developments.

Exam Probability: **High**

34. *Answer choices:*

(see index for correct answer)

- a. Total Worker Health
- b. Crisis plan
- c. Planning
- d. Professional performances

Guidance: level 1

:: Income ::

In business and accounting, net income is an entity`s income minus cost of goods sold, expenses and taxes for an accounting period. It is computed as the residual of all revenues and gains over all expenses and losses for the period, and has also been defined as the net increase in shareholders` equity that results from a company`s operations. In the context of the presentation of financial statements, the IFRS Foundation defines net income as synonymous with profit and loss. The difference between revenue and the cost of making a product or providing a service, before deducting overheads, payroll, taxation, and interest payments. This is different from operating income .

Exam Probability: **High**

35. *Answer choices:*

(see index for correct answer)

- a. Real income
- b. Salary inversion
- c. Windfall gain
- d. Bottom line

Guidance: level 1

:: Legal terms ::

__________ is a type of meaning in which a phrase, statement or resolution is not explicitly defined, making several interpretations plausible. A common aspect of __________ is uncertainty. It is thus an attribute of any idea or statement whose intended meaning cannot be definitively resolved according to a rule or process with a finite number of steps.

Exam Probability: **Medium**

36. *Answer choices:*

(see index for correct answer)

- a. Deed of gift
- b. Ambiguity
- c. Prerogative
- d. Jurisprudence constante

Guidance: level 1

:: Commercial item transport and distribution ::

In commerce, supply-chain management , the management of the flow of goods and services, involves the movement and storage of raw materials, of work-in-process inventory, and of finished goods from point of origin to point of consumption. Interconnected or interlinked networks, channels and node businesses combine in the provision of products and services required by end customers in a supply chain. Supply-chain management has been defined as the "design, planning, execution, control, and monitoring of supply-chain activities with the objective of creating net value, building a competitive infrastructure, leveraging worldwide logistics, synchronizing supply with demand and measuring performance globally."SCM practice draws heavily from the areas of industrial engineering, systems engineering, operations management, logistics, procurement, information technology, and marketing and strives for an integrated approach. Marketing channels play an important role in supply-chain management. Current research in supply-chain management is concerned with topics related to sustainability and risk management, among others. Some suggest that the "people dimension" of SCM, ethical issues, internal integration, transparency/visibility, and human capital/talent management are topics that have, so far, been underrepresented on the research agenda.

Exam Probability: **Medium**

37. *Answer choices:*

(see index for correct answer)

- a. EPCglobal Network
- b. Shuttle tanker
- c. Oversize load
- d. Supply chain management

Guidance: level 1

:: Management ::

__________ is a process by which entities review the quality of all factors involved in production. ISO 9000 defines __________ as "A part of quality management focused on fulfilling quality requirements".

Exam Probability: **Medium**

38. *Answer choices:*

(see index for correct answer)

- a. Business value
- b. Complementary assets
- c. Quality control
- d. Strategic management

Guidance: level 1

:: Marketing ::

A __________ is an overall experience of a customer that distinguishes an organization or product from its rivals in the eyes of the customer. __________ s are used in business, marketing, and advertising. Name __________ s are sometimes distinguished from generic or store __________ s.

Exam Probability: **Medium**

39. *Answer choices:*

(see index for correct answer)

- a. Franchising
- b. Customer lifetime value
- c. Breakthrough Moments
- d. Brand

Guidance: level 1

:: ::

A __________ is a professional who provides expert advice in a particular area such as security , management, education, accountancy, law, human resources, marketing , finance, engineering, science or any of many other specialized fields.

Exam Probability: **Medium**

40. *Answer choices:*

(see index for correct answer)

- a. open system
- b. hierarchical perspective
- c. Consultant
- d. process perspective

Guidance: level 1

:: Rhetoric ::

__________ is the pattern of narrative development that aims to make vivid a place, object, character, or group. __________ is one of four rhetorical modes , along with exposition, argumentation, and narration. In practice it would be difficult to write literature that drew on just one of the four basic modes.

Exam Probability: **High**

41. *Answer choices:*

(see index for correct answer)

- a. Trope
- b. Magnanimity
- c. Pleonasm
- d. Description

Guidance: level 1

:: Marketing ::

__________ , in marketing, manufacturing, call centres and management, is the use of flexible computer-aided manufacturing systems to produce custom output. Such systems combine the low unit costs of mass production processes with the flexibility of individual customization.

Exam Probability: **Medium**

42. *Answer choices:*

(see index for correct answer)

- a. Movie gimmick
- b. Mass customization
- c. Adobe Media Optimizer
- d. Customer newsletter service

Guidance: level 1

:: Labour relations ::

__________ is a field of study that can have different meanings depending on the context in which it is used. In an international context, it is a subfield of labor history that studies the human relations with regard to work – in its broadest sense – and how this connects to questions of social inequality. It explicitly encompasses unregulated, historical, and non-Western forms of labor. Here, __________ define "for or with whom one works and under what rules. These rules determine the type of work, type and amount of remuneration, working hours, degrees of physical and psychological strain, as well as the degree of freedom and autonomy associated with the work."

Exam Probability: **Medium**

43. *Answer choices:*

(see index for correct answer)

- a. Boulwarism
- b. Scranton Declaration
- c. Eurocadres
- d. Labor relations

Guidance: level 1

:: Industrial Revolution ::

The ________, now also known as the First ________, was the transition to new manufacturing processes in Europe and the US, in the period from about 1760 to sometime between 1820 and 1840. This transition included going from hand production methods to machines, new chemical manufacturing and iron production processes, the increasing use of steam power and water power, the development of machine tools and the rise of the mechanized factory system. The ________ also led to an unprecedented rise in the rate of population growth.

Exam Probability: **Medium**

44. *Answer choices:*

(see index for correct answer)

- a. Bowling Iron Works

- b. The Condition of the Working Class in England
- c. Industrial Revolution
- d. Factory system

Guidance: level 1

:: ::

_________ is an evaluative or corrective exercise that can occur in any area of human life. _________ can therefore take many different forms . How people go about criticizing, can vary a great deal. In specific areas of human endeavour, the form of _________ can be highly specialized and technical; it often requires professional knowledge to appreciate the _________ . For subject-specific information, see the Varieties of _________ page.

Exam Probability: **Low**

45. *Answer choices:*

(see index for correct answer)

- a. personal values
- b. hierarchical
- c. open system
- d. Criticism

Guidance: level 1

:: Management ::

In organizational studies, _________ is the efficient and effective development of an organization`s resources when they are needed. Such resources may include financial resources, inventory, human skills, production resources, or information technology and natural resources.

Exam Probability: **Low**

46. *Answer choices:*

(see index for correct answer)

- a. Best current practice
- b. Quick response manufacturing
- c. Kata
- d. Resource management

Guidance: level 1

:: Marketing ::

_________ or stock is the goods and materials that a business holds for the ultimate goal of resale .

Exam Probability: **Low**

47. *Answer choices:*

(see index for correct answer)

- a. Product marketing
- b. Customer dynamics
- c. Marketing brochure
- d. Buy one, get one free

Guidance: level 1

:: Outsourcing ::

_________ is the relocation of a business process from one country to another—typically an operational process, such as manufacturing, or supporting processes, such as accounting. Typically this refers to a company business, although state governments may also employ _________. More recently, technical and administrative services have been offshored.

Exam Probability: **Low**

48. *Answer choices:*

(see index for correct answer)

- a. Affiliated Computer Services
- b. Managed security service
- c. Offshoring
- d. Virtual Staff Finder

Guidance: level 1

:: ::

In business strategy, _________ is establishing a competitive advantage by having the lowest cost of operation in the industry. _________ is often driven by company efficiency, size, scale, scope and cumulative experience .A _________ strategy aims to exploit scale of production, well-defined scope and other economies , producing highly standardized products, using advanced technology.In recent years, more and more companies have chosen a strategic mix to achieve market leadership. These patterns consist of simultaneous _________ , superior customer service and product leadership. Walmart has succeeded across the world due to its _________ strategy. The company has cut down on exesses at every point of production and thus are able to provide the consumers with quality products at low prices.

Exam Probability: **High**

49. *Answer choices:*

(see index for correct answer)

- a. hierarchical
- b. process perspective
- c. Cost leadership
- d. surface-level diversity

Guidance: level 1

:: Unemployment ::

In economics, a _________ is a business cycle contraction when there is a general decline in economic activity. Macroeconomic indicators such as GDP , investment spending, capacity utilization, household income, business profits, and inflation fall, while bankruptcies and the unemployment rate rise. In the United Kingdom, it is defined as a negative economic growth for two consecutive quarters.

Exam Probability: **Low**

50. *Answer choices:*

(see index for correct answer)

- a. Short time
- b. Employment protection legislation
- c. JobBridge
- d. Recession

Guidance: level 1

:: Production and manufacturing ::

_________ is a set of techniques and tools for process improvement. Though as a shortened form it may be found written as 6S, it should not be confused with the methodology known as 6S .

Exam Probability: **Medium**

51. *Answer choices:*

(see index for correct answer)

- a. Verband der Automobilindustrie
- b. Continuous production
- c. Bill of resources
- d. Six Sigma

Guidance: level 1

:: Management ::

A _________ describes the rationale of how an organization creates, delivers, and captures value, in economic, social, cultural or other contexts. The process of _________ construction and modification is also called _________ innovation and forms a part of business strategy.

Exam Probability: **High**

52. *Answer choices:*

(see index for correct answer)

- a. Responsible autonomy
- b. One in, one out policy
- c. Business model

- d. Corporate recovery

Guidance: level 1

:: Budgets ::

A _________ is a financial plan for a defined period, often one year. It may also include planned sales volumes and revenues, resource quantities, costs and expenses, assets, liabilities and cash flows. Companies, governments, families and other organizations use it to express strategic plans of activities or events in measurable terms.

Exam Probability: **Medium**

53. *Answer choices:*

(see index for correct answer)

- a. Budgeted cost of work scheduled
- b. Participatory budgeting
- c. Film budgeting
- d. Budget

Guidance: level 1

:: Business models ::

_________ es are privately owned corporations, partnerships, or sole proprietorships that have fewer employees and/or less annual revenue than a regular-sized business or corporation. Businesses are defined as "small" in terms of being able to apply for government support and qualify for preferential tax policy varies depending on the country and industry. _________ es range from fifteen employees under the Australian Fair Work Act 2009, fifty employees according to the definition used by the European Union, and fewer than five hundred employees to qualify for many U.S. _________ Administration programs. While _________ es can also be classified according to other methods, such as annual revenues, shipments, sales, assets, or by annual gross or net revenue or net profits, the number of employees is one of the most widely used measures.

Exam Probability: **High**

54. *Answer choices:*

(see index for correct answer)

- a. Professional open source
- b. Subsidiary
- c. Small business
- d. Inclusive business model

Guidance: level 1

:: Credit cards ::

The __________ Company, also known as Amex, is an American multinational financial services corporation headquartered in Three World Financial Center in New York City. The company was founded in 1850 and is one of the 30 components of the Dow Jones Industrial Average. The company is best known for its charge card, credit card, and traveler's cheque businesses.

Exam Probability: **Low**

55. *Answer choices:*

(see index for correct answer)

- a. American Express
- b. PayAnywhere
- c. Access
- d. Barclaycard

Guidance: level 1

:: Generally Accepted Accounting Principles ::

In accounting, _________ is the income that a business have from its normal business activities, usually from the sale of goods and services to customers. _________ is also referred to as sales or turnover.Some companies receive _________ from interest, royalties, or other fees. _________ may refer to business income in general, or it may refer to the amount, in a monetary unit, earned during a period of time, as in "Last year, Company X had _________ of $42 million". Profits or net income generally imply total _________ minus total expenses in a given period. In accounting, in the balance statement it is a subsection of the Equity section and _________ increases equity, it is often referred to as the "top line" due to its position on the income statement at the very top. This is to be contrasted with the "bottom line" which denotes net income .

Exam Probability: **Medium**

56. *Answer choices:*

(see index for correct answer)

- a. Revenue
- b. Cost pool
- c. Depreciation
- d. deferred revenue

Guidance: level 1

:: ::

According to Torrington, a __________ is usually developed by conducting a job analysis, which includes examining the tasks and sequences of tasks necessary to perform the job. The analysis considers the areas of knowledge and skills needed for the job. A job usually includes several roles. According to Hall, the __________ might be broadened to form a person specification or may be known as "terms of reference". The person/job specification can be presented as a stand-alone document, but in practice it is usually included within the __________. A __________ is often used by employers in the recruitment process.

Exam Probability: **Low**

57. *Answer choices:*

(see index for correct answer)

- a. similarity-attraction theory
- b. functional perspective
- c. open system
- d. process perspective

Guidance: level 1

:: E-commerce ::

__________ is the activity of buying or selling of products on online services or over the Internet. Electronic commerce draws on technologies such as mobile commerce, electronic funds transfer, supply chain management, Internet marketing, online transaction processing, electronic data interchange , inventory management systems, and automated data collection systems.

Exam Probability: **Medium**

58. *Answer choices:*

(see index for correct answer)

- a. PaySafe
- b. Primecoin
- c. Eurocheque
- d. E-commerce

Guidance: level 1

:: Behaviorism ::

In behavioral psychology, _________ is a consequence applied that will strengthen an organism`s future behavior whenever that behavior is preceded by a specific antecedent stimulus. This strengthening effect may be measured as a higher frequency of behavior , longer duration , greater magnitude , or shorter latency . There are two types of _________ , known as positive _________ and negative _________ ; positive is where by a reward is offered on expression of the wanted behaviour and negative is taking away an undesirable element in the persons environment whenever the desired behaviour is achieved.

Exam Probability: **High**

59. *Answer choices:*

(see index for correct answer)

- a. Matching Law
- b. Systematic desensitization
- c. contingency management
- d. Programmed instruction

Guidance: level 1

Business law

Corporate law (also known as business law) is the body of law governing the rights, relations, and conduct of persons, companies, organizations and businesses. It refers to the legal practice relating to, or the theory of corporations. Corporate law often describes the law relating to matters which derive directly from the life-cycle of a corporation. It thus encompasses the formation, funding, governance, and death of a corporation.

:: United States federal public corruption crime ::

Mail fraud and _________ are federal crimes in the United States that involve mailing or electronically transmitting something associated with fraud. Jurisdiction is claimed by the federal government if the illegal activity crosses interstate or international borders.

Exam Probability: **Medium**

1. *Answer choices:*

(see index for correct answer)

- a. Wire fraud
- b. RICO Act

Guidance: level 1

:: Real estate valuation ::

_________ or OMV is the price at which an asset would trade in a competitive auction setting. _________ is often used interchangeably with open _________, fair value or fair _________, although these terms have distinct definitions in different standards, and may or may not differ in some circumstances.

Exam Probability: **Low**

2. *Answer choices:*

(see index for correct answer)

- a. Royal Institution of Chartered Surveyors
- b. Market value
- c. Days on market
- d. Real estate appraisal

Guidance: level 1

:: Legal terms ::

An __________ is a legal and equitable remedy in the form of a special court order that compels a party to do or refrain from specific acts. "When a court employs the extraordinary remedy of __________, it directs the conduct of a party, and does so with the backing of its full coercive powers." A party that fails to comply with an __________ faces criminal or civil penalties, including possible monetary sanctions and even imprisonment. They can also be charged with contempt of court. Counter __________ s are __________ s that stop or reverse the enforcement of another __________ .

Exam Probability: **Low**

3. *Answer choices:*

(see index for correct answer)

- a. Pain and suffering
- b. Injunction
- c. Due process
- d. Gross floor area

Guidance: level 1

:: ::

A contract is a legally-binding agreement which recognises and governs the rights and duties of the parties to the agreement. A contract is legally enforceable because it meets the requirements and approval of the law. An agreement typically involves the exchange of goods, services, money, or promises of any of those. In the event of breach of contract, the law awards the injured party access to legal remedies such as damages and cancellation.

Exam Probability: **Low**

4. *Answer choices:*

(see index for correct answer)

- a. functional perspective
- b. imperative
- c. Sarbanes-Oxley act of 2002
- d. information systems assessment

Guidance: level 1

:: ::

A concept of English law, a _________ is an untrue or misleading statement of fact made during negotiations by one party to another, the statement then inducing that other party into the contract. The misled party may normally rescind the contract, and sometimes may be awarded damages as well .

Exam Probability: **Low**

5. *Answer choices:*

(see index for correct answer)

- a. Sarbanes-Oxley act of 2002
- b. process perspective

- c. Misrepresentation
- d. functional perspective

Guidance: level 1

:: ::

An __________ is a contingent motivator. Traditional __________ s are extrinsic motivators which reward actions to yield a desired outcome. The effectiveness of traditional __________ s has changed as the needs of Western society have evolved. While the traditional __________ model is effective when there is a defined procedure and goal for a task, Western society started to require a higher volume of critical thinkers, so the traditional model became less effective. Institutions are now following a trend in implementing strategies that rely on intrinsic motivations rather than the extrinsic motivations that the traditional __________ s foster.

Exam Probability: **Medium**

6. *Answer choices:*

(see index for correct answer)

- a. Incentive
- b. personal values
- c. functional perspective
- d. information systems assessment

Guidance: level 1

:: Real property law ::

_________ is the judicial process whereby a will is "proved" in a court of law and accepted as a valid public document that is the true last testament of the deceased, or whereby the estate is settled according to the laws of intestacy in the state of residence [or real property] of the deceased at time of death in the absence of a legal will.

Exam Probability: **Low**

7. *Answer choices:*

(see index for correct answer)

- a. Probate
- b. Habous
- c. Land grant
- d. Good guy clause

Guidance: level 1

:: Actuarial science ::

_________ is the possibility of losing something of value. Values can be gained or lost when taking _________ resulting from a given action or inaction, foreseen or unforeseen . _________ can also be defined as the intentional interaction with uncertainty. Uncertainty is a potential, unpredictable, and uncontrollable outcome; _________ is a consequence of action taken in spite of uncertainty.

Exam Probability: **High**

8. *Answer choices:*

(see index for correct answer)

- a. Cohort
- b. Mathematical statistics
- c. Anders Lindstedt
- d. Model risk

Guidance: level 1

:: Legal doctrines and principles ::

In the common law of torts, _________ loquitur is a doctrine that infers negligence from the very nature of an accident or injury in the absence of direct evidence on how any defendant behaved. Although modern formulations differ by jurisdiction, common law originally stated that the accident must satisfy the necessary elements of negligence: duty, breach of duty, causation, and injury. In _________ loquitur, the elements of duty of care, breach, and causation are inferred from an injury that does not ordinarily occur without negligence.

Exam Probability: **High**

9. *Answer choices:*

(see index for correct answer)

- a. unconscionable contract
- b. Abstention doctrine
- c. Assumption of risk
- d. Respondeat superior

Guidance: level 1

:: Contract law ::

A _________ cannot be enforced by law. _________ s are different from voidable contracts, which are contracts that may be nullified. However, when a contract is being written and signed, there is no automatic mechanism available in every situation that can be utilized to detect the validity or enforceability of that contract. Practically, a contract can be declared to be void by a court of law. So the main question is that under what conditions can a contract be deemed as void

Exam Probability: **Medium**

10. *Answer choices:*

(see index for correct answer)

- a. Void contract

- b. Franchisor
- c. Drop dead date
- d. Multimarket contact

Guidance: level 1

:: ::

__________ is property that is movable. In common law systems, __________ may also be called chattels or personalty. In civil law systems, __________ is often called movable property or movables – any property that can be moved from one location to another.

Exam Probability: **Low**

11. *Answer choices:*

(see index for correct answer)

- a. Personal property
- b. corporate values
- c. Sarbanes-Oxley act of 2002
- d. functional perspective

Guidance: level 1

:: Legal doctrines and principles ::

_________ , land acquisition , compulsory purchase , resumption , resumption/compulsory acquisition , or expropriation is the power of a state, provincial, or national government to take private property for public use. However, this power can be legislatively delegated by the state to municipalities, government subdivisions, or even to private persons or corporations, when they are authorized by the legislature to exercise the functions of public character.

Exam Probability: **Medium**

12. *Answer choices:*

(see index for correct answer)

- a. Act of state
- b. Eminent domain
- c. Act of state doctrine
- d. compulsory purchase

Guidance: level 1

:: ::

Competition law is a law that promotes or seeks to maintain market competition by regulating anti-competitive conduct by companies. Competition law is implemented through public and private enforcement. Competition law is known as " _________ law" in the United States for historical reasons, and as "anti-monopoly law" in China and Russia. In previous years it has been known as trade practices law in the United Kingdom and Australia. In the European Union, it is referred to as both _________ and competition law.

Exam Probability: **High**

13. *Answer choices:*

(see index for correct answer)

- a. Antitrust
- b. surface-level diversity
- c. hierarchical perspective
- d. imperative

Guidance: level 1

:: ::

In English law, a __________ or __________ absolute is an estate in land, a form of freehold ownership. It is a way that real estate and land may be owned in common law countries, and is the highest possible ownership interest that can be held in real property. Allodial title is reserved to governments under a civil law structure. The rights of the __________ owner are limited by government powers of taxation, compulsory purchase, police power, and escheat, and it could also be limited further by certain encumbrances or conditions in the deed, such as, for example, a condition that required the land to be used as a public park, with a reversion interest in the grantor if the condition fails; this is a __________ conditional.

Exam Probability: **Medium**

14. *Answer choices:*

(see index for correct answer)

- a. imperative
- b. corporate values
- c. hierarchical
- d. hierarchical perspective

Guidance: level 1

:: ::

__________ , often abbreviated cert. in the United States, is a process for seeking judicial review and a writ issued by a court that agrees to review. A __________ is issued by a superior court, directing an inferior court, tribunal, or other public authority to send the record of a proceeding for review.

Exam Probability: **High**

15. *Answer choices:*

(see index for correct answer)

- a. Certiorari
- b. information systems assessment
- c. imperative
- d. functional perspective

Guidance: level 1

:: Legal terms ::

A _________ is any "lesser" criminal act in some common law legal systems. _________ s are generally punished less severely than felonies, but theoretically more so than administrative infractions and regulatory offences. Many _________ s are punished with monetary fines.

Exam Probability: **Medium**

16. *Answer choices:*

(see index for correct answer)

- a. Officious intermeddler
- b. Adjudication
- c. First impression
- d. Affray

Guidance: level 1

:: ::

A _________ is monetary compensation paid by an employer to an employee in exchange for work done. Payment may be calculated as a fixed amount for each task completed , or at an hourly or daily rate , or based on an easily measured quantity of work done.

Exam Probability: **Medium**

17. *Answer choices:*

(see index for correct answer)

- a. Wage
- b. interpersonal communication
- c. information systems assessment
- d. surface-level diversity

Guidance: level 1

:: Contract law ::

In contract law, _________ is an excuse for the nonperformance of duties under a contract, based on a change in circumstances , the nonoccurrence of which was an underlying assumption of the contract, that makes performance of the contract literally impossible.

Exam Probability: **Medium**

18. *Answer choices:*

(see index for correct answer)

- a. Culpa in contrahendo
- b. End-user license agreement
- c. Heads of loss
- d. Last shot

Guidance: level 1

:: Latin legal terms ::

In law and government, __________ describes practices that are legally recognised, regardless whether the practice exists in reality. In contrast, de facto describes situations that exist in reality, even if not legally recognised. The terms are often used to contrast different scenarios: for a colloquial example, "I know that, __________, this is supposed to be a parking lot, but now that the flood has left four feet of water here, it`s a de facto swimming pool". To further explain, even if the signs around the flooded parking lot say "Parking Lot" it is "in fact" a swimming pool .

Exam Probability: **Medium**

19. *Answer choices:*

(see index for correct answer)

- a. pari delicto
- b. De jure
- c. Nolo contendere
- d. Quid pro quo

Guidance: level 1

:: Insolvency ::

__________ is the state of being unable to pay the money owed, by a person or company, on time; those in a state of __________ are said to be insolvent. There are two forms: cash-flow __________ and balance-sheet __________ .

Exam Probability: **High**

20. *Answer choices:*

(see index for correct answer)

- a. Insolvency
- b. Official Committee of Equity Security Holders
- c. Liquidation
- d. Conservatorship

Guidance: level 1

:: ::

__________ is the assignment of any responsibility or authority to another person to carry out specific activities. It is one of the core concepts of management leadership. However, the person who delegated the work remains accountable for the outcome of the delegated work. __________ empowers a subordinate to make decisions, i.e. it is a shifting of decision-making authority from one organizational level to a lower one. __________, if properly done, is not fabrication. The opposite of effective __________ is micromanagement, where a manager provides too much input, direction, and review of delegated work. In general, __________ is good and can save money and time, help in building skills, and motivate people. On the other hand, poor __________ might cause frustration and confusion to all the involved parties. Some agents, however, do not favour a __________ and consider the power of making a decision rather burdensome.

Exam Probability: **Medium**

21. *Answer choices:*

(see index for correct answer)

- a. hierarchical
- b. empathy
- c. cultural
- d. similarity-attraction theory

Guidance: level 1

:: Contract law ::

__________ is the act of recall or annulment. It is the cancelling of an act, the recalling of a grant or privilege, or the making void of some deed previously existing.

Exam Probability: **Medium**

22. *Answer choices:*

(see index for correct answer)

- a. Pactum de quota litis
- b. Extended warranty
- c. Meeting of the minds
- d. Franchisor

Guidance: level 1

:: Criminal procedure ::

__________ is the adjudication process of the criminal law. While __________ differs dramatically by jurisdiction, the process generally begins with a formal criminal charge with the person on trial either being free on bail or incarcerated, and results in the conviction or acquittal of the defendant. __________ can be either in form of inquisitorial or adversarial __________ .

Exam Probability: **Medium**

23. *Answer choices:*

(see index for correct answer)

- a. Exoneration
- b. Criminal procedure

Guidance: level 1

:: ::

_________ is an abstract concept of management of complex systems according to a set of rules and trends. In systems theory, these types of rules exist in various fields of biology and society, but the term has slightly different meanings according to context. For example.

Exam Probability: **High**

24. *Answer choices:*

(see index for correct answer)

- a. Regulation
- b. imperative
- c. Sarbanes-Oxley act of 2002
- d. interpersonal communication

Guidance: level 1

:: ::

__________ is a process whereby a person assumes the parenting of another, usually a child, from that person`s biological or legal parent or parents. Legal __________ s permanently transfers all rights and responsibilities, along with filiation, from the biological parent or parents.

Exam Probability: **High**

25. *Answer choices:*

(see index for correct answer)

- a. hierarchical perspective
- b. open system
- c. process perspective
- d. Adoption

Guidance: level 1

:: ::

In the law of evidence, a __________ of a particular fact can be made without the aid of proof in some situations. The invocation of a __________ shifts the burden of proof from one party to the opposing party in a court trial.

Exam Probability: **Low**

26. *Answer choices:*

(see index for correct answer)

- a. hierarchical perspective
- b. personal values
- c. Presumption
- d. interpersonal communication

Guidance: level 1

:: Financial regulatory authorities of the United States ::

The _________ is the revenue service of the United States federal government. The government agency is a bureau of the Department of the Treasury, and is under the immediate direction of the Commissioner of Internal Revenue, who is appointed to a five-year term by the President of the United States. The IRS is responsible for collecting taxes and administering the Internal Revenue Code, the main body of federal statutory tax law of the United States. The duties of the IRS include providing tax assistance to taxpayers and pursuing and resolving instances of erroneous or fraudulent tax filings. The IRS has also overseen various benefits programs, and enforces portions of the Affordable Care Act.

Exam Probability: **Medium**

27. *Answer choices:*

(see index for correct answer)

- a. Internal Revenue Service

- b. Office of the Comptroller of the Currency
- c. Office of Thrift Supervision
- d. Farm Credit Administration

Guidance: level 1

:: Commerce ::

_________ relates to "the exchange of goods and services, especially on a large scale". It includes legal, economic, political, social, cultural and technological systems that operate in a country or in international trade.

Exam Probability: **Medium**

28. *Answer choices:*

(see index for correct answer)

- a. Commerce
- b. Customs broking
- c. Recommerce
- d. GT Nexus

Guidance: level 1

:: Information technology audit ::

_________ is the act of using a computer to take or alter electronic data, or to gain unlawful use of a computer or system. In the United States, _________ is specifically proscribed by the _________ and Abuse Act, which criminalizes computer-related acts under federal jurisdiction. Types of _________ include.

Exam Probability: **High**

29. *Answer choices:*

(see index for correct answer)

- a. ACL
- b. Computer fraud
- c. Host protected area
- d. SekChek Local

Guidance: level 1

:: Labour relations ::

_________ is a field of study that can have different meanings depending on the context in which it is used. In an international context, it is a subfield of labor history that studies the human relations with regard to work – in its broadest sense – and how this connects to questions of social inequality. It explicitly encompasses unregulated, historical, and non-Western forms of labor. Here, _________ define "for or with whom one works and under what rules. These rules determine the type of work, type and amount of remuneration, working hours, degrees of physical and psychological strain, as well as the degree of freedom and autonomy associated with the work."

Exam Probability: **Low**

30. *Answer choices:*

(see index for correct answer)

- a. Review Body
- b. United Students Against Sweatshops
- c. Labor relations
- d. Acas

Guidance: level 1

:: Advertising ::

In law, _________ is speech or writing on behalf of a business with the intent of earning revenue or a profit. It is economic in nature and usually attempts to persuade consumers to purchase the business's product or service. The Supreme Court of the United States defines _________ as speech that "proposes a commercial transaction".

Exam Probability: **Low**

31. *Answer choices:*

(see index for correct answer)

- a. MyThings
- b. Logojet

- c. Kids club
- d. Commercial speech

Guidance: level 1

:: International trade ::

_________ involves the transfer of goods or services from one person or entity to another, often in exchange for money. A system or network that allows _________ is called a market.

Exam Probability: **High**

32. *Answer choices:*

(see index for correct answer)

- a. End-use certificate
- b. Effective rate of protection
- c. Trade
- d. Concertina model

Guidance: level 1

:: ::

In law, a __________ is a coming together of parties to a dispute, to present information in a tribunal, a formal setting with the authority to adjudicate claims or disputes. One form of tribunal is a court. The tribunal, which may occur before a judge, jury, or other designated trier of fact, aims to achieve a resolution to their dispute.

Exam Probability: **Low**

33. *Answer choices:*

(see index for correct answer)

- a. deep-level diversity
- b. Character
- c. cultural
- d. Trial

Guidance: level 1

:: Law ::

__________ is a body of law which defines the role, powers, and structure of different entities within a state, namely, the executive, the parliament or legislature, and the judiciary; as well as the basic rights of citizens and, in federal countries such as the United States and Canada, the relationship between the central government and state, provincial, or territorial governments.

Exam Probability: **High**

34. *Answer choices:*

(see index for correct answer)

- a. Comparative law
- b. Legal case

Guidance: level 1

:: Trade secrets ::

The _________ of 1996 was a 6 title Act of Congress dealing with a wide range of issues, including not only industrial espionage , but the insanity defense, matters regarding the Boys & Girls Clubs of America, requirements for presentence investigation reports, and the United States Sentencing Commission reports regarding encryption or scrambling technology, and other technical and minor amendments.

Exam Probability: **Low**

35. *Answer choices:*

(see index for correct answer)

- a. Economic Espionage Act
- b. Economic Espionage Act of 1996
- c. Biswamohan Pani
- d. Confidential Information

Guidance: level 1

:: Insurance terms ::

A _________ in the broadest sense is a natural person or other legal entity who receives money or other benefits from a benefactor. For example, the _________ of a life insurance policy is the person who receives the payment of the amount of insurance after the death of the insured.

Exam Probability: **Low**

36. *Answer choices:*

(see index for correct answer)

- a. Gross premiums written
- b. Insurance bad faith
- c. Adjustment clause
- d. Cash value

Guidance: level 1

:: Arbitration law ::

The United States Arbitration Act , more commonly referred to as the _________ or FAA, is an act of Congress that provides for judicial facilitation of private dispute resolution through arbitration. It applies in both state courts and federal courts, as was held constitutional in Southland Corp. v. Keating. It applies where the transaction contemplated by the parties "involves" interstate commerce and is predicated on an exercise of the Commerce Clause powers granted to Congress in the U.S. Constitution.

Exam Probability: **Medium**

37. *Answer choices:*

(see index for correct answer)

- a. Federal Arbitration Act
- b. Kompetenz-kompetenz
- c. Convention on the Recognition and Enforcement of Foreign Arbitral Awards
- d. UNCITRAL Model Law on International Commercial Arbitration

Guidance: level 1

:: Business ::

_________ is a trade policy that does not restrict imports or exports; it can also be understood as the free market idea applied to international trade. In government, _________ is predominantly advocated by political parties that hold liberal economic positions while economically left-wing and nationalist political parties generally support protectionism, the opposite of _________ .

Exam Probability: **Medium**

38. *Answer choices:*

(see index for correct answer)

- a. Lean dynamics
- b. Intangible asset finance
- c. Free trade
- d. Procurement PunchOut

Guidance: level 1

:: ::

In financial markets, a share is a unit used as mutual funds, limited partnerships, and real estate investment trusts. The owner of _________ in the corporation/company is a shareholder of the corporation. A share is an indivisible unit of capital, expressing the ownership relationship between the company and the shareholder. The denominated value of a share is its face value, and the total of the face value of issued _________ represent the capital of a company, which may not reflect the market value of those _________ .

Exam Probability: **Medium**

39. *Answer choices:*

(see index for correct answer)

- a. Shares
- b. levels of analysis
- c. process perspective
- d. Character

Guidance: level 1

:: ::

A _________ is a sworn body of people convened to render an impartial verdict officially submitted to them by a court, or to set a penalty or judgment. Modern juries tend to be found in courts to ascertain the guilt or lack thereof in a crime. In Anglophone jurisdictions, the verdict may be guilty or not guilty . The old institution of grand juries still exists in some places, particularly the United States, to investigate whether enough evidence of a crime exists to bring someone to trial.

Exam Probability: **Medium**

40. *Answer choices:*

(see index for correct answer)

- a. surface-level diversity
- b. functional perspective
- c. hierarchical
- d. Jury

Guidance: level 1

:: ::

Credit is the trust which allows one party to provide money or resources to another party wherein the second party does not reimburse the first party immediately , but promises either to repay or return those resources at a later date. In other words, credit is a method of making reciprocity formal, legally enforceable, and extensible to a large group of unrelated people.

Exam Probability: **Low**

41. *Answer choices:*

(see index for correct answer)

- a. Consumer credit
- b. personal values
- c. hierarchical
- d. functional perspective

Guidance: level 1

:: Data management ::

_________ is a form of intellectual property that grants the creator of an original creative work an exclusive legal right to determine whether and under what conditions this original work may be copied and used by others, usually for a limited term of years. The exclusive rights are not absolute but limited by limitations and exceptions to _________ law, including fair use. A major limitation on _________ on ideas is that _________ protects only the original expression of ideas, and not the underlying ideas themselves.

Exam Probability: **Low**

42. *Answer choices:*

(see index for correct answer)

- a. WCF Data Services
- b. Information integration
- c. Metadata controller
- d. Copyright

Guidance: level 1

:: Patent law ::

A _________ is generally any statement intended to specify or delimit the scope of rights and obligations that may be exercised and enforced by parties in a legally recognized relationship. In contrast to other terms for legally operative language, the term _________ usually implies situations that involve some level of uncertainty, waiver, or risk.

Exam Probability: **Medium**

43. *Answer choices:*

(see index for correct answer)

- a. First to file and first to invent
- b. Disclaimer
- c. Prosecution history estoppel
- d. Patent infringement

Guidance: level 1

:: ::

In law, an _________ is the process in which cases are reviewed, where parties request a formal change to an official decision. _________ s function both as a process for error correction as well as a process of clarifying and interpreting law. Although appellate courts have existed for thousands of years, common law countries did not incorporate an affirmative right to _________ into their jurisprudence until the 19th century.

Exam Probability: **High**

44. *Answer choices:*

(see index for correct answer)

- a. Appeal
- b. deep-level diversity

- c. interpersonal communication
- d. hierarchical

Guidance: level 1

:: ::

An ________ , for United States federal income tax, is a closely held corporation that makes a valid election to be taxed under Subchapter S of Chapter 1 of the Internal Revenue Code. In general, ________ s do not pay any income taxes. Instead, the corporation`s income or losses are divided among and passed through to its shareholders. The shareholders must then report the income or loss on their own individual income tax returns.

Exam Probability: **Medium**

45. *Answer choices:*

(see index for correct answer)

- a. empathy
- b. personal values
- c. open system
- d. surface-level diversity

Guidance: level 1

:: Intention ::

_________ is the mental element of a person's intention to commit a crime; or knowledge that one's action or lack of action would cause a crime to be committed. It is a necessary element of many crimes.

Exam Probability: **High**

46. *Answer choices:*

(see index for correct answer)

- a. Letter of Intent
- b. bona fide

Guidance: level 1

:: Business law ::

A _________ is a form of partnership similar to a general partnership except that while a general partnership must have at least two general partners , a _________ must have at least one GP and at least one limited partner.

Exam Probability: **High**

47. *Answer choices:*

(see index for correct answer)

- a. Forged endorsement

- b. Limited partnership
- c. Holder
- d. Bulk sale

Guidance: level 1

:: Project management ::

_________ is the right to exercise power, which can be formalized by a state and exercised by way of judges, appointed executives of government, or the ecclesiastical or priestly appointed representatives of a God or other deities.

Exam Probability: **Medium**

48. *Answer choices:*

(see index for correct answer)

- a. Axelos
- b. Big Hairy Audacious Goal
- c. Cone of Uncertainty
- d. Theme-centered interaction

Guidance: level 1

:: Business law ::

The term is used to designate a range of diverse, if often kindred, concepts. These have historically been addressed in a number of discrete disciplines, notably mathematics, physics, chemistry, ethics, aesthetics, ontology, and theology.

Exam Probability: **Low**

49. *Answer choices:*

(see index for correct answer)

- a. Ladenschlussgesetz
- b. Unfair business practices
- c. Contract A
- d. Turnkey

Guidance: level 1

:: Business models ::

A _________, _________ company or daughter company is a company that is owned or controlled by another company, which is called the parent company, parent, or holding company. The _________ can be a company, corporation, or limited liability company. In some cases it is a government or state-owned enterprise. In some cases, particularly in the music and book publishing industries, subsidiaries are referred to as imprints.

Exam Probability: **High**

50. *Answer choices:*

(see index for correct answer)

- a. Paid To Click
- b. Parent company
- c. Collective business system
- d. Subsidiary

Guidance: level 1

:: Finance ::

_________ is the investigation or exercise of care that a reasonable business or person is expected to take before entering into an agreement or contract with another party, or an act with a certain standard of care.

Exam Probability: **High**

51. *Answer choices:*

(see index for correct answer)

- a. Margin
- b. Due diligence
- c. Portfolio optimization
- d. Rule of 78s

Guidance: level 1

:: Legal terms ::

_________ , or exemplary damages, are damages assessed in order to punish the defendant for outrageous conduct and/or to reform or deter the defendant and others from engaging in conduct similar to that which formed the basis of the lawsuit. Although the purpose of _________ is not to compensate the plaintiff, the plaintiff will receive all or some of the _________ award.

Exam Probability: **Low**

52. *Answer choices:*

(see index for correct answer)

- a. Preliminary injunction
- b. Agreement in principle
- c. vacant possession
- d. Punitive damages

Guidance: level 1

:: Contract law ::

An _________ —or acceleration covenant— in the law of contracts, is a term that fully matures the performance due from a party upon a breach of the contract. Such clauses are most prevalent in mortgages and similar contracts to purchase real estate in installments.

Exam Probability: **Low**

53. *Answer choices:*

(see index for correct answer)

- a. Performance Based Contracting
- b. Collateral contract
- c. Subcontractor
- d. Acceleration clause

Guidance: level 1

:: Contract law ::

_________ , in human interactions, is a sincere intention to be fair, open, and honest, regardless of the outcome of the interaction. While some Latin phrases lose their literal meaning over centuries, this is not the case with bona fides; it is still widely used and interchangeable with its generally accepted modern-day English translation of _________ . It is an important concept within law and business. The opposed concepts are bad faith, mala fides and perfidy . In contemporary English, the usage of bona fides is synonymous with credentials and identity. The phrase is sometimes used in job advertisements, and should not be confused with the bona fide occupational qualifications or the employer`s _________ effort, as described below.

Exam Probability: **Medium**

54. *Answer choices:*

(see index for correct answer)

- a. Contra proferentem
- b. Expectation damages
- c. Good faith
- d. Neo-classical contract

Guidance: level 1

:: Treaties ::

A __________ is an agreement under international law entered into by actors in international law, namely sovereign states and international organizations. A __________ may also be known as an agreement, protocol, covenant, convention, pact, or exchange of letters, among other terms. Regardless of terminology, all of these forms of agreements are, under international law, equally considered treaties and the rules are the same.

Exam Probability: **Low**

55. *Answer choices:*

(see index for correct answer)

- a. Clausula rebus sic stantibus
- b. Secret treaty
- c. Investor state dispute settlement
- d. Treaty

Guidance: level 1

:: ::

__________ is widespread, interconnected digital technology. The term entered the popular culture from science fiction and the arts but is now used by technology strategists, security professionals, government, military and industry leaders and entrepreneurs to describe the domain of the global technology environment. Others consider __________ to be just a notional environment in which communication over computer networks occurs. The word became popular in the 1990s when the uses of the Internet, networking, and digital communication were all growing dramatically and the term " __________ " was able to represent the many new ideas and phenomena that were emerging. It has been called the largest unregulated and uncontrolled domain in the history of mankind, and is also unique because it is a domain created by people vice the traditional physical domains.

Exam Probability: **Medium**

56. *Answer choices:*

(see index for correct answer)

- a. Sarbanes-Oxley act of 2002
- b. hierarchical perspective
- c. empathy
- d. Cyberspace

Guidance: level 1

:: Debt ::

_________ , in finance and economics, is payment from a borrower or deposit-taking financial institution to a lender or depositor of an amount above repayment of the principal sum , at a particular rate. It is distinct from a fee which the borrower may pay the lender or some third party. It is also distinct from dividend which is paid by a company to its shareholders from its profit or reserve, but not at a particular rate decided beforehand, rather on a pro rata basis as a share in the reward gained by risk taking entrepreneurs when the revenue earned exceeds the total costs.

Exam Probability: **Low**

57. *Answer choices:*

(see index for correct answer)

- a. Interest
- b. Museum of Foreign Debt
- c. Medical debt
- d. Floating charge

Guidance: level 1

:: Stock market ::

_________ is freedom from, or resilience against, potential harm caused by others. Beneficiaries of _________ may be of persons and social groups, objects and institutions, ecosystems or any other entity or phenomenon vulnerable to unwanted change by its environment.

Exam Probability: **High**

58. *Answer choices:*

(see index for correct answer)

- a. House stock
- b. Matchbook FX
- c. Security
- d. Secondary market offering

Guidance: level 1

:: ::

_________ is the study and management of exchange relationships. _________ is the business process of creating relationships with and satisfying customers. With its focus on the customer, _________ is one of the premier components of business management.

Exam Probability: **Low**

59. *Answer choices:*

(see index for correct answer)

- a. empathy
- b. hierarchical perspective
- c. Marketing

- d. Sarbanes-Oxley act of 2002

Guidance: level 1

Finance

Finance is a field that is concerned with the allocation (investment) of assets and liabilities over space and time, often under conditions of risk or uncertainty. Finance can also be defined as the science of money management. Participants in the market aim to price assets based on their risk level, fundamental value, and their expected rate of return. Finance can be split into three sub-categories: public finance, corporate finance and personal finance.

:: Accounting source documents ::

A _________ or account statement is a summary of financial transactions which have occurred over a given period on a bank account held by a person or business with a financial institution.

Exam Probability: **Low**

1. *Answer choices:*

(see index for correct answer)

- a. Bank statement
- b. Parcel audit
- c. Invoice
- d. Credit memorandum

Guidance: level 1

:: Income taxes ::

An _________ is a tax imposed on individuals or entities that varies with respective income or profits . _________ generally is computed as the product of a tax rate times taxable income. Taxation rates may vary by type or characteristics of the taxpayer.

Exam Probability: **Low**

2. *Answer choices:*

(see index for correct answer)

- a. Income Tax Act 2007
- b. State income tax
- c. Income taxes in Canada

- d. Income tax

Guidance: level 1

:: ::

An ________ , for United States federal income tax, is a closely held corporation that makes a valid election to be taxed under Subchapter S of Chapter 1 of the Internal Revenue Code. In general, ________ s do not pay any income taxes. Instead, the corporation`s income or losses are divided among and passed through to its shareholders. The shareholders must then report the income or loss on their own individual income tax returns.

Exam Probability: **Low**

3. *Answer choices:*

(see index for correct answer)

- a. S corporation
- b. hierarchical
- c. functional perspective
- d. corporate values

Guidance: level 1

:: ::

_________ involves decision making. It can include judging the merits of multiple options and selecting one or more of them. One can make a _________ between imagined options or between real options followed by the corresponding action. For example, a traveler might choose a route for a journey based on the preference of arriving at a given destination as soon as possible. The preferred route can then follow from information such as the length of each of the possible routes, traffic conditions, etc. The arrival at a _________ can include more complex motivators such as cognition, instinct, and feeling.

Exam Probability: **High**

4. *Answer choices:*

(see index for correct answer)

- a. process perspective
- b. imperative
- c. deep-level diversity
- d. Choice

Guidance: level 1

:: Generally Accepted Accounting Principles ::

The first published description of the process is found in Luca Pacioli`s 1494 work Summa de arithmetica, in the section titled Particularis de Computis et Scripturis. Although he did not use the term, he essentially prescribed a technique similar to a post-closing _________ .

Exam Probability: **Low**

5. *Answer choices:*

(see index for correct answer)

- a. Construction in progress
- b. Operating income
- c. Cost pool
- d. Deprival value

Guidance: level 1

:: Management accounting ::

__________ , or dollar contribution per unit, is the selling price per unit minus the variable cost per unit. "Contribution" represents the portion of sales revenue that is not consumed by variable costs and so contributes to the coverage of fixed costs. This concept is one of the key building blocks of break-even analysis.

Exam Probability: **High**

6. *Answer choices:*

(see index for correct answer)

- a. Process costing
- b. Overhead

- c. Institute of Cost and Management Accountants of Bangladesh
- d. Contribution margin

Guidance: level 1

:: Inventory ::

_________ is the amount of inventory a company has in stock at the end of its fiscal year. It is closely related with _________ cost, which is the amount of money spent to get these goods in stock. It should be calculated at the lower of cost or market.

Exam Probability: **Low**

7. *Answer choices:*

(see index for correct answer)

- a. Ending inventory
- b. Safety stock
- c. Inventory bounce
- d. Inventory control problem

Guidance: level 1

:: Global systemically important banks ::

_________ Inc. or Citi is an American multinational investment bank and financial services corporation headquartered in New York City. The company was formed by the merger of banking giant Citicorp and financial conglomerate Travelers Group in 1998; Travelers was subsequently spun off from the company in 2002. _________ owns Citicorp, the holding company for Citibank, as well as several international subsidiaries.

Exam Probability: **Medium**

8. *Answer choices:*

(see index for correct answer)

- a. Citigroup
- b. Morgan Stanley
- c. BNP Paribas
- d. Groupe BPCE

Guidance: level 1

:: ::

_________ is the collection of techniques, skills, methods, and processes used in the production of goods or services or in the accomplishment of objectives, such as scientific investigation. _________ can be the knowledge of techniques, processes, and the like, or it can be embedded in machines to allow for operation without detailed knowledge of their workings. Systems applying _________ by taking an input, changing it according to the system`s use, and then producing an outcome are referred to as _________ systems or technological systems.

Exam Probability: **Medium**

9. *Answer choices:*

(see index for correct answer)

- a. process perspective
- b. Sarbanes-Oxley act of 2002
- c. empathy
- d. similarity-attraction theory

Guidance: level 1

:: Valuation (finance) ::

_________ refers to an assessment of the viability, stability, and profitability of a business, sub-business or project.

Exam Probability: **Low**

10. *Answer choices:*

(see index for correct answer)

- a. Financial analysis
- b. Business valuation standard
- c. Institution of Valuers
- d. Overtrading

Guidance: level 1

:: Financial ratios ::

_________ is a measure of how revenue growth translates into growth in operating income. It is a measure of leverage, and of how risky, or volatile, a company`s operating income is.

Exam Probability: **Low**

11. *Answer choices:*

(see index for correct answer)

- a. Price/cash flow ratio
- b. Net interest spread
- c. Operating leverage
- d. Interest coverage ratio

Guidance: level 1

:: Banking ::

A _________ is a financial account maintained by a bank for a customer. A _________ can be a deposit account, a credit card account, a current account, or any other type of account offered by a financial institution, and represents the funds that a customer has entrusted to the financial institution and from which the customer can make withdrawals. Alternatively, accounts may be loan accounts in which case the customer owes money to the financial institution.

Exam Probability: **Low**

12. *Answer choices:*

(see index for correct answer)

- a. Bank account
- b. Correlation swap
- c. MSI 20000
- d. Village banking

Guidance: level 1

:: ::

In the field of analysis of algorithms in computer science, the _________ is a method of amortized analysis based on accounting. The _________ often gives a more intuitive account of the amortized cost of an operation than either aggregate analysis or the potential method. Note, however, that this does not guarantee such analysis will be immediately obvious; often, choosing the correct parameters for the _________ requires as much knowledge of the problem and the complexity bounds one is attempting to prove as the other two methods.

Exam Probability: **High**

13. *Answer choices:*

(see index for correct answer)

- a. Sarbanes-Oxley act of 2002
- b. levels of analysis
- c. functional perspective
- d. empathy

Guidance: level 1

:: Planning ::

_________ is a high level plan to achieve one or more goals under conditions of uncertainty. In the sense of the "art of the general," which included several subsets of skills including tactics, siegecraft, logistics etc., the term came into use in the 6th century C.E. in East Roman terminology, and was translated into Western vernacular languages only in the 18th century. From then until the 20th century, the word " _________ " came to denote "a comprehensive way to try to pursue political ends, including the threat or actual use of force, in a dialectic of wills" in a military conflict, in which both adversaries interact.

Exam Probability: **Low**

14. *Answer choices:*

(see index for correct answer)

- a. Strategy
- b. Interactive planning
- c. Default effect
- d. BLUF

Guidance: level 1

:: Stock market ::

_________ is a form of stock which may have any combination of features not possessed by common stock including properties of both an equity and a debt instrument, and is generally considered a hybrid instrument. _________ s are senior to common stock, but subordinate to bonds in terms of claim and may have priority over common stock in the payment of dividends and upon liquidation. Terms of the _________ are described in the issuing company`s articles of association or articles of incorporation.

Exam Probability: **Medium**

15. *Answer choices:*

(see index for correct answer)

- a. Mosaic theory
- b. Squeeze out
- c. Reverse stock split
- d. Preferred stock

Guidance: level 1

:: ::

_________ officially refers to an administrative area of the Principality of Monaco, specifically the ward of _________ /Spélugues, where the _________ Casino is located. Informally the name also refers to a larger district, the _________ Quarter , which besides _________ /Spélugues also includes the wards of La Rousse/Saint Roman, Larvotto/Bas Moulins, and Saint Michel. The permanent population of the ward of _________ is about 3,500, while that of the quarter is about 15,000. Monaco has four traditional quarters. From west to east they are: Fontvieille , Monaco-Ville , La Condamine, and _________ .

Exam Probability: **Low**

16. *Answer choices:*

(see index for correct answer)

- a. corporate values
- b. imperative
- c. interpersonal communication
- d. Monte Carlo

Guidance: level 1

:: Market research ::

_________ , an acronym for Information through Disguised Experimentation is an annual market research fair conducted by the students of IIM-Lucknow. Students create games and use various other simulated environments to capture consumers' subconscious thoughts. This innovative method of market research removes the sensitization effect that might bias peoples answers to questions. This ensures that the most truthful answers are captured to research questions. The games are designed in such a way that the observers can elicit all the required information just by observing and noting down the behaviour and the responses of the participants.

Exam Probability: **Medium**

17. *Answer choices:*

(see index for correct answer)

- a. DigitalMR
- b. Advertising Research Foundation
- c. Cambashi
- d. IModerate

Guidance: level 1

:: Stock market ::

A share price is the price of a single share of a number of saleable stocks of a company, derivative or other financial asset.In layman's terms, the _________ is the highest amount someone is willing to pay for the stock, or the lowest amount that it can be bought for.

Exam Probability: **High**

18. *Answer choices:*

(see index for correct answer)

- a. Stock price
- b. Alternative display facility
- c. Chi-X Global
- d. Witching hour

Guidance: level 1

:: Interest rates ::

An _________ is the amount of interest due per period, as a proportion of the amount lent, deposited or borrowed . The total interest on an amount lent or borrowed depends on the principal sum, the _________ , the compounding frequency, and the length of time over which it is lent, deposited or borrowed.

Exam Probability: **High**

19. *Answer choices:*

(see index for correct answer)

- a. Time preference
- b. Interest rate
- c. Annual effective discount rate

- d. Effective annual interest rate

Guidance: level 1

:: Materials ::

A _________ , also known as a feedstock, unprocessed material, or primary commodity, is a basic material that is used to produce goods, finished products, energy, or intermediate materials which are feedstock for future finished products. As feedstock, the term connotes these materials are bottleneck assets and are highly important with regard to producing other products. An example of this is crude oil, which is a _________ and a feedstock used in the production of industrial chemicals, fuels, plastics, and pharmaceutical goods; lumber is a _________ used to produce a variety of products including all types of furniture. The term " _________ " denotes materials in minimally processed or unprocessed in states; e.g., raw latex, crude oil, cotton, coal, raw biomass, iron ore, air, logs, or water i.e. "...any product of agriculture, forestry, fishing and any other mineral that is in its natural form or which has undergone the transformation required to prepare it for internationally marketing in substantial volumes."

Exam Probability: **Medium**

20. *Answer choices:*

(see index for correct answer)

- a. Raw material
- b. Mineral wool
- c. Nanophase material
- d. Refractory

Guidance: level 1

:: Bonds (finance) ::

In finance, a _________ or convertible note or convertible debt is a type of bond that the holder can convert into a specified number of shares of common stock in the issuing company or cash of equal value. It is a hybrid security with debt- and equity-like features. It originated in the mid-19th century, and was used by early speculators such as Jacob Little and Daniel Drew to counter market cornering.

Exam Probability: **Medium**

21. *Answer choices:*

(see index for correct answer)

- a. Salomon BIG
- b. Prize Bond
- c. Convertible bond
- d. Eurobond

Guidance: level 1

:: ::

An _________ is a systematic and independent examination of books, accounts, statutory records, documents and vouchers of an organization to ascertain how far the financial statements as well as non-financial disclosures present a true and fair view of the concern. It also attempts to ensure that the books of accounts are properly maintained by the concern as required by law. _________ ing has become such a ubiquitous phenomenon in the corporate and the public sector that academics started identifying an " _________ Society". The _________ or perceives and recognises the propositions before them for examination, obtains evidence, evaluates the same and formulates an opinion on the basis of his judgement which is communicated through their _________ ing report.

Exam Probability: **Low**

22. *Answer choices:*

(see index for correct answer)

- a. Sarbanes-Oxley act of 2002
- b. interpersonal communication
- c. Audit
- d. hierarchical perspective

Guidance: level 1

:: ::

An __________ is a comprehensive report on a company`s activities throughout the preceding year. __________ s are intended to give shareholders and other interested people information about the company`s activities and financial performance. They may be considered as grey literature. Most jurisdictions require companies to prepare and disclose __________ s, and many require the __________ to be filed at the company`s registry. Companies listed on a stock exchange are also required to report at more frequent intervals .

Exam Probability: **High**

23. *Answer choices:*

(see index for correct answer)

- a. imperative
- b. Character
- c. corporate values
- d. hierarchical perspective

Guidance: level 1

:: Business ethics ::

In accounting and in most Schools of economic thought, __________ is a rational and unbiased estimate of the potential market price of a good, service, or asset. It takes into account such objectivity factors as.

Exam Probability: **High**

24. *Answer choices:*

(see index for correct answer)

- a. Fair value
- b. Precarity
- c. Conspiracy of Fools
- d. Corporate behaviour

Guidance: level 1

:: Basel II ::

All businesses take risks based on two factors: the probability an adverse circumstance will come about and the cost of such adverse circumstance.Risk management is the study of how to control risks and balance the possibility of gains.

Exam Probability: **Low**

25. *Answer choices:*

(see index for correct answer)

- a. Credit risk
- b. Legal risk
- c. Advanced IRB
- d. Foundation IRB

Guidance: level 1

:: Investment ::

In finance, the benefit from an _________ is called a return. The return may consist of a gain realised from the sale of property or an _________, unrealised capital appreciation , or _________ income such as dividends, interest, rental income etc., or a combination of capital gain and income. The return may also include currency gains or losses due to changes in foreign currency exchange rates.

Exam Probability: **Low**

26. *Answer choices:*

(see index for correct answer)

- a. MarketSmith
- b. Greater fool
- c. Investment
- d. Investing online

Guidance: level 1

:: Commerce ::

A __________ , is a document acknowledging that a person has received money or property in payment following a sale or other transfer of goods or provision of a service. All __________ s must have the date of purchase on them. If the recipient of the payment is legally required to collect sales tax or VAT from the customer, the amount would be added to the __________ and the collection would be deemed to have been on behalf of the relevant tax authority. In many countries, a retailer is required to include the sales tax or VAT in the displayed price of goods sold, from which the tax amount would be calculated at point of sale and remitted to the tax authorities in due course. Similarly, amounts may be deducted from amounts payable, as in the case of wage withholding taxes. On the other hand, tips or other gratuities given by a customer, for example in a restaurant, would not form part of the payment amount or appear on the __________ .

Exam Probability: **Medium**

27. *Answer choices:*

(see index for correct answer)

- a. Kiosk
- b. Country commercial guides
- c. Gumball machine
- d. Receipt

Guidance: level 1

:: Income ::

__________ is a ratio between the net profit and cost of investment resulting from an investment of some resources. A high ROI means the investment`s gains favorably to its cost. As a performance measure, ROI is used to evaluate the efficiency of an investment or to compare the efficiencies of several different investments. In purely economic terms, it is one way of relating profits to capital invested. __________ is a performance measure used by businesses to identify the efficiency of an investment or number of different investments.

Exam Probability: **Low**

28. *Answer choices:*

(see index for correct answer)

- a. IRD asset
- b. Mandatory tipping
- c. Return on investment
- d. Net national income

Guidance: level 1

:: ::

_________ is a political and social philosophy promoting traditional social institutions in the context of culture and civilization. The central tenets of _________ include tradition, human imperfection, organic society, hierarchy, authority, and property rights. Conservatives seek to preserve a range of institutions such as religion, parliamentary government, and property rights, with the aim of emphasizing social stability and continuity. The more traditional elements—reactionaries—oppose modernism and seek a return to "the way things were".

Exam Probability: **Medium**

29. *Answer choices:*

(see index for correct answer)

- a. interpersonal communication
- b. open system
- c. functional perspective
- d. Conservatism

Guidance: level 1

:: Commerce ::

Continuation of an entity as a _________ is presumed as the basis for financial reporting unless and until the entity`s liquidation becomes imminent. Preparation of financial statements under this presumption is commonly referred to as the _________ basis of accounting. If and when an entity`s liquidation becomes imminent, financial statements are prepared under the liquidation basis of accounting .

Exam Probability: **Medium**

30. *Answer choices:*

(see index for correct answer)

- a. TradeCard
- b. Social dumping
- c. Fixed price
- d. Custom house

Guidance: level 1

:: Management accounting ::

In economics, __________ s, indirect costs or overheads are business expenses that are not dependent on the level of goods or services produced by the business. They tend to be time-related, such as interest or rents being paid per month, and are often referred to as overhead costs. This is in contrast to variable costs, which are volume-related and unknown at the beginning of the accounting year. For a simple example, such as a bakery, the monthly rent for the baking facilities, and the monthly payments for the security system and basic phone line are __________ s, as they do not change according to how much bread the bakery produces and sells. On the other hand, the wage costs of the bakery are variable, as the bakery will have to hire more workers if the production of bread increases. Economists reckon __________ as a entry barrier for new entrepreneurs.

Exam Probability: **Low**

31. *Answer choices:*

(see index for correct answer)

- a. Net present value
- b. Grenzplankostenrechnung
- c. Total benefits of ownership
- d. Fixed cost

Guidance: level 1

:: Elementary geometry ::

The _________ is the front of an animal`s head that features three of the head`s sense organs, the eyes, nose, and mouth, and through which animals express many of their emotions. The _________ is crucial for human identity, and damage such as scarring or developmental deformities affects the psyche adversely.

Exam Probability: **Medium**

32. *Answer choices:*

(see index for correct answer)

- a. Hypotenuse
- b. Face
- c. Golden rectangle
- d. Parallel postulate

Guidance: level 1

:: Options (finance) ::

In finance, a put or _________ is a stock market device which gives the owner the right, but not the obligation, to sell an asset , at a specified price , by a predetermined date to a given party . The purchase of a _________ is interpreted as a negative sentiment about the future value of theunderlying stock. The term "put" comes from the fact that the owner has the right to "put up for sale" the stock or index.

Exam Probability: **High**

33. *Answer choices:*

(see index for correct answer)

- a. Naked put
- b. Rainbow option
- c. Mountain range
- d. Real options valuation

Guidance: level 1

:: Financial risk ::

The _________ on a financial investment is the expected value of its return . It is a measure of the center of the distribution of the random variable that is the return.

Exam Probability: **Low**

34. *Answer choices:*

(see index for correct answer)

- a. Expected return
- b. Diversification
- c. Discounted maximum loss
- d. Consistent pricing process

Guidance: level 1

:: Bonds (finance) ::

An _________ is a legal contract that reflects or covers a debt or purchase obligation. It specifically refers to two types of practices: in historical usage, an _________ d servant status, and in modern usage, it is an instrument used for commercial debt or real estate transaction.

Exam Probability: **Low**

35. *Answer choices:*

(see index for correct answer)

- a. Perpetual bond
- b. Kimchi bond
- c. LECOP
- d. Indenture

Guidance: level 1

:: Taxation ::

In a tax system, the _________ is the ratio at which a business or person is taxed. There are several methods used to present a _________ : statutory, average, marginal, and effective. These rates can also be presented using different definitions applied to a tax base: inclusive and exclusive.

Exam Probability: **Medium**

36. *Answer choices:*

(see index for correct answer)

- a. Tax cap
- b. Tax rate
- c. Indirect tax
- d. Tax investigation

Guidance: level 1

:: Asset ::

In accounting, a _________ is any asset which can reasonably be expected to be sold, consumed, or exhausted through the normal operations of a business within the current fiscal year or operating cycle . Typical _________ s include cash, cash equivalents, short-term investments , accounts receivable, stock inventory, supplies, and the portion of prepaid liabilities which will be paid within a year.In simple words, assets which are held for a short period are known as _________ s. Such assets are expected to be realised in cash or consumed during the normal operating cycle of the business.

Exam Probability: **Medium**

37. *Answer choices:*

(see index for correct answer)

- a. Current asset
- b. Fixed asset

Guidance: level 1

:: ::

A _________ is the process of presenting a topic to an audience. It is typically a demonstration, introduction, lecture, or speech meant to inform, persuade, inspire, motivate, or to build good will or to present a new idea or product. The term can also be used for a formal or ritualized introduction or offering, as with the _________ of a debutante. _________ s in certain formats are also known as keynote address.

Exam Probability: **Low**

38. *Answer choices:*

(see index for correct answer)

- a. deep-level diversity
- b. hierarchical perspective
- c. corporate values
- d. levels of analysis

Guidance: level 1

:: Financial regulatory authorities of the United States ::

The __________ is the revenue service of the United States federal government. The government agency is a bureau of the Department of the Treasury, and is under the immediate direction of the Commissioner of Internal Revenue, who is appointed to a five-year term by the President of the United States. The IRS is responsible for collecting taxes and administering the Internal Revenue Code, the main body of federal statutory tax law of the United States. The duties of the IRS include providing tax assistance to taxpayers and pursuing and resolving instances of erroneous or fraudulent tax filings. The IRS has also overseen various benefits programs, and enforces portions of the Affordable Care Act.

Exam Probability: **Low**

39. *Answer choices:*

(see index for correct answer)

- a. Federal Reserve Board
- b. Commodity Futures Trading Commission
- c. Consumer Financial Protection Bureau
- d. Federal Deposit Insurance Corporation

Guidance: level 1

:: Financial accounting ::

_________ refers to any one of several methods by which a company, for `financial accounting` or tax purposes, depreciates a fixed asset in such a way that the amount of depreciation taken each year is higher during the earlier years of an asset's life. For financial accounting purposes, _________ is expected to be much more productive during its early years, so that depreciation expense will more accurately represent how much of an asset's usefulness is being used up each year. For tax purposes, _________ provides a way of deferring corporate income taxes by reducing taxable income in current years, in exchange for increased taxable income in future years. This is a valuable tax incentive that encourages businesses to purchase new assets.

Exam Probability: **Medium**

40. *Answer choices:*

(see index for correct answer)

- a. Asset swap
- b. Accelerated depreciation
- c. Working capital
- d. Book value

Guidance: level 1

:: Funds ::

_________ value is the value of an entity`s assets minus the value of its liabilities, often in relation to open-end or mutual funds, since shares of such funds registered with the U.S. Securities and Exchange Commission are redeemed at their _________ value. It is also a key figure with regard to hedge funds and venture capital funds when calculating the value of the underlying investments in these funds by investors. This may also be the same as the book value or the equity value of a business. _________ value may represent the value of the total equity, or it may be divided by the number of shares outstanding held by investors, thereby representing the _________ value per share.

Exam Probability: **Low**

41. *Answer choices:*

(see index for correct answer)

- a. Icapital.biz Berhad
- b. Glacier National Park Fund
- c. China-Africa Development Fund
- d. Film Musicians Secondary Markets Fund

Guidance: level 1

:: Costs ::

In microeconomic theory, the _________ , or alternative cost, of making a particular choice is the value of the most valuable choice out of those that were not taken. In other words, opportunity that will require sacrifices.

Exam Probability: **Low**

42. *Answer choices:*

(see index for correct answer)

- a. Further processing cost
- b. Manufacturing cost
- c. Prospective costs
- d. Joint cost

Guidance: level 1

:: Financial markets ::

A _________ is a market in which people trade financial securities and derivatives such as futures and options at low transaction costs. Securities include stocks and bonds, and precious metals.

Exam Probability: **High**

43. *Answer choices:*

(see index for correct answer)

- a. Financial market
- b. Market depth
- c. Global Industry Classification Standard
- d. Options Price Reporting Authority

Guidance: level 1

:: Financial risk ::

_________ is any of various types of risk associated with financing, including financial transactions that include company loans in risk of default. Often it is understood to include only downside risk, meaning the potential for financial loss and uncertainty about its extent.

Exam Probability: **Low**

44. *Answer choices:*

(see index for correct answer)

- a. Age at risk
- b. Financial risk
- c. Operational risk management
- d. Interest rate risk

Guidance: level 1

:: Inventory ::

Costs are associated with particular goods using one of the several formulas, including specific identification, first-in first-out , or average cost. Costs include all costs of purchase, costs of conversion and other costs that are incurred in bringing the inventories to their present location and condition. Costs of goods made by the businesses include material, labor, and allocated overhead. The costs of those goods which are not yet sold are deferred as costs of inventory until the inventory is sold or written down in value.

Exam Probability: **Medium**

45. *Answer choices:*

(see index for correct answer)

- a. Perpetual inventory
- b. Stock obsolescence
- c. Cost of goods sold
- d. Stock demands

Guidance: level 1

:: Financial ratios ::

The _________ shows the percentage of how profitable a company`s assets are in generating revenue.

Exam Probability: **Low**

46. *Answer choices:*

(see index for correct answer)

- a. Days in inventory
- b. Information ratio
- c. Return on assets
- d. Dividend payout ratio

Guidance: level 1

:: Contract law ::

A _________ is a legally-binding agreement which recognises and governs the rights and duties of the parties to the agreement. A _________ is legally enforceable because it meets the requirements and approval of the law. An agreement typically involves the exchange of goods, services, money, or promises of any of those. In the event of breach of _________, the law awards the injured party access to legal remedies such as damages and cancellation.

Exam Probability: **High**

47. *Answer choices:*

(see index for correct answer)

- a. Nudum pactum
- b. Contract

- c. Material transfer agreement
- d. Essentialia negotii

Guidance: level 1

:: ::

A _________ , in the word`s original meaning, is a sheet of paper on which one performs work. They come in many forms, most commonly associated with children`s school work assignments, tax forms, and accounting or other business environments. Software is increasingly taking over the paper-based _________ .

Exam Probability: **Low**

48. *Answer choices:*

(see index for correct answer)

- a. levels of analysis
- b. open system
- c. information systems assessment
- d. similarity-attraction theory

Guidance: level 1

:: Marketing ::

A __________ is something that is necessary for an organism to live a healthy life. __________ s are distinguished from wants in that, in the case of a __________ , a deficiency causes a clear adverse outcome: a dysfunction or death. In other words, a __________ is something required for a safe, stable and healthy life while a want is a desire, wish or aspiration. When __________ s or wants are backed by purchasing power, they have the potential to become economic demands.

Exam Probability: **High**

49. *Answer choices:*

(see index for correct answer)

- a. Product literature
- b. Existing visitor optimisation
- c. Hakan Okay
- d. Marketing spending

Guidance: level 1

:: Financial accounting ::

__________ is the value of all the non-financial and financial assets owned by an institutional unit or sector minus the value of all its outstanding liabilities. Since financial assets minus outstanding liabilities equal net financial assets, __________ can also be conveniently expressed as non-financial assets plus net financial assets. __________ can apply to companies, individuals, governments or economic sectors such as the sector of financial corporations or to entire countries.

Exam Probability: **High**

50. *Answer choices:*

(see index for correct answer)

- a. Controlling interest
- b. Money measurement
- c. Intangibles
- d. Net worth

Guidance: level 1

:: Capital gains taxes ::

A __________ refers to profit that results from a sale of a capital asset, such as stock, bond or real estate, where the sale price exceeds the purchase price. The gain is the difference between a higher selling price and a lower purchase price. Conversely, a capital loss arises if the proceeds from the sale of a capital asset are less than the purchase price.

Exam Probability: **Medium**

51. *Answer choices:*

(see index for correct answer)

- a. Capital gains tax
- b. Capital gain

- c. Capital Cost Allowance

Guidance: level 1

:: ::

In financial markets, a share is a unit used as mutual funds, limited partnerships, and real estate investment trusts. The owner of _________ in the corporation/company is a shareholder of the corporation. A share is an indivisible unit of capital, expressing the ownership relationship between the company and the shareholder. The denominated value of a share is its face value, and the total of the face value of issued _________ represent the capital of a company, which may not reflect the market value of those _________.

Exam Probability: **Low**

52. *Answer choices:*

(see index for correct answer)

- a. Shares
- b. levels of analysis
- c. interpersonal communication
- d. Character

Guidance: level 1

:: ::

_________ is the administration of an organization, whether it is a business, a not-for-profit organization, or government body. _________ includes the activities of setting the strategy of an organization and coordinating the efforts of its employees to accomplish its objectives through the application of available resources, such as financial, natural, technological, and human resources. The term " _________ " may also refer to those people who manage an organization.

Exam Probability: **Low**

53. *Answer choices:*

(see index for correct answer)

- a. deep-level diversity
- b. process perspective
- c. co-culture
- d. Management

Guidance: level 1

:: Fixed income market ::

In finance, the _________ is a curve showing several yields or interest rates across different contract lengths for a similar debt contract. The curve shows the relation between the interest rate and the time to maturity, known as the "term", of the debt for a given borrower in a given currency. For example, the U.S. dollar interest rates paid on U.S. Treasury securities for various maturities are closely watched by many traders, and are commonly plotted on a graph such as the one on the right which is informally called "the _________ ". More formal mathematical descriptions of this relation are often called the term structure of interest rates.

Exam Probability: **High**

54. *Answer choices:*

(see index for correct answer)

- a. Yield curve
- b. Inter-dealer broker
- c. Bond market
- d. Bond Exchange of South Africa

Guidance: level 1

:: Financial ratios ::

The _________ is a liquidity ratio that measures whether a firm has enough resources to meet its short-term obligations. It compares a firm's current assets to its current liabilities, and is expressed as follows.

Exam Probability: **Medium**

55. *Answer choices:*

(see index for correct answer)

- a. Current ratio
- b. PB ratio
- c. Cost accrual ratio
- d. Earnings yield

Guidance: level 1

:: Generally Accepted Accounting Principles ::

_________ , or non-current liabilities, are liabilities that are due beyond a year or the normal operation period of the company. The normal operation period is the amount of time it takes for a company to turn inventory into cash. On a classified balance sheet, liabilities are separated between current and _________ to help users assess the company`s financial standing in short-term and long-term periods. _________ give users more information about the long-term prosperity of the company, while current liabilities inform the user of debt that the company owes in the current period. On a balance sheet, accounts are listed in order of liquidity, so _________ come after current liabilities. In addition, the specific long-term liability accounts are listed on the balance sheet in order of liquidity. Therefore, an account due within eighteen months would be listed before an account due within twenty-four months. Examples of _________ are bonds payable, long-term loans, capital leases, pension liabilities, post-retirement healthcare liabilities, deferred compensation, deferred revenues, deferred income taxes, and derivative liabilities.

Exam Probability: **Medium**

56. *Answer choices:*

(see index for correct answer)

- a. Earnings before interest and taxes
- b. Shares outstanding
- c. Liability
- d. Long-term liabilities

Guidance: level 1

:: Finance ::

The _________ of a corporation is the accumulated net income of the corporation that is retained by the corporation at a particular point of time, such as at the end of the reporting period. At the end of that period, the net income at that point is transferred from the Profit and Loss Account to the _________ account. If the balance of the _________ account is negative it may be called accumulated losses, retained losses or accumulated deficit, or similar terminology.

Exam Probability: **Low**

57. *Answer choices:*

(see index for correct answer)

- a. Retained earnings

- b. Dedicated Portfolio Theory
- c. Periodic deposit
- d. Value investing

Guidance: level 1

:: Accounting ::

_________ is a process of providing relief to shared service organization`s cost centers that provide a product or service. In turn, the associated expense is assigned to internal clients` cost centers that consume the products and services. For example, the CIO may provide all IT services within the company and assign the costs back to the business units that consume each offering.

Exam Probability: **Medium**

58. *Answer choices:*

(see index for correct answer)

- a. Legal cashier
- b. Cost allocation
- c. ACSOI
- d. Professional services networks

Guidance: level 1

:: ::

__________ is the production of products for use or sale using labour and machines, tools, chemical and biological processing, or formulation. The term may refer to a range of human activity, from handicraft to high tech, but is most commonly applied to industrial design, in which raw materials are transformed into finished goods on a large scale. Such finished goods may be sold to other manufacturers for the production of other, more complex products, such as aircraft, household appliances, furniture, sports equipment or automobiles, or sold to wholesalers, who in turn sell them to retailers, who then sell them to end users and consumers.

Exam Probability: **Low**

59. *Answer choices:*

(see index for correct answer)

- a. Manufacturing
- b. Character
- c. levels of analysis
- d. functional perspective

Guidance: level 1

Human resource management

Human resource (HR) management is the strategic approach to the effective management of organization workers so that they help the business gain a competitive advantage. It is designed to maximize employee performance in service of an employer's strategic objectives. HR is primarily concerned with the management of people within organizations, focusing on policies and on systems. HR departments are responsible for overseeing employee-benefits design, employee recruitment, training and development, performance appraisal, and rewarding (e.g., managing pay and benefit systems). HR also concerns itself with organizational change and industrial relations, that is, the balancing of organizational practices with requirements arising from collective bargaining and from governmental laws.

:: Employment ::

_________ is measuring the output of a particular business process or procedure, then modifying the process or procedure to increase the output, increase efficiency, or increase the effectiveness of the process or procedure. _________ can be applied to either individual performance such as an athlete or organizational performance such as a racing team or a commercial business.

Exam Probability: **High**

1. *Answer choices:*

(see index for correct answer)

- a. Cyberloafing
- b. Contingent employment
- c. Academic job market
- d. Performance improvement

Guidance: level 1

:: Employment compensation ::

A __________ is a type of employee benefit plan offered in the United States pursuant to Section 125 of the Internal Revenue Code. Its name comes from the earliest such plans that allowed employees to choose between different types of benefits, similar to the ability of a customer to choose among available items in a cafeteria. Qualified __________ s are excluded from gross income. To qualify, a __________ must allow employees to choose from two or more benefits consisting of cash or qualified benefit plans. The Internal Revenue Code explicitly excludes deferred compensation plans from qualifying as a __________ subject to a gross income exemption. Section 125 also provides two exceptions.

Exam Probability: **Low**

2. *Answer choices:*

(see index for correct answer)

- a. IDS Pay Report
- b. Cafeteria plan
- c. Take-home vehicle
- d. Equal Pay Act 1970

Guidance: level 1

:: Employment compensation ::

Generally PTO hours cover everything from planned vacations to sick days, and are becoming more prevalent in the field of human resource management. Unlike more traditional leave plans, PTO plans don`t distinguish employee absences from personal days, vacation days, or sick days. Upon employment, the company determines how many PTO hours will be allotted per year and a "rollover" policy. Some companies let PTO hours accumulate for only a year, and unused hours disappear at year-end. Some PTO plans may also accommodate unexpected or unforeseeable circumstances such as jury duty, military duty, and bereavement leave. PTO bank plans typically do not include short-term or long-term disability leave, workers compensation, family and medical leave, sabbatical, or community service leave.

Exam Probability: **High**

3. *Answer choices:*

(see index for correct answer)

- a. Duvet day
- b. Scanlon plan
- c. Equal Pay Act of 1963
- d. Paid time off

Guidance: level 1

:: United States federal labor legislation ::

The _________ of 1967 is a US labor law that forbids employment discrimination against anyone at least 40 years of age in the United States . In 1967, the bill was signed into law by President Lyndon B. Johnson. The ADEA prevents age discrimination and provides equal employment opportunity under conditions that were not explicitly covered in Title VII of the Civil Rights Act of 1964. It also applies to the standards for pensions and benefits provided by employers, and requires that information concerning the needs of older workers be provided to the general public.

Exam Probability: **Low**

4. *Answer choices:*

(see index for correct answer)

- a. National Whistleblowers Center
- b. Adamson Act
- c. Anti-Pinkerton Act
- d. Federal Emergency Relief Administration

Guidance: level 1

:: ::

The U.S. _________ is a federal agency that administers and enforces civil rights laws against workplace discrimination. The EEOC investigates discrimination complaints based on an individual`s race, children, national origin, religion, sex, age, disability, sexual orientation, gender identity, genetic information, and retaliation for reporting, participating in, and/or opposing a discriminatory practice.

Exam Probability: **High**

5. *Answer choices:*

(see index for correct answer)

- a. empathy
- b. Equal Employment Opportunity Commission
- c. surface-level diversity
- d. functional perspective

Guidance: level 1

:: Labour relations ::

__________ is a form of protest in which people congregate outside a place of work or location where an event is taking place. Often, this is done in an attempt to dissuade others from going in , but it can also be done to draw public attention to a cause. Picketers normally endeavor to be non-violent. It can have a number of aims, but is generally to put pressure on the party targeted to meet particular demands or cease operations. This pressure is achieved by harming the business through loss of customers and negative publicity, or by discouraging or preventing workers or customers from entering the site and thereby preventing the business from operating normally.

Exam Probability: **Medium**

6. *Answer choices:*

(see index for correct answer)

- a. Broad left
- b. Global union federation
- c. Union shop
- d. Picketing

Guidance: level 1

:: United States employment discrimination case law ::

__________ , 490 U.S. 228 , was an important decision by the United States Supreme Court on the issues of prescriptive sex discrimination and employer liability for sex discrimination. The employee, Ann Hopkins, sued her former employer, the accounting firm Price Waterhouse. She argued that the firm denied her partnership because she didn`t fit the partners` idea of what a female employee should look like and act like. The employer failed to prove that it would have denied her partnership anyway, and the Court held that constituted sex discrimination under Title VII of the Civil Rights Act of 1964. The significance of the Supreme Court`s ruling was twofold. First, it established that gender stereotyping is actionable as sex discrimination. Second, it established the mixed-motive framework that enables employees to prove discrimination when other, lawful reasons for the adverse employment action exist alongside discriminatory motivations or reasons.

Exam Probability: **Low**

7. *Answer choices:*

(see index for correct answer)

- a. Bundy v. Jackson
- b. Price Waterhouse v. Hopkins

- c. Ricci v. DeStefano
- d. Hosanna-Tabor Evangelical Lutheran Church and School v. Equal Employment Opportunity Commission

Guidance: level 1

:: United States employment discrimination case law ::

_________ , 557 U.S. 557 , is a US labor law case of the United States Supreme Court on unlawful discrimination through disparate impact under the Civil Rights Act of 1964.

Exam Probability: **Low**

8. *Answer choices:*

(see index for correct answer)

- a. Gross v. FBL Financial Services, Inc.
- b. Glenn v. Brumby
- c. McDonnell Douglas Corp. v. Green
- d. Shyamala Rajender v. University of Minnesota

Guidance: level 1

:: ::

A trade union is an association of workers forming a legal unit or legal personhood, usually called a "bargaining unit", which acts as bargaining agent and legal representative for a unit of employees in all matters of law or right arising from or in the administration of a collective agreement. Labour unions typically fund the formal organisation, head office, and legal team functions of the labour union through regular fees or union dues. The delegate staff of the labour union representation in the workforce are made up of workplace volunteers who are appointed by members in democratic elections.

Exam Probability: **Medium**

9. *Answer choices:*

(see index for correct answer)

- a. Labor union
- b. hierarchical perspective
- c. empathy
- d. deep-level diversity

Guidance: level 1

:: Human resource management ::

__________ is a method of job analysis that was developed by the Employment and Training Administration of the United States Department of Labor. FJA produces standardized occupational information specific to the performance of the work and the performer.

Exam Probability: **Medium**

10. *Answer choices:*

(see index for correct answer)

- a. Appreciative inquiry
- b. Co-determination
- c. Functional job analysis
- d. Attendance management

Guidance: level 1

:: Business ethics ::

A _________ is a person who exposes any kind of information or activity that is deemed illegal, unethical, or not correct within an organization that is either private or public. The information of alleged wrongdoing can be classified in many ways: violation of company policy/rules, law, regulation, or threat to public interest/national security, as well as fraud, and corruption. Those who become _________ s can choose to bring information or allegations to surface either internally or externally. Internally, a _________ can bring his/her accusations to the attention of other people within the accused organization such as an immediate supervisor. Externally, a _________ can bring allegations to light by contacting a third party outside of an accused organization such as the media, government, law enforcement, or those who are concerned. _________ s, however, take the risk of facing stiff reprisal and retaliation from those who are accused or alleged of wrongdoing.

Exam Probability: **Medium**

11. *Answer choices:*

(see index for correct answer)

- a. Rules of the garage
- b. Whistleblower
- c. Institute of Business Ethics
- d. Smart casual

Guidance: level 1

:: Offshoring ::

A _________ is the temporary suspension or permanent termination of employment of an employee or, more commonly, a group of employees for business reasons, such as personnel management or downsizing an organization. Originally, _________ referred exclusively to a temporary interruption in work, or employment but this has evolved to a permanent elimination of a position in both British and US English, requiring the addition of "temporary" to specify the original meaning of the word. A _________ is not to be confused with wrongful termination. Laid off workers or displaced workers are workers who have lost or left their jobs because their employer has closed or moved, there was insufficient work for them to do, or their position or shift was abolished . Downsizing in a company is defined to involve the reduction of employees in a workforce. Downsizing in companies became a popular practice in the 1980s and early 1990s as it was seen as a way to deliver better shareholder value as it helps to reduce the costs of employers . Indeed, recent research on downsizing in the U.S., UK, and Japan suggests that downsizing is being regarded by management as one of the preferred routes to help declining organizations, cutting unnecessary costs, and improve organizational performance. Usually a _________ occurs as a cost cutting measure.

Exam Probability: **Medium**

12. *Answer choices:*

(see index for correct answer)

- a. Offshore custom software development
- b. Offshore outsourcing
- c. Global labor arbitrage
- d. Avasant

Guidance: level 1

:: Sexual harassment in the United States ::

In law, a _________ , reasonable man, or the man on the Clapham omnibus is a hypothetical person of legal fiction crafted by the courts and communicated through case law and jury instructions.

Exam Probability: **Low**

13. *Answer choices:*

(see index for correct answer)

- a. Reasonable person
- b. Fitzgerald v. Barnstable School Committee
- c. Sandy Gallin
- d. Hostile Advances

Guidance: level 1

:: Asset ::

In financial accounting, an _________ is any resource owned by the business. Anything tangible or intangible that can be owned or controlled to produce value and that is held by a company to produce positive economic value is an _________ . Simply stated, _________ s represent value of ownership that can be converted into cash . The balance sheet of a firm records the monetary value of the _________ s owned by that firm. It covers money and other valuables belonging to an individual or to a business.

Exam Probability: **High**

14. *Answer choices:*

(see index for correct answer)

- a. Fixed asset
- b. Current asset

Guidance: level 1

:: Employment compensation ::

In government contracting, a _________ is defined as the hourly wage, usual benefits and overtime, paid to the majority of workers, laborers, and mechanics within a particular area. This is usually the union wage.

Exam Probability: **Medium**

15. *Answer choices:*

(see index for correct answer)

- a. Prevailing wage
- b. Uninsured employer
- c. Open compensation plan
- d. Personal income

Guidance: level 1

:: ::

_________, also known as alcohol use disorder , is a broad term for any drinking of alcohol that results in mental or physical health problems. The disorder was previously divided into two types: alcohol abuse and alcohol dependence. In a medical context, _________ is said to exist when two or more of the following conditions are present: a person drinks large amounts of alcohol over a long time period, has difficulty cutting down, acquiring and drinking alcohol takes up a great deal of time, alcohol is strongly desired, usage results in not fulfilling responsibilities, usage results in social problems, usage results in health problems, usage results in risky situations, withdrawal occurs when stopping, and alcohol tolerance has occurred with use. Risky situations include drinking and driving or having unsafe sex, among other things. Alcohol use can affect all parts of the body, but it particularly affects the brain, heart, liver, pancreas and immune system. This can result in mental illness, Wernicke–Korsakoff syndrome, irregular heartbeat, an impaired immune response, liver cirrhosis and increased cancer risk, among other diseases. Drinking during pregnancy can cause damage to the baby resulting in fetal alcohol spectrum disorders. Women are generally more sensitive than men to the harmful physical and mental effects of alcohol.

Exam Probability: **Low**

16. *Answer choices:*

(see index for correct answer)

- a. Alcoholism
- b. Character
- c. empathy
- d. open system

Guidance: level 1

:: Design of experiments ::

In the design of experiments, treatments are applied to experimental units in the treatment group. In comparative experiments, members of the complementary group, the _________ , receive either no treatment or a standard treatment.

Exam Probability: **Medium**

17. *Answer choices:*

(see index for correct answer)

- a. Spectrum bias
- b. Provocation test
- c. Resentful demoralization
- d. Control group

Guidance: level 1

:: Sociological theories ::

A _________ is a systematic process for determining and addressing needs, or "gaps" between current conditions and desired conditions or "wants". The discrepancy between the current condition and wanted condition must be measured to appropriately identify the need. The need can be a desire to improve current performance or to correct a deficiency.

Exam Probability: **High**

18. *Answer choices:*

(see index for correct answer)

- a. Needs assessment
- b. resource mobilization
- c. comfort zone
- d. Compliance gaining

Guidance: level 1

:: Employment compensation ::

_________ is a notional derivative of a Health Reimbursement Arrangement , a type of US employer-funded health benefit plan that reimburses employees for out-of-pocket medical expenses and, in limited cases, to pay for health insurance plan premiums.

Exam Probability: **High**

19. *Answer choices:*

(see index for correct answer)

- a. New York Disability Benefits Law
- b. Golden boot compensation
- c. Health Reimbursement Account
- d. Employee stock purchase plan

Guidance: level 1

:: Employment compensation ::

Employee stock ownership, or employee share ownership, is an ownership interest in a company held by the company`s workforce. The ownership interest may be facilitated by the company as part of employees` remuneration or incentive compensation for work performed, or the company itself may be employee owned.

Exam Probability: **High**

20. *Answer choices:*

(see index for correct answer)

- a. Pay Bands
- b. Golden parachute
- c. Employee stock ownership plan
- d. Merit pay

Guidance: level 1

:: Social psychology ::

In social psychology, _________ is the phenomenon of a person exerting less effort to achieve a goal when he or she works in a group than when working alone. This is seen as one of the main reasons groups are sometimes less productive than the combined performance of their members working as individuals, but should be distinguished from the accidental coordination problems that groups sometimes experience.

Exam Probability: **High**

21. *Answer choices:*

(see index for correct answer)

- a. coercive persuasion
- b. objectification
- c. sociometer
- d. Social character

Guidance: level 1

:: Trade unions in the United States ::

_________ is a labor union in the United States and Canada with roughly 300,000 active members. The union's members work predominantly in the hotel, food service, laundry, warehouse, and casino gaming industries. The union was formed in 2004 by the merger of Union of Needletrades, Industrial, and Textile Employees and Hotel Employees and Restaurant Employees Union .

Exam Probability: **Low**

22. *Answer choices:*

(see index for correct answer)

- a. Allied Pilots Association
- b. Pennsylvania Association of Staff Nurses and Allied Professionals
- c. UNITE HERE
- d. National Border Patrol Council

Guidance: level 1

:: ::

A _________ contract is a form of employment that carries fewer hours per week than a full-time job. They work in shifts. The shifts are often rotational. Workers are considered to be _________ if they commonly work fewer than 30 hours per week. According to the International Labour Organization, the number of _________ workers has increased from one-fourth to a half in the past 20 years in most developed countries, excluding the United States. There are many reasons for working _________, including the desire to do so, having one`s hours cut back by an employer and being unable to find a full-time job. The International Labour Organisation Convention 175 requires that _________ workers be treated no less favourably than full-time workers.

Exam Probability: **Medium**

23. *Answer choices:*

(see index for correct answer)

- a. surface-level diversity
- b. cultural
- c. Sarbanes-Oxley act of 2002
- d. functional perspective

Guidance: level 1

:: Learning methods ::

_________ is an approach to problem solving. It involves taking action and reflecting upon the results. This helps improve the problem-solving process as well as simplify the solutions developed by the team.

Exam Probability: **Medium**

24. *Answer choices:*

(see index for correct answer)

- a. Audience response system
- b. Double-loop learning
- c. double loop learning
- d. Action learning

Guidance: level 1

:: Survey methodology ::

An _________ is a conversation where questions are asked and answers are given. In common parlance, the word " _________ " refers to a one-on-one conversation between an _________ er and an _________ ee. The _________ er asks questions to which the _________ ee responds, usually so information may be transferred from _________ ee to _________ er . Sometimes, information can be transferred in both directions. It is a communication, unlike a speech, which produces a one-way flow of information.

Exam Probability: **Medium**

25. *Answer choices:*

(see index for correct answer)

- a. Inverse probability weighting
- b. Census
- c. Group concept mapping
- d. Computer-assisted survey information collection

Guidance: level 1

:: Human resource management ::

_________ is a sub-discipline of human resources, focused on employee _________ policy-making. While _________ are tangible, there are intangible rewards such as recognition, work-life and development. Combined, these are referred to as total rewards . The term " _________ " refers to the discipline as well as the rewards themselves.

Exam Probability: **Medium**

26. *Answer choices:*

(see index for correct answer)

- a. Job enlargement
- b. Senior management
- c. Compensation and benefits
- d. Workforce planning

Guidance: level 1

:: Project management ::

Some scenarios associate "this kind of planning" with learning "life skills". _________ s are necessary, or at least useful, in situations where individuals need to know what time they must be at a specific location to receive a specific service, and where people need to accomplish a set of goals within a set time period.

Exam Probability: **Medium**

27. *Answer choices:*

(see index for correct answer)

- a. Concept note
- b. Case competition

- c. Schedule
- d. Mandated lead arranger

Guidance: level 1

:: ::

On December 31, 2016, Xerox separated its business process service operations into a new publicly traded company, Conduent. Xerox focuses on its document technology and document outsourcing business, and continues to trade on the NYSE. On January 31, 2018, Xerox announced that it would sell a controlling stake to Fujifilm, which has maintained a joint venture in the Asia-Pacific region known as Fuji Xerox.

Exam Probability: **Low**

28. *Answer choices:*

(see index for correct answer)

- a. Xerox Corporation
- b. functional perspective
- c. similarity-attraction theory
- d. co-culture

Guidance: level 1

:: Behavior ::

__________ refers to behavior-change procedures that were employed during the 1970s and early 1980s. Based on methodological behaviorism, overt behavior was modified with presumed consequences, including artificial positive and negative reinforcement contingencies to increase desirable behavior, or administering positive and negative punishment and/or extinction to reduce problematic behavior. For the treatment of phobias, habituation and punishment were the basic principles used in flooding, a subcategory of desensitization.

Exam Probability: **Medium**

29. *Answer choices:*

(see index for correct answer)

- a. theory of reasoned action
- b. theory of planned behavior

Guidance: level 1

:: ::

In business strategy, _________ is establishing a competitive advantage by having the lowest cost of operation in the industry. _________ is often driven by company efficiency, size, scale, scope and cumulative experience .A _________ strategy aims to exploit scale of production, well-defined scope and other economies , producing highly standardized products, using advanced technology.In recent years, more and more companies have chosen a strategic mix to achieve market leadership. These patterns consist of simultaneous _________ , superior customer service and product leadership. Walmart has succeeded across the world due to its _________ strategy. The company has cut down on exesses at every point of production and thus are able to provide the consumers with quality products at low prices.

Exam Probability: **Medium**

30. *Answer choices:*

(see index for correct answer)

- a. cultural
- b. Cost leadership
- c. personal values
- d. Sarbanes-Oxley act of 2002

Guidance: level 1

:: Business process ::

Outsourcing is an agreement in which one company hires another company to be responsible for a planned or existing activity that is or could be done internally,and sometimes involves transferring employees and assets from one firm to another.

Exam Probability: **High**

31. *Answer choices:*

(see index for correct answer)

- a. Feasibility study
- b. Order processing
- c. Business process outsourcing
- d. Business process reengineering

Guidance: level 1

:: Business ::

_________ is a trade policy that does not restrict imports or exports; it can also be understood as the free market idea applied to international trade. In government, _________ is predominantly advocated by political parties that hold liberal economic positions while economically left-wing and nationalist political parties generally support protectionism, the opposite of _________ .

Exam Probability: **Low**

32. *Answer choices:*

(see index for correct answer)

- a. Counter trade
- b. Staff and line
- c. Door-to-door
- d. Free Trade

Guidance: level 1

:: ::

A __________ seeks to further a particular profession, the interests of individuals engaged in that profession and the public interest. In the United States, such an association is typically a nonprofit organization for tax purposes.

Exam Probability: **Low**

33. *Answer choices:*

(see index for correct answer)

- a. Professional association
- b. hierarchical perspective
- c. cultural
- d. similarity-attraction theory

Guidance: level 1

:: Socialism ::

In sociology, _________ is the process of internalizing the norms and ideologies of society. _________ encompasses both learning and teaching and is thus "the means by which social and cultural continuity are attained".

Exam Probability: **Medium**

34. *Answer choices:*

(see index for correct answer)

- a. UAR Socialist Youth Organization
- b. Eco-communalism
- c. Socialization
- d. Socialist fraternal kiss

Guidance: level 1

:: ::

__________ is an experience a person may have when one moves to a cultural environment which is different from one`s own; it is also the personal disorientation a person may feel when experiencing an unfamiliar way of life due to immigration or a visit to a new country, a move between social environments, or simply transition to another type of life. One of the most common causes of __________ involves individuals in a foreign environment. __________ can be described as consisting of at least one of four distinct phases: honeymoon, negotiation, adjustment, and adaptation.

Exam Probability: **High**

35. *Answer choices:*

(see index for correct answer)

- a. personal values
- b. Culture shock
- c. empathy
- d. similarity-attraction theory

Guidance: level 1

:: Psychometrics ::

A __________ is a set of categories designed to elicit information about a quantitative or a qualitative attribute. In the social sciences, particularly psychology, common examples are the Likert response scale and 1-10 __________s in which a person selects the number which is considered to reflect the perceived quality of a product.

Exam Probability: **Medium**

36. *Answer choices:*

(see index for correct answer)

- a. Rating scale
- b. Quantitative psychology
- c. Reaction time
- d. Mental age

Guidance: level 1

:: Occupational safety and health ::

Note: Parts of this article are written from the perspective of aircraft safety analysis techniques and definitions; these may not represent current best practice and the article needs to be updated to represent a more generic description of _________ and discussion of more modern standards and techniques.

Exam Probability: **Low**

37. *Answer choices:*

(see index for correct answer)

- a. Hazard analysis
- b. Electric shock

- c. Code of safe working practices
- d. Safety Jackpot

Guidance: level 1

:: Human resource management ::

_________ involves improving the effectiveness of organizations and the individuals and teams within them. Training may be viewed as related to immediate changes in organizational effectiveness via organized instruction, while development is related to the progress of longer-term organizational and employee goals. While _________ technically have differing definitions, the two are oftentimes used interchangeably and/or together. _________ has historically been a topic within applied psychology but has within the last two decades become closely associated with human resources management, talent management, human resources development, instructional design, human factors, and knowledge management.

Exam Probability: **Low**

38. *Answer choices:*

(see index for correct answer)

- a. Human resource management
- b. On-ramping
- c. Workforce modeling
- d. Training and development

Guidance: level 1

:: Industrial agreements ::

A ________, in labor relations, is a group of employees with a clear and identifiable community of interests who are represented by a single labor union in collective bargaining and other dealings with management. Examples would be non-management professors, law enforcement professionals, blue-collar workers, clerical and administrative employees, etc. Geographic location as well as the number of facilities included in ________ s can be at issue during representation cases.

Exam Probability: **Low**

39. *Answer choices:*

(see index for correct answer)

- a. Bargaining unit
- b. Common rule awards
- c. In Place of Strife
- d. Workplace Authority

Guidance: level 1

:: Television terminology ::

Distance education or long- _________ is the education of students who may not always be physically present at a school. Traditionally, this usually involved correspondence courses wherein the student corresponded with the school via post. Today it involves online education. Courses that are conducted are either hybrid, blended or 100% _________ . Massive open online courses , offering large-scale interactive participation and open access through the World Wide Web or other network technologies, are recent developments in distance education. A number of other terms are used roughly synonymously with distance education.

Exam Probability: **Medium**

40. *Answer choices:*

(see index for correct answer)

- a. multiplexing
- b. Distance learning
- c. nonprofit
- d. Satellite television

Guidance: level 1

:: Employment compensation ::

A _________ is pay and benefits employees receive when they leave employment at a company unwillfully. In addition to their remaining regular pay, it may include some of the following.

Exam Probability: **Medium**

41. *Answer choices:*

(see index for correct answer)

- a. Australian Fair Pay Commission
- b. Severance package
- c. Equal Pay Act of 1963
- d. Federal Salary Council

Guidance: level 1

:: Fundamental analysis ::

_________ , also known as letter stock or restricted securities, is stock of a company that is not fully transferable until certain conditions have been met. Upon satisfaction of those conditions, the stock is no longer restricted, and becomes transferable to the person holding the award. _________ is often used as a form of employee compensation, in which case it typically becomes transferrable upon the satisfaction of certain conditions, such as continued employment for a period of time or the achievement of particular product-development milestones, earnings per share goals or other financial targets. _________ is a popular alternative to stock options, particularly for executives, due to favorable accounting rules and income tax treatment.

Exam Probability: **Medium**

42. *Answer choices:*

(see index for correct answer)

- a. Restricted stock
- b. Terminal value
- c. Goldman Sachs asset management factor model
- d. Growth stock

Guidance: level 1

:: Employment compensation ::

Compensation and benefits is a sub-discipline of human resources, focused on employee compensation and benefits policy-making. While compensation and benefits are tangible, there are intangible rewards such as recognition, work-life and development. Combined, these are referred to as _________ s . The term "compensation and benefits" refers to the discipline as well as the rewards themselves.

Exam Probability: **Low**

43. *Answer choices:*

(see index for correct answer)

- a. Federal Wage System
- b. Law Enforcement Availability Pay
- c. Labour law
- d. Reservation wage

Guidance: level 1

:: Human resource management ::

__________ is a core function of human resource management and it is related to the specification of contents, methods and relationship of jobs in order to satisfy technological and organizational requirements as well as the social and personal requirements of the job holder or the employee. Its principles are geared towards how the nature of a person`s job affects their attitudes and behavior at work, particularly relating to characteristics such as skill variety and autonomy. The aim of a __________ is to improve job satisfaction, to improve through-put, to improve quality and to reduce employee problems .

Exam Probability: **Medium**

44. *Answer choices:*

(see index for correct answer)

- a. Job design
- b. E-HRM
- c. Workplace mentoring
- d. Income bracket

Guidance: level 1

:: Human resource management ::

A __________ is an outsourcing firm which provides services to small and medium sized businesses . Typically, the PEO offering may include human resource consulting, safety and risk mitigation services, payroll processing, employer payroll tax filing, workers` compensation insurance, health benefits, employers` practice and liability insurance , retirement vehicles , regulatory compliance assistance, workforce management technology, and training and development. The PEO enters into a contractual co-employment agreement with its clientele. Through co-employment, the PEO becomes the employer of record for tax purposes through filing payroll taxes under its own tax identification numbers.

Exam Probability: **Medium**

45. *Answer choices:*

(see index for correct answer)

- a. Salary
- b. Human resources
- c. Sham peer review
- d. Professional employer organization

Guidance: level 1

:: Majority–minority relations ::

__________ , also known as reservation in India and Nepal, positive discrimination / action in the United Kingdom, and employment equity in Canada and South Africa, is the policy of promoting the education and employment of members of groups that are known to have previously suffered from discrimination. Historically and internationally, support for __________ has sought to achieve goals such as bridging inequalities in employment and pay, increasing access to education, promoting diversity, and redressing apparent past wrongs, harms, or hindrances.

Exam Probability: **Low**

46. *Answer choices:*

(see index for correct answer)

- a. cultural Relativism
- b. cultural dissonance
- c. Affirmative action

Guidance: level 1

:: ::

_________ refers to the overall process of attracting, shortlisting, selecting and appointing suitable candidates for jobs within an organization. _________ can also refer to processes involved in choosing individuals for unpaid roles. Managers, human resource generalists and _________ specialists may be tasked with carrying out _________, but in some cases public-sector employment agencies, commercial _________ agencies, or specialist search consultancies are used to undertake parts of the process. Internet-based technologies which support all aspects of _________ have become widespread.

Exam Probability: **High**

47. *Answer choices:*

(see index for correct answer)

- a. similarity-attraction theory
- b. open system
- c. corporate values
- d. surface-level diversity

Guidance: level 1

:: Developmental psychology ::

_________ behavior refers to behavior that enables a person to get along in his or her environment with greatest success and least conflict with others. This is a term used in the areas of psychology and special education. _________ behavior relates to every day skills or tasks that the average person is able to complete, similar to the term life skills.

Exam Probability: **Medium**

48. *Answer choices:*

(see index for correct answer)

- a. Cognitive development
- b. Adaptive

Guidance: level 1

:: Survey methodology ::

_________ is often used to assess thoughts, opinions, and feelings. Surveys can be specific and limited, or they can have more global, widespread goals. Psychologists and sociologists often use surveys to analyze behavior, while it is also used to meet the more pragmatic needs of the media, such as, in evaluating political candidates, public health officials, professional organizations, and advertising and marketing directors. A survey consists of a predetermined set of questions that is given to a sample. With a representative sample, that is, one that is representative of the larger population of interest, one can describe the attitudes of the population from which the sample was drawn. Further, one can compare the attitudes of different populations as well as look for changes in attitudes over time. A good sample selection is key as it allows one to generalize the findings from the sample to the population, which is the whole purpose of _________ .

Exam Probability: **Low**

49. *Answer choices:*

(see index for correct answer)

- a. Group concept mapping
- b. Inverse probability weighting
- c. Public opinion
- d. Survey research

Guidance: level 1

:: Validity (statistics) ::

In psychometrics, __________ refers to the extent to which a measure represents all facets of a given construct. For example, a depression scale may lack __________ if it only assesses the affective dimension of depression but fails to take into account the behavioral dimension. An element of subjectivity exists in relation to determining __________, which requires a degree of agreement about what a particular personality trait such as extraversion represents. A disagreement about a personality trait will prevent the gain of a high __________.

Exam Probability: **Medium**

50. *Answer choices:*

(see index for correct answer)

- a. Convergent validity
- b. Content validity
- c. Ecological validity
- d. Incremental validity

Guidance: level 1

:: Business terms ::

A _________ is a short statement of why an organization exists, what its overall goal is, identifying the goal of its operations: what kind of product or service it provides, its primary customers or market, and its geographical region of operation. It may include a short statement of such fundamental matters as the organization`s values or philosophies, a business`s main competitive advantages, or a desired future state—the "vision".

Exam Probability: **Low**

51. *Answer choices:*

(see index for correct answer)

- a. front office
- b. organizational capital
- c. strategic plan
- d. Mission statement

Guidance: level 1

:: Human resource management ::

__________ are transactions in which the ownership of companies, other business organizations, or their operating units are transferred or consolidated with other entities. As an aspect of strategic management, M&A can allow enterprises to grow or downsize, and change the nature of their business or competitive position.

Exam Probability: **Medium**

52. *Answer choices:*

(see index for correct answer)

- a. Managerial assessment of proficiency
- b. Workforce sciences
- c. Progress, plans, problems
- d. Functional job analysis

Guidance: level 1

:: Financial statements ::

In financial accounting, a __________ or statement of financial position or statement of financial condition is a summary of the financial balances of an individual or organization, whether it be a sole proprietorship, a business partnership, a corporation, private limited company or other organization such as Government or not-for-profit entity. Assets, liabilities and ownership equity are listed as of a specific date, such as the end of its financial year. A __________ is often described as a "snapshot of a company`s financial condition". Of the four basic financial statements, the __________ is the only statement which applies to a single point in time of a business` calendar year.

Exam Probability: **Low**

53. *Answer choices:*

(see index for correct answer)

- a. Statement on Auditing Standards No. 70: Service Organizations
- b. quarterly report
- c. Statements on auditing standards
- d. Government financial statements

Guidance: level 1

:: Employment compensation ::

A ________ , also known as a flexible spending arrangement, is one of a number of tax-advantaged financial accounts, resulting in payroll tax savings. Before the Patient Protection and Affordable Care Act, one significant disadvantage to using an FSA was that funds not used by the end of the plan year were forfeited to the employer, known as the "use it or lose it" rule. Under the terms of the Affordable Care Act, a plan may permit an employee to carry over up to $500 into the following year without losing the funds.

Exam Probability: **High**

54. *Answer choices:*

(see index for correct answer)

- a. Performance-related pay
- b. Flexible spending account
- c. Salary calculator
- d. Crowell v. Benson

Guidance: level 1

:: ::

The ________ of 1938 29 U.S.C. § 203 is a United States labor law that creates the right to a minimum wage, and "time-and-a-half" overtime pay when people work over forty hours a week. It also prohibits most employment of minors in "oppressive child labor". It applies to employees engaged in interstate commerce or employed by an enterprise engaged in commerce or in the production of goods for commerce, unless the employer can claim an exemption from coverage.

Exam Probability: **Medium**

55. *Answer choices:*

(see index for correct answer)

- a. open system
- b. empathy
- c. Fair Labor Standards Act
- d. imperative

Guidance: level 1

:: ::

__________ is overt or covert, often harmful, social interaction with the intention of inflicting damage or other unpleasantness upon another individual. It may occur either reactively or without provocation. In humans, frustration due to blocked goals can cause __________ . Human __________ can be classified into direct and indirect __________ ; whilst the former is characterized by physical or verbal behavior intended to cause harm to someone, the latter is characterized by behavior intended to harm the social relations of an individual or group.

Exam Probability: **Medium**

56. *Answer choices:*

(see index for correct answer)

- a. co-culture
- b. open system
- c. Aggression
- d. hierarchical perspective

Guidance: level 1

:: Office work ::

The _________ is a concept in management developed by Laurence J. Peter, which observes that people in a hierarchy tend to rise to their "level of incompetence". In other words, an employee is promoted based on their success in previous jobs until they reach a level at which they are no longer competent, as skills in one job do not necessarily translate to another. The concept was elucidated in the 1969 book The _________ by Peter and Raymond Hull.

Exam Probability: **Low**

57. *Answer choices:*

(see index for correct answer)

- a. Career woman
- b. Service bureau
- c. Clerk
- d. Mobile office

Guidance: level 1

:: ::

__________ , also known as drug abuse, is a patterned use of a drug in which the user consumes the substance in amounts or with methods which are harmful to themselves or others, and is a form of substance-related disorder. Widely differing definitions of drug abuse are used in public health, medical and criminal justice contexts. In some cases criminal or anti-social behaviour occurs when the person is under the influence of a drug, and long term personality changes in individuals may occur as well. In addition to possible physical, social, and psychological harm, use of some drugs may also lead to criminal penalties, although these vary widely depending on the local jurisdiction.

Exam Probability: **Medium**

58. *Answer choices:*

(see index for correct answer)

- a. hierarchical
- b. levels of analysis
- c. Substance abuse
- d. interpersonal communication

Guidance: level 1

:: Human resource management ::

An _________ is a diagram that shows the structure of an organization and the relationships and relative ranks of its parts and positions/jobs. The term is also used for similar diagrams, for example ones showing the different elements of a field of knowledge or a group of languages.

Exam Probability: **Medium**

59. *Answer choices:*

(see index for correct answer)

- a. Adaptive performance
- b. Organizational chart
- c. Person specification
- d. Talent supply chain management

Guidance: level 1

Information systems

Information systems (IS) are formal, sociotechnical, organizational systems designed to collect, process, store, and distribute information. In a sociotechnical perspective Information Systems are composed by four components: technology, process, people and organizational structure.

:: Management ::

_________ is the identification of an organization`s assets , followed by the development, documentation, and implementation of policies and procedures for protecting these assets.

Exam Probability: **High**

1. *Answer choices:*

(see index for correct answer)

- a. Project management information system
- b. Supply chain optimization
- c. Extended enterprise
- d. Security management

Guidance: level 1

:: ::

_________ is a brand name associated with the development of the _________ web browser. It is now owned by Verizon Media, a subsidiary of Verizon. The brand belonged to the _________ Communications Corporation , an independent American computer services company, whose headquarters were in Mountain View, California, and later Dulles, Virginia. The browser was once dominant but lost to Internet Explorer and other competitors after the so-called first browser war, its market share falling from more than 90 percent in the mid-1990s to less than 1 percent in 2006.

Exam Probability: **Low**

2. *Answer choices:*

(see index for correct answer)

- a. corporate values
- b. Netscape

- c. co-culture
- d. hierarchical perspective

Guidance: level 1

:: Database theory ::

_________ is the organisation of data according to a database model. The designer determines what data must be stored and how the data elements interrelate. With this information, they can begin to fit the data to the database model.

Exam Probability: **Medium**

3. *Answer choices:*

(see index for correct answer)

- a. Database design
- b. Full table scan
- c. Dependency theory
- d. Relational database

Guidance: level 1

:: Stochastic processes ::

_________ in its modern meaning is a "new idea, creative thoughts, new imaginations in form of device or method". _________ is often also viewed as the application of better solutions that meet new requirements, unarticulated needs, or existing market needs. Such _________ takes place through the provision of more-effective products, processes, services, technologies, or business models that are made available to markets, governments and society. An _________ is something original and more effective and, as a consequence, new, that "breaks into" the market or society. _________ is related to, but not the same as, invention, as _________ is more apt to involve the practical implementation of an invention to make a meaningful impact in the market or society, and not all _________ s require an invention. _________ often manifests itself via the engineering process, when the problem being solved is of a technical or scientific nature. The opposite of _________ is exnovation.

Exam Probability: **High**

4. *Answer choices:*

(see index for correct answer)

- a. Skorokhod problem
- b. Quadratic variation
- c. Markov model
- d. Innovation

Guidance: level 1

:: Automatic identification and data capture ::

__________ is the trademark for a type of matrix barcode first designed in 1994 for the automotive industry in Japan. A barcode is a machine-readable optical label that contains information about the item to which it is attached. In practice, __________ s often contain data for a locator, identifier, or tracker that points to a website or application. A __________ uses four standardized encoding modes to store data efficiently; extensions may also be used.

Exam Probability: **Low**

5. *Answer choices:*

(see index for correct answer)

- a. Wireless identification and sensing platform
- b. Mobile data terminal
- c. HipVoice
- d. Track and trace

Guidance: level 1

:: Information technology management ::

__________ s or pop-ups are forms of online advertising on the World Wide Web. A pop-up is a graphical user interface display area, usually a small window, that suddenly appears in the foreground of the visual interface. The pop-up window containing an advertisement is usually generated by JavaScript that uses cross-site scripting , sometimes with a secondary payload that uses Adobe Flash. They can also be generated by other vulnerabilities/security holes in browser security.

Exam Probability: **Low**

6. *Answer choices:*

(see index for correct answer)

- a. Enterprise portal
- b. Socitm
- c. HP FutureSmart firmware
- d. Capability Maturity Model

Guidance: level 1

:: Behavioral and social facets of systemic risk ::

__________ is the difficulty in understanding an issue and effectively making decisions when one has too much information about that issue. Generally, the term is associated with the excessive quantity of daily information. __________ most likely originated from information theory, which are studies in the storage, preservation, communication, compression, and extraction of information. The term, __________ , was first used in Bertram Gross` 1964 book, The Managing of Organizations, and it was further popularized by Alvin Toffler in his bestselling 1970 book Future Shock. Speier et al. stated.

Exam Probability: **Medium**

7. *Answer choices:*

(see index for correct answer)

- a. Continuous partial attention
- b. Latent human error
- c. Crowd psychology
- d. Information overload

Guidance: level 1

:: Automatic identification and data capture ::

_________ is human–computer interaction in which a computer is expected to be transported during normal usage, which allows for transmission of data, voice and video. _________ involves mobile communication, mobile hardware, and mobile software. Communication issues include ad hoc networks and infrastructure networks as well as communication properties, protocols, data formats and concrete technologies. Hardware includes mobile devices or device components. Mobile software deals with the characteristics and requirements of mobile applications.

Exam Probability: **High**

8. *Answer choices:*

(see index for correct answer)

- a. CyberCode
- b. Forms processing
- c. Mobile computing
- d. IBeacon

Guidance: level 1

:: Content management systems ::

_________ is the textual, visual, or aural content that is encountered as part of the user experience on websites. It may include—among other things—text, images, sounds, videos, and animations.

Exam Probability: **Low**

9. *Answer choices:*

(see index for correct answer)

- a. MediaValet
- b. EduWave
- c. CcHost
- d. Web content

Guidance: level 1

:: Costs ::

In economics, _________ is the total economic cost of production and is made up of variable cost, which varies according to the quantity of a good produced and includes inputs such as labour and raw materials, plus fixed cost, which is independent of the quantity of a good produced and includes inputs that cannot be varied in the short term: fixed costs such as buildings and machinery, including sunk costs if any. Since cost is measured per unit of time, it is a flow variable.

Exam Probability: **High**

10. *Answer choices:*

(see index for correct answer)

- a. Road Logistics Costing in South Africa
- b. Further processing cost
- c. Total cost
- d. Cost overrun

Guidance: level 1

:: Computing input devices ::

In computing, an _________ is a piece of computer hardware equipment used to provide data and control signals to an information processing system such as a computer or information appliance. Examples of _________ s include keyboards, mouse, scanners, digital cameras and joysticks. Audio _________ s may be used for purposes including speech recognition. Many companies are utilizing speech recognition to help assist users to use their device.

Exam Probability: **Low**

11. *Answer choices:*

(see index for correct answer)

- a. Keyboard controller
- b. Cyber Snipa
- c. Griffin PowerMate
- d. Manual pulse generator

Guidance: level 1

:: Virtual reality ::

_________ is an experience taking place within simulated and immersive environments that can be similar to or completely different from the real world. Applications of _________ can include entertainment and educational purposes . Other, distinct types of VR style technology include augmented reality and mixed reality.

Exam Probability: **Low**

12. *Answer choices:*

(see index for correct answer)

- a. Social presence theory
- b. Virtual reality

- c. Virtual engineering
- d. Polynomial texture mapping

Guidance: level 1

:: Intelligence (information gathering) ::

_________ comprises the strategies and technologies used by enterprises for the data analysis of business information. BI technologies provide historical, current and predictive views of business operations. Common functions of _________ technologies include reporting, online analytical processing, analytics, data mining, process mining, complex event processing, business performance management, benchmarking, text mining, predictive analytics and prescriptive analytics. BI technologies can handle large amounts of structured and sometimes unstructured data to help identify, develop and otherwise create new strategic business opportunities. They aim to allow for the easy interpretation of these big data. Identifying new opportunities and implementing an effective strategy based on insights can provide businesses with a competitive market advantage and long-term stability.

Exam Probability: **Medium**

13. *Answer choices:*

(see index for correct answer)

- a. Advanced Technical Intelligence Center
- b. Criminal intelligence
- c. Business intelligence
- d. Intelligence requirement

Guidance: level 1

:: Marketing ::

__________ is the percentage of a market accounted for by a specific entity. In a survey of nearly 200 senior marketing managers, 67% responded that they found the revenue- "dollar __________ " metric very useful, while 61% found "unit __________ " very useful.

Exam Probability: **High**

14. *Answer choices:*

(see index for correct answer)

- a. NauticExpo
- b. Market share
- c. Meta marketing
- d. Mandatory labelling

Guidance: level 1

:: Computing output devices ::

An __________ is any piece of computer hardware equipment which converts information into human-readable form.

Exam Probability: **High**

15. *Answer choices:*

(see index for correct answer)

- a. Vinyl cutter
- b. DR37-P
- c. GammaFax
- d. Powerwall

Guidance: level 1

:: Data analysis ::

_________ is a process of inspecting, cleansing, transforming, and modeling data with the goal of discovering useful information, informing conclusions, and supporting decision-making. _________ has multiple facets and approaches, encompassing diverse techniques under a variety of names, and is used in different business, science, and social science domains. In today`s business world, _________ plays a role in making decisions more scientific and helping businesses operate more effectively.

Exam Probability: **Low**

16. *Answer choices:*

(see index for correct answer)

- a. Data analysis

- b. Aggregative Contingent Estimation
- c. Grouped data
- d. Missing data

Guidance: level 1

:: Customer relationship management software ::

_________ Software Corporation is a Global Business Software company based in Austin, TX and was founded in 1972. Its products are aimed at the manufacturing, distribution, retail and services industries.

Exam Probability: **Low**

17. *Answer choices:*

(see index for correct answer)

- a. GoldMine
- b. Comm100
- c. Entellium
- d. Vocalcom

Guidance: level 1

:: Payment systems ::

_________ is a mobile phone-based money transfer, financing and microfinancing service, launched in 2007 by Vodafone for Safaricom and Vodacom, the largest mobile network operators in Kenya and Tanzania. It has since expanded to Afghanistan, South Africa, India and in 2014 to Romania and in 2015 to Albania. _________ allows users to deposit, withdraw, transfer money and pay for goods and services easily with a mobile device.

Exam Probability: **Low**

18. *Answer choices:*

(see index for correct answer)

- a. Certified Payment-Card Industry Security Implementer
- b. Substitute check
- c. PayPoint
- d. Ready Financial

Guidance: level 1

:: Enterprise modelling ::

_________ are large-scale application software packages that support business processes, information flows, reporting, and data analytics in complex organizations. While ES are generally packaged enterprise application software systems they can also be bespoke, custom developed systems created to support a specific organization`s needs.

Exam Probability: **Low**

19. *Answer choices:*

(see index for correct answer)

- a. Enterprise engineering
- b. Enterprise systems
- c. Event-driven process chain
- d. Integrated enterprise modeling

Guidance: level 1

:: Cryptography ::

In cryptography, __________ is the process of encoding a message or information in such a way that only authorized parties can access it and those who are not authorized cannot. __________ does not itself prevent interference, but denies the intelligible content to a would-be interceptor. In an __________ scheme, the intended information or message, referred to as plaintext, is encrypted using an __________ algorithm – a cipher – generating ciphertext that can be read only if decrypted. For technical reasons, an __________ scheme usually uses a pseudo-random __________ key generated by an algorithm. It is in principle possible to decrypt the message without possessing the key, but, for a well-designed __________ scheme, considerable computational resources and skills are required. An authorized recipient can easily decrypt the message with the key provided by the originator to recipients but not to unauthorized users.

Exam Probability: **Low**

20. *Answer choices:*

(see index for correct answer)

- a. cryptosystem
- b. Anonymous matching
- c. Encryption
- d. plaintext

Guidance: level 1

:: ::

A __________ is a telecommunications network that extends over a large geographical distance for the primary purpose of computer networking. __________ s are often established with leased telecommunication circuits.

Exam Probability: **High**

21. *Answer choices:*

(see index for correct answer)

- a. Wide Area Network
- b. hierarchical
- c. levels of analysis
- d. Character

Guidance: level 1

:: ::

A __________ is a structure / access pattern specific to data warehouse environments, used to retrieve client-facing data. The __________ is a subset of the data warehouse and is usually oriented to a specific business line or team. Whereas data warehouses have an enterprise-wide depth, the information in __________s pertains to a single department. In some deployments, each department or business unit is considered the owner of its __________ including all the hardware, software and data. This enables each department to isolate the use, manipulation and development of their data. In other deployments where conformed dimensions are used, this business unit ownership will not hold true for shared dimensions like customer, product, etc.

Exam Probability: **High**

22. *Answer choices:*

(see index for correct answer)

- a. empathy
- b. Character
- c. Data mart
- d. interpersonal communication

Guidance: level 1

:: ::

A database is an organized collection of data, generally stored and accessed electronically from a computer system. Where databases are more complex they are often developed using formal design and modeling techniques.

Exam Probability: **Low**

23. *Answer choices:*

(see index for correct answer)

- a. Database management system
- b. surface-level diversity
- c. Character
- d. deep-level diversity

Guidance: level 1

:: Global Positioning System ::

A __________ is a mechanism for determining the location of an object in space. Technologies for this task exist ranging from worldwide coverage with meter accuracy to workspace coverage with sub-millimetre accuracy.

Exam Probability: **Medium**

24. *Answer choices:*

(see index for correct answer)

- a. OmniSTAR
- b. StarFire
- c. SK-42 reference system
- d. Positioning system

Guidance: level 1

:: Market research ::

_________ s are many different distantly related animals that typically have a long cylindrical tube-like body and no limbs. _________ s vary in size from microscopic to over 1 metre in length for marine polychaete _________ s , 6.7 metres for the African giant earth _________ , Microchaetus rappi, and 58 metres for the marine nemertean _________ , Lineus longissimus. Various types of _________ occupy a small variety of parasitic niches, living inside the bodies of other animals. Free-living _________ species do not live on land, but instead, live in marine or freshwater environments, or underground by burrowing.In biology, " _________ " refers to an obsolete taxon, vermes, used by Carolus Linnaeus and Jean-Baptiste Lamarck for all non-arthropod invertebrate animals, now seen to be paraphyletic. The name stems from the Old English word wyrm. Most animals called " _________ s" are invertebrates, but the term is also used for the amphibian caecilians and the slow _________ Anguis, a legless burrowing lizard. Invertebrate animals commonly called " _________ s" include annelids , nematodes , platyhelminthes , marine nemertean _________ s , marine Chaetognatha , priapulid _________ s, and insect larvae such as grubs and maggots.

Exam Probability: **High**

25. *Answer choices:*

(see index for correct answer)

- a. Market research
- b. Nielsen VideoScan
- c. New economic order
- d. Worm

Guidance: level 1

:: Data security ::

__________ , sometimes shortened to InfoSec, is the practice of preventing unauthorized access, use, disclosure, disruption, modification, inspection, recording or destruction of information. The information or data may take any form, e.g. electronic or physical. __________ `s primary focus is the balanced protection of the confidentiality, integrity and availability of data while maintaining a focus on efficient policy implementation, all without hampering organization productivity. This is largely achieved through a multi-step risk management process that identifies assets, threat sources, vulnerabilities, potential impacts, and possible controls, followed by assessment of the effectiveness of the risk management plan.

Exam Probability: **Medium**

26. *Answer choices:*

(see index for correct answer)

- a. Blancco
- b. Offline private key
- c. NIST RBAC model
- d. Information security

Guidance: level 1

:: Production economics ::

_________ is a way of producing goods and services that relies on self-organizing communities of individuals. In such communities, the labor of a large number of people is coordinated towards a shared outcome.

Exam Probability: **Low**

27. *Answer choices:*

(see index for correct answer)

- a. Hicks-neutral technical change
- b. Isoquant
- c. Peer production
- d. Economies of scale

Guidance: level 1

:: Financial markets ::

The _________ business model is a business model in which a customer must pay a recurring price at regular intervals for access to a product or service. The model was pioneered by publishers of books and periodicals in the 17th century, and is now used by many businesses and websites.

Exam Probability: **Medium**

28. *Answer choices:*

(see index for correct answer)

- a. Market impact
- b. Financial signal processing
- c. Secondary market
- d. Subscription

Guidance: level 1

:: Network theory ::

A _________ is a social structure made up of a set of social actors , sets of dyadic ties, and other social interactions between actors. The _________ perspective provides a set of methods for analyzing the structure of whole social entities as well as a variety of theories explaining the patterns observed in these structures. The study of these structures uses _________ analysis to identify local and global patterns, locate influential entities, and examine network dynamics.

Exam Probability: **High**

29. *Answer choices:*

(see index for correct answer)

- a. Social network
- b. Strategic Network Formation
- c. Agent network topology
- d. Evolving networks

Guidance: level 1

:: Procurement practices ::

_________ or commercially available off-the-shelf products are packaged solutions which are then adapted to satisfy the needs of the purchasing organization, rather than the commissioning of custom-made, or bespoke, solutions. A related term, Mil-COTS, refers to COTS products for use by the U.S. military.

Exam Probability: **Medium**

30. *Answer choices:*

(see index for correct answer)

- a. Commercial off-the-shelf
- b. Construction by configuration

Guidance: level 1

:: E-commerce ::

The phrase _________ was originally coined in 1997 by Kevin Duffey at the launch of the Global _________ Forum, to mean "the delivery of electronic commerce capabilities directly into the consumer's hand, anywhere, via wireless technology." Many choose to think of _________ as meaning "a retail outlet in your customer's pocket."

Exam Probability: **Low**

31. *Answer choices:*

(see index for correct answer)

- a. Online marketplace
- b. Live banner
- c. ITransact
- d. Mobile commerce

Guidance: level 1

:: Internet marketing ::

_________ is the process of increasing the quality and quantity of website traffic, increasing visibility of a website or a web page to users of a web search engine.SEO refers to the improvement of unpaid results , and excludes the purchase of paid placement.

Exam Probability: **High**

32. *Answer choices:*

(see index for correct answer)

- a. Quality Score
- b. Post-click marketing
- c. Pre-popping
- d. Search engine optimization

Guidance: level 1

:: Strategic management ::

__________ is a management term for an element that is necessary for an organization or project to achieve its mission. Alternative terms are key result area and key success factor .

Exam Probability: **Medium**

33. *Answer choices:*

(see index for correct answer)

- a. Critical success factor
- b. Keiretsu
- c. TmsEKP
- d. customer lock-in

Guidance: level 1

:: Transaction processing ::

In _________ , information systems typically facilitate and manage transaction-oriented applications.

Exam Probability: **Low**

34. *Answer choices:*

(see index for correct answer)

- a. Westi
- b. Transactional NTFS
- c. Pseudoconversational transaction
- d. Online transaction processing

Guidance: level 1

:: Finance ::

_________ is a financial estimate intended to help buyers and owners determine the direct and indirect costs of a product or system. It is a management accounting concept that can be used in full cost accounting or even ecological economics where it includes social costs.

Exam Probability: **Medium**

35. *Answer choices:*

(see index for correct answer)

- a. Swing trading
- b. Total cost of ownership
- c. Asset purchase agreement
- d. Periodic deposit

Guidance: level 1

:: Data management ::

_________ involves combining data residing in different sources and providing users with a unified view of them. This process becomes significant in a variety of situations, which include both commercial and scientific domains. _________ appears with increasing frequency as the volume and the need to share existing data explodes. It has become the focus of extensive theoretical work, and numerous open problems remain unsolved. _________ encourages collaboration between internal as well as external users

Exam Probability: **Low**

36. *Answer choices:*

(see index for correct answer)

- a. Holos
- b. Dynamic knowledge repository
- c. Operational historian

- d. Data integration

Guidance: level 1

:: Domain name system ::

__________ , Inc. is an American company based in Reston, Virginia, United States that operates a diverse array of network infrastructure, including two of the Internet's thirteen root nameservers, the authoritative registry for the .com, .net, and .name generic top-level domains and the .cc and .tv country-code top-level domains, and the back-end systems for the .jobs, .gov, and .edu top-level domains. __________ also offers a range of security services, including managed DNS, distributed denial-of-service attack mitigation and cyber-threat reporting.

Exam Probability: **Low**

37. *Answer choices:*

(see index for correct answer)

- a. Vanity domain
- b. Zone file
- c. Verisign
- d. DNS spoofing

Guidance: level 1

:: ::

A _________ is a discussion or informational website published on the World Wide Web consisting of discrete, often informal diary-style text entries . Posts are typically displayed in reverse chronological order, so that the most recent post appears first, at the top of the web page. Until 2009, _________ s were usually the work of a single individual, occasionally of a small group, and often covered a single subject or topic. In the 2010s, "multi-author _________ s" emerged, featuring the writing of multiple authors and sometimes professionally edited. MABs from newspapers, other media outlets, universities, think tanks, advocacy groups, and similar institutions account for an increasing quantity of _________ traffic. The rise of Twitter and other "micro _________ ging" systems helps integrate MABs and single-author _________ s into the news media. _________ can also be used as a verb, meaning to maintain or add content to a _________ .

Exam Probability: **Medium**

38. *Answer choices:*

(see index for correct answer)

- a. Blog
- b. personal values
- c. hierarchical perspective
- d. open system

Guidance: level 1

:: Database management systems ::

A _________ is a type of data model that determines the logical structure of a database and fundamentally determines in which manner data can be stored, organized and manipulated. The most popular example of a _________ is the relational model, which uses a table-based format.

Exam Probability: **Medium**

39. *Answer choices:*

(see index for correct answer)

- a. Database dump
- b. Valid time
- c. Object Exchange Model
- d. Data retrieval

Guidance: level 1

:: Fault tolerance ::

_________ is the property that enables a system to continue operating properly in the event of the failure of some of its components. If its operating quality decreases at all, the decrease is proportional to the severity of the failure, as compared to a naively designed system, in which even a small failure can cause total breakdown. _________ is particularly sought after in high-availability or life-critical systems. The ability of maintaining functionality when portions of a system break down is referred to as graceful degradation.

Exam Probability: **Medium**

40. *Answer choices:*

(see index for correct answer)

- a. Recovery procedure
- b. Repetition code
- c. Fault-tolerant software
- d. Elegant degradation

Guidance: level 1

:: ::

_________ is a kind of action that occur as two or more objects have an effect upon one another. The idea of a two-way effect is essential in the concept of _________ , as opposed to a one-way causal effect. A closely related term is interconnectivity, which deals with the _________ s of _________ s within systems: combinations of many simple _________ s can lead to surprising emergent phenomena. _________ has different tailored meanings in various sciences. Changes can also involve _________ .

Exam Probability: **Low**

41. *Answer choices:*

(see index for correct answer)

- a. similarity-attraction theory

- b. Interaction
- c. surface-level diversity
- d. hierarchical perspective

Guidance: level 1

:: E-commerce ::

__________ generally refer to payment services operated under financial regulation and performed from or via a mobile device. Instead of paying with cash, cheque, or credit cards, a consumer can use a mobile to pay for a wide range of services and digital or hard goods. Although the concept of using non-coin-based currency systems has a long history, it is only recently that the technology to support such systems has become widely available.

Exam Probability: **High**

42. *Answer choices:*

(see index for correct answer)

- a. SwapSimple
- b. Helpling
- c. ICOCA
- d. Mobile payment

Guidance: level 1

:: Information systems ::

A _________ manages the creation and modification of digital content. It typically supports multiple users in a collaborative environment.

Exam Probability: **High**

43. *Answer choices:*

(see index for correct answer)

- a. Internal Market Information System
- b. Content management system
- c. Sticky information
- d. Sales force management system

Guidance: level 1

:: Commerce ::

_________ , Inc. is an American media-services provider headquartered in Los Gatos, California, founded in 1997 by Reed Hastings and Marc Randolph in Scotts Valley, California. The company`s primary business is its subscription-based streaming OTT service which offers online streaming of a library of films and television programs, including those produced in-house. As of April 2019, _________ had over 148 million paid subscriptions worldwide, including 60 million in the United States, and over 154 million subscriptions total including free trials. It is available almost worldwide except in mainland China as well as Syria, North Korea, and Crimea . The company also has offices in the Netherlands, Brazil, India, Japan, and South Korea. _________ is a member of the Motion Picture Association of America .

Exam Probability: **High**

44. *Answer choices:*

(see index for correct answer)

- a. Requisition
- b. Netflix
- c. Uttarapatha
- d. Fast track

Guidance: level 1

:: Teams ::

A _________ usually refers to a group of individuals who work together from different geographic locations and rely on communication technology such as email, FAX, and video or voice conferencing services in order to collaborate. The term can also refer to groups or teams that work together asynchronously or across organizational levels. Powell, Piccoli and Ives define _________ s as "groups of geographically, organizationally and/or time dispersed workers brought together by information and telecommunication technologies to accomplish one or more organizational tasks." According to Ale Ebrahim et. al. , _________ s can also be defined as "small temporary groups of geographically, organizationally and/or time dispersed knowledge workers who coordinate their work predominantly with electronic information and communication technologies in order to accomplish one or more organization tasks."

Exam Probability: **Medium**

45. *Answer choices:*

(see index for correct answer)

- a. Virtual team
- b. team composition

Guidance: level 1

:: Information technology ::

__________ is the reorientation of product and service designs to focus on the end user as an individual consumer, in contrast with an earlier era of only organization-oriented offerings . Technologies whose first commercialization was at the inter-organization level thus have potential for later __________ . The emergence of the individual consumer as the primary driver of product and service design is most commonly associated with the IT industry, as large business and government organizations dominated the early decades of computer usage and development. Thus the microcomputer revolution, in which electronic computing moved from exclusively enterprise and government use to include personal computing, is a cardinal example of __________ . But many technology-based products, such as calculators and mobile phones, have also had their origins in business markets, and only over time did they become dominated by high-volume consumer usage, as these products commoditized and prices fell. An example of enterprise software that became consumer software is optical character recognition software, which originated with banks and postal systems but eventually became personal productivity software.

Exam Probability: **Low**

46. *Answer choices:*

(see index for correct answer)

- a. IT industry competitiveness index
- b. Consumerization
- c. Omniview technology
- d. Information technology

Guidance: level 1

:: ::

_________ is a free email service developed by Google. Users can access _________ on the web and using third-party programs that synchronize email content through POP or IMAP protocols. _________ started as a limited beta release on April 1, 2004 and ended its testing phase on July 7, 2009.

Exam Probability: **High**

47. *Answer choices:*

(see index for correct answer)

- a. cultural
- b. imperative
- c. Character
- d. Gmail

Guidance: level 1

:: E-commerce ::

_________ , and its now-deprecated predecessor, Secure Sockets Layer , are cryptographic protocols designed to provide communications security over a computer network. Several versions of the protocols find widespread use in applications such as web browsing, email, instant messaging, and voice over IP . Websites can use TLS to secure all communications between their servers and web browsers.

Exam Probability: **High**

48. *Answer choices:*

(see index for correct answer)

- a. Centricom
- b. Digital certificate
- c. Multichannel retailing
- d. Online locator service

Guidance: level 1

:: Types of marketing ::

In microeconomics and management, _________ is an arrangement in which the supply chain of a company is owned by that company. Usually each member of the supply chain produces a different product or service, and the products combine to satisfy a common need. It is contrasted with horizontal integration, wherein a company produces several items which are related to one another. _________ has also described management styles that bring large portions of the supply chain not only under a common ownership, but also into one corporation .

Exam Probability: **Medium**

49. *Answer choices:*

(see index for correct answer)

- a. Vertical integration
- b. Customerization
- c. Multi-domestic strategy

- d. Secret brand

Guidance: level 1

:: Data management ::

__________ is a set of processes and technologies that supports the collection, managing, and publishing of information in any form or medium. When stored and accessed via computers, this information may be more specifically referred to as digital content, or simply as content.

Exam Probability: **Low**

50. *Answer choices:*

(see index for correct answer)

- a. Microsoft Office PerformancePoint Server
- b. Database schema
- c. Content management
- d. Lean integration

Guidance: level 1

:: Data transmission ::

In telecommunication a ________ is the means of connecting one location to another for the purpose of transmitting and receiving digital information. It can also refer to a set of electronics assemblies, consisting of a transmitter and a receiver and the interconnecting data telecommunication circuit. These are governed by a link protocol enabling digital data to be transferred from a data source to a data sink.

Exam Probability: **Low**

51. *Answer choices:*

(see index for correct answer)

- a. Protocol data unit
- b. Percept
- c. Ultra-wideband
- d. Tape relay

Guidance: level 1

:: Information systems ::

_________ is a process used in the life cycle area of the dynamic systems development method to collect business requirements while developing new information systems for a company. "The JAD process also includes approaches for enhancing user participation, expediting development, and improving the quality of specifications." It consists of a workshop where "knowledge workers and IT specialists meet, sometimes for several days, to define and review the business requirements for the system." The attendees include high level management officials who will ensure the product provides the needed reports and information at the end. This acts as "a management process which allows Corporate Information Services departments to work more effectively with users in a shorter time frame".

Exam Probability: **High**

52. *Answer choices:*

(see index for correct answer)

- a. VAT Information Exchange System
- b. Joint application design
- c. Credit bureau
- d. Master of Business Systems

Guidance: level 1

:: ::

A _________ is a computer file which stores data to be used by a computer application or system, including input and output data. A _________ usually does not contain instructions or code to be executed .

Exam Probability: **High**

53. *Answer choices:*

(see index for correct answer)

- a. Data file
- b. open system
- c. empathy
- d. surface-level diversity

Guidance: level 1

:: Data management ::

__________ is a data management concept concerning the capability that enables an organization to ensure that high data quality exists throughout the complete lifecycle of the data. The key focus areas of __________ include availability, usability, consistency, data integrity and data security and includes establishing processes to ensure effective data management throughout the enterprise such as accountability for the adverse effects of poor data quality and ensuring that the data which an enterprise has can be used by the entire organization.

Exam Probability: **Low**

54. *Answer choices:*

(see index for correct answer)

- a. Learning object
- b. Dynamic knowledge repository
- c. ROOT
- d. Data governance

Guidance: level 1

:: Information science ::

_________ is the resolution of uncertainty; it is that which answers the question of "what an entity is" and thus defines both its essence and nature of its characteristics. _________ relates to both data and knowledge, as data is meaningful _________ representing values attributed to parameters, and knowledge signifies understanding of a concept. _________ is uncoupled from an observer, which is an entity that can access _________ and thus discern what it specifies; _________ exists beyond an event horizon for example. In the case of knowledge, the _________ itself requires a cognitive observer to be obtained.

Exam Probability: **High**

55. *Answer choices:*

(see index for correct answer)

- a. Information
- b. Conceptions of Library and Information Science
- c. Exploratory search
- d. Information professional

Guidance: level 1

:: Management ::

The __________ is a strategy performance management tool – a semi-standard structured report, that can be used by managers to keep track of the execution of activities by the staff within their control and to monitor the consequences arising from these actions.

Exam Probability: **Low**

56. *Answer choices:*

(see index for correct answer)

- a. Project cost management
- b. Balanced scorecard
- c. Manager Tools Podcast
- d. Concept of the Corporation

Guidance: level 1

:: ::

A _________ is an abstract model that organizes elements of data and standardizes how they relate to one another and to properties of the real world entities. For instance, a _________ may specify that the data element representing a car be composed of a number of other elements which, in turn, represent the color and size of the car and define its owner.

Exam Probability: **High**

57. *Answer choices:*

(see index for correct answer)

- a. Sarbanes-Oxley act of 2002
- b. cultural
- c. Data model
- d. personal values

Guidance: level 1

:: Data security ::

In information technology, a _________ , or data _________ , or the process of backing up, refers to the copying into an archive file of computer data that is already in secondary storage—so that it may be used to restore the original after a data loss event. The verb form is "back up" , whereas the noun and adjective form is " _________ ".

Exam Probability: **Medium**

58. *Answer choices:*

(see index for correct answer)

- a. Rublon
- b. Jericho Forum Commandments
- c. Backup
- d. Security convergence

Guidance: level 1

:: Information and communication technologies for development ::

__________ is a non-profit initiative established with the goal of transforming education for children around the world; this goal was to be achieved by creating and distributing educational devices for the developing world, and by creating software and content for those devices.

Exam Probability: **Low**

59. *Answer choices:*

(see index for correct answer)

- a. Declaration of Helsinki
- b. United Nations Information and Communication Technologies Task Force
- c. Ma3bar
- d. Ghana-India Kofi Annan Centre of Excellence in ICT

Guidance: level 1

Marketing

Marketing is the study and management of exchange relationships. Marketing is the business process of creating relationships with and satisfying customers. With its focus on the customer, marketing is one of the premier components of business management.

Marketing is defined by the American Marketing Association as "the activity, set of institutions, and processes for creating, communicating, delivering, and exchanging offerings that have value for customers, clients, partners, and society at large."

The term __________ refers to measures designed to increase the degree of autonomy and self-determination in people and in communities in order to enable them to represent their interests in a responsible and self-determined way, acting on their own authority. It is the process of becoming stronger and more confident, especially in controlling one`s life and claiming one`s rights. __________ as action refers both to the process of self- __________ and to professional support of people, which enables them to overcome their sense of powerlessness and lack of influence, and to recognize and use their resources. To do work with power.

Exam Probability: **Low**

1. *Answer choices:*

(see index for correct answer)

- a. Supplier performance management
- b. Organizational conflict
- c. Outrage constraint
- d. Business plan

Guidance: level 1

:: Marketing ::

_________ is "commercial competition characterized by the repeated cutting of prices below those of competitors". One competitor will lower its price, then others will lower their prices to match. If one of them reduces their price again, a new round of reductions starts. In the short term, _________ s are good for buyers, who can take advantage of lower prices. Often they are not good for the companies involved because the lower prices reduce profit margins and can threaten their survival.

Exam Probability: **Low**

2. *Answer choices:*

(see index for correct answer)

- a. Advertising media selection
- b. Fan loyalty
- c. Inventory
- d. Masstige

Guidance: level 1

:: ::

A _________ or sample _________ is a single measure of some attribute of a sample . It is calculated by applying a function to the values of the items of the sample, which are known together as a set of data.

Exam Probability: **Low**

3. *Answer choices:*

(see index for correct answer)

- a. hierarchical
- b. Statistic
- c. imperative
- d. deep-level diversity

Guidance: level 1

:: Marketing ::

_________ is research conducted for a problem that has not been studied more clearly, intended to establish priorities, develop operational definitions and improve the final research design. _________ helps determine the best research design, data-collection method and selection of subjects. It should draw definitive conclusions only with extreme caution. Given its fundamental nature, _________ often relies on techniques such as.

Exam Probability: **High**

4. *Answer choices:*

(see index for correct answer)

- a. Impulse buying
- b. Franchise fee
- c. Gambling advertising
- d. Pricing objectives

Guidance: level 1

:: Marketing terminology ::

_________ is used in marketing to describe the inability to assess the value gained from engaging in an activity using any tangible evidence. It is often used to describe services where there is no tangible product that the customer can purchase, that can be seen or touched.

Exam Probability: **Low**

5. *Answer choices:*

(see index for correct answer)

- a. Intangibility
- b. Marketing exposure
- c. Arrow information paradox
- d. sponsored link

Guidance: level 1

:: Supply chain management ::

_________ is the removal of intermediaries in economics from a supply chain, or cutting out the middlemen in connection with a transaction or a series of transactions. Instead of going through traditional distribution channels, which had some type of intermediary , companies may now deal with customers directly, for example via the Internet. Hence, the use of factory direct and direct from the factory to mean the same thing.

Exam Probability: **Medium**

6. *Answer choices:*

(see index for correct answer)

- a. Netchain analysis
- b. Design for logistics
- c. Certified Supply Chain Professional
- d. Disintermediation

Guidance: level 1

:: Data management ::

_________ is a form of intellectual property that grants the creator of an original creative work an exclusive legal right to determine whether and under what conditions this original work may be copied and used by others, usually for a limited term of years. The exclusive rights are not absolute but limited by limitations and exceptions to _________ law, including fair use. A major limitation on _________ on ideas is that _________ protects only the original expression of ideas, and not the underlying ideas themselves.

Exam Probability: **Low**

7. *Answer choices:*

(see index for correct answer)

- a. Copyright
- b. Enterprise data management
- c. Storage block
- d. World Wide Molecular Matrix

Guidance: level 1

:: Decision theory ::

Within economics the concept of _________ is used to model worth or value, but its usage has evolved significantly over time. The term was introduced initially as a measure of pleasure or satisfaction within the theory of utilitarianism by moral philosophers such as Jeremy Bentham and John Stuart Mill. But the term has been adapted and reapplied within neoclassical economics, which dominates modern economic theory, as a _________ function that represents a consumer`s preference ordering over a choice set. As such, it is devoid of its original interpretation as a measurement of the pleasure or satisfaction obtained by the consumer from that choice.

Exam Probability: **Medium**

8. *Answer choices:*

(see index for correct answer)

- a. Recognition primed decision
- b. Institutionalism
- c. Rational planning model
- d. Utility

Guidance: level 1

:: ::

_________ is a term frequently used in marketing. It is a measure of how products and services supplied by a company meet or surpass customer expectation. _________ is defined as "the number of customers, or percentage of total customers, whose reported experience with a firm, its products, or its services exceeds specified satisfaction goals."

Exam Probability: **High**

9. *Answer choices:*

(see index for correct answer)

- a. imperative
- b. process perspective
- c. hierarchical perspective
- d. interpersonal communication

Guidance: level 1

:: Project management ::

_________ is the right to exercise power, which can be formalized by a state and exercised by way of judges, appointed executives of government, or the ecclesiastical or priestly appointed representatives of a God or other deities.

Exam Probability: **Low**

10. *Answer choices:*

(see index for correct answer)

- a. Defense Acquisition Workforce Improvement Act
- b. Authority
- c. Expected commercial value
- d. Decision table

Guidance: level 1

:: ::

_________ is a means of protection from financial loss. It is a form of risk management, primarily used to hedge against the risk of a contingent or uncertain loss

Exam Probability: **Medium**

11. *Answer choices:*

(see index for correct answer)

- a. open system
- b. deep-level diversity
- c. Insurance
- d. Sarbanes-Oxley act of 2002

Guidance: level 1

:: Market research ::

__________ is the action of defining, gathering, analyzing, and distributing intelligence about products, customers, competitors, and any aspect of the environment needed to support executives and managers in strategic decision making for an organization.

Exam Probability: **High**

12. *Answer choices:*

(see index for correct answer)

- a. Competitive intelligence
- b. Early adopter
- c. The Ehrenberg-Bass Institute for Marketing Science
- d. Focus group

Guidance: level 1

:: Supply chain management terms ::

In business and finance, _________ is a system of organizations, people, activities, information, and resources involved inmoving a product or service from supplier to customer. _________ activities involve the transformation of natural resources, raw materials, and components into a finished product that is delivered to the end customer. In sophisticated _________ systems, used products may re-enter the _________ at any point where residual value is recyclable. _________ s link value chains.

Exam Probability: **Medium**

13. *Answer choices:*

(see index for correct answer)

- a. Widget
- b. Price look-up code
- c. Most valuable customers
- d. Last mile

Guidance: level 1

:: Promotion and marketing communications ::

Advertising mail, also known as _________ , junk mail , mailshot or admail, is the delivery of advertising material to recipients of postal mail. The delivery of advertising mail forms a large and growing service for many postal services, and direct-mail marketing forms a significant portion of the direct marketing industry. Some organizations attempt to help people opt out of receiving advertising mail, in many cases motivated by a concern over its negative environmental impact.

Exam Probability: **Medium**

14. *Answer choices:*

(see index for correct answer)

- a. Direct mail
- b. CollarCard
- c. Social network advertising
- d. Custom media

Guidance: level 1

:: ::

_________ is both a research area and a practical skill encompassing the ability of an individual or organization to "lead" or guide other individuals, teams, or entire organizations. Specialist literature debates various viewpoints, contrasting Eastern and Western approaches to _________ , and also United States versus European approaches. U.S. academic environments define _________ as "a process of social influence in which a person can enlist the aid and support of others in the accomplishment of a common task".

Exam Probability: **Low**

15. *Answer choices:*

(see index for correct answer)

- a. corporate values
- b. levels of analysis
- c. Leadership
- d. Character

Guidance: level 1

:: ::

_________ is a process whereby a person assumes the parenting of another, usually a child, from that person`s biological or legal parent or parents. Legal _________ s permanently transfers all rights and responsibilities, along with filiation, from the biological parent or parents.

Exam Probability: **Low**

16. *Answer choices:*

(see index for correct answer)

- a. co-culture
- b. cultural
- c. hierarchical perspective

- d. Adoption

Guidance: level 1

:: ::

_________ , known in Europe as research and technological development , refers to innovative activities undertaken by corporations or governments in developing new services or products, or improving existing services or products. _________ constitutes the first stage of development of a potential new service or the production process.

Exam Probability: **High**

17. *Answer choices:*

(see index for correct answer)

- a. Research and development
- b. process perspective
- c. information systems assessment
- d. Character

Guidance: level 1

:: Brand management ::

In marketing, _________ is the analysis and planning on how a brand is perceived in the market. Developing a good relationship with the target market is essential for _________ . Tangible elements of _________ include the product itself; its look, price, and packaging, etc. The intangible elements are the experiences that the consumers share with the brand, and also the relationships they have with the brand. A brand manager would oversee all aspects of the consumer`s brand association as well as relationships with members of the supply chain.

Exam Probability: **High**

18. *Answer choices:*

(see index for correct answer)

- a. Status brand
- b. Operator logo
- c. Brand aversion
- d. Brand management

Guidance: level 1

:: Cultural appropriation ::

_________ is a social and economic order that encourages the acquisition of goods and services in ever-increasing amounts. With the industrial revolution, but particularly in the 20th century, mass production led to an economic crisis: there was overproduction—the supply of goods would grow beyond consumer demand, and so manufacturers turned to planned obsolescence and advertising to manipulate consumer spending. In 1899, a book on _________ published by Thorstein Veblen, called The Theory of the Leisure Class, examined the widespread values and economic institutions emerging along with the widespread "leisure time" in the beginning of the 20th century. In it Veblen "views the activities and spending habits of this leisure class in terms of conspicuous and vicarious consumption and waste. Both are related to the display of status and not to functionality or usefulness."

Exam Probability: **Medium**

19. *Answer choices:*

(see index for correct answer)

- a. Hollywood Indian
- b. Cool
- c. National-Anarchism
- d. Consumerism

Guidance: level 1

:: Information technology ::

__________ is the use of computers to store, retrieve, transmit, and manipulate data, or information, often in the context of a business or other enterprise. IT is considered to be a subset of information and communications technology . An __________ system is generally an information system, a communications system or, more specifically speaking, a computer system – including all hardware, software and peripheral equipment – operated by a limited group of users.

Exam Probability: **High**

20. *Answer choices:*

(see index for correct answer)

- a. United States v. Ivanov
- b. Geeks Without Bounds
- c. ActivEcho
- d. Information infrastructure

Guidance: level 1

:: Project management ::

Contemporary business and science treat as a __________ any undertaking, carried out individually or collaboratively and possibly involving research or design, that is carefully planned to achieve a particular aim.

Exam Probability: **Low**

21. *Answer choices:*

(see index for correct answer)

- a. Project
- b. Logical framework approach
- c. Market requirements document
- d. Assumption-based planning

Guidance: level 1

:: Survey methodology ::

An _________ is a conversation where questions are asked and answers are given. In common parlance, the word " _________ " refers to a one-on-one conversation between an _________ er and an _________ ee. The _________ er asks questions to which the _________ ee responds, usually so information may be transferred from _________ ee to _________ er . Sometimes, information can be transferred in both directions. It is a communication, unlike a speech, which produces a one-way flow of information.

Exam Probability: **Medium**

22. *Answer choices:*

(see index for correct answer)

- a. Self-report study
- b. Group concept mapping
- c. American Association for Public Opinion Research

- d. Interview

Guidance: level 1

:: Types of marketing ::

_________ was first defined as a form of marketing developed from direct response marketing campaigns which emphasizes customer retention and satisfaction, rather than a focus on sales transactions.

Exam Probability: **Medium**

23. *Answer choices:*

(see index for correct answer)

- a. Alliance marketing
- b. Cause marketing
- c. Direct response
- d. Limited edition candy

Guidance: level 1

:: ::

_________ Corporation is an American multinational technology company with headquarters in Redmond, Washington. It develops, manufactures, licenses, supports and sells computer software, consumer electronics, personal computers, and related services. Its best known software products are the _________ Windows line of operating systems, the _________ Office suite, and the Internet Explorer and Edge Web browsers. Its flagship hardware products are the Xbox video game consoles and the _________ Surface lineup of touchscreen personal computers. As of 2016, it is the world's largest software maker by revenue, and one of the world's most valuable companies. The word " _________ " is a portmanteau of "microcomputer" and "software". _________ is ranked No. 30 in the 2018 Fortune 500 rankings of the largest United States corporations by total revenue.

Exam Probability: **High**

24. *Answer choices:*

(see index for correct answer)

- a. hierarchical perspective
- b. Sarbanes-Oxley act of 2002
- c. Microsoft
- d. functional perspective

Guidance: level 1

:: ::

__________ is the means to see, hear, or become aware of something or someone through our fundamental senses. The term __________ derives from the Latin word perceptio, and is the organization, identification, and interpretation of sensory information in order to represent and understand the presented information, or the environment.

Exam Probability: **High**

25. *Answer choices:*

(see index for correct answer)

- a. Character
- b. information systems assessment
- c. cultural
- d. Perception

Guidance: level 1

:: ::

In business and engineering, new _________ covers the complete process of bringing a new product to market. A central aspect of NPD is product design, along with various business considerations. New _________ is described broadly as the transformation of a market opportunity into a product available for sale. The product can be tangible or intangible , though sometimes services and other processes are distinguished from "products." NPD requires an understanding of customer needs and wants, the competitive environment, and the nature of the market.Cost, time and quality are the main variables that drive customer needs. Aiming at these three variables, innovative companies develop continuous practices and strategies to better satisfy customer requirements and to increase their own market share by a regular development of new products. There are many uncertainties and challenges which companies must face throughout the process. The use of best practices and the elimination of barriers to communication are the main concerns for the management of the NPD .

Exam Probability: **Medium**

26. *Answer choices:*

(see index for correct answer)

- a. information systems assessment
- b. imperative
- c. empathy
- d. Product development

Guidance: level 1

:: Consumer theory ::

_________ is the quantity of a good that consumers are willing and able to purchase at various prices during a given period of time.

Exam Probability: **Low**

27. *Answer choices:*

(see index for correct answer)

- a. End-of-life
- b. Autonomous consumption
- c. Marshallian demand function
- d. Demand

Guidance: level 1

:: Product development ::

In business and engineering, _________ covers the complete process of bringing a new product to market. A central aspect of NPD is product design, along with various business considerations. _________ is described broadly as the transformation of a market opportunity into a product available for sale. The product can be tangible or intangible , though sometimes services and other processes are distinguished from "products." NPD requires an understanding of customer needs and wants, the competitive environment, and the nature of the market.Cost, time and quality are the main variables that drive customer needs. Aiming at these three variables, innovative companies develop continuous practices and strategies to better satisfy customer requirements and to increase their own market share by a regular development of new products. There are many uncertainties and challenges which companies must face throughout the process. The use of best practices and the elimination of barriers to communication are the main concerns for the management of the NPD .

Exam Probability: **Medium**

28. *Answer choices:*

(see index for correct answer)

- a. Walter Heidenfels
- b. New product development
- c. Minimum viable product
- d. Specification tree

Guidance: level 1

:: ::

In production, research, retail, and accounting, a _________ is the value of money that has been used up to produce something or deliver a service, and hence is not available for use anymore. In business, the _________ may be one of acquisition, in which case the amount of money expended to acquire it is counted as _________. In this case, money is the input that is gone in order to acquire the thing. This acquisition _________ may be the sum of the _________ of production as incurred by the original producer, and further _________s of transaction as incurred by the acquirer over and above the price paid to the producer. Usually, the price also includes a mark-up for profit over the _________ of production.

Exam Probability: **Low**

29. *Answer choices:*

(see index for correct answer)

- a. information systems assessment
- b. levels of analysis
- c. co-culture
- d. surface-level diversity

Guidance: level 1

:: Business law ::

A __________ is an arrangement where parties, known as partners, agree to cooperate to advance their mutual interests. The partners in a __________ may be individuals, businesses, interest-based organizations, schools, governments or combinations. Organizations may partner to increase the likelihood of each achieving their mission and to amplify their reach. A __________ may result in issuing and holding equity or may be only governed by a contract.

Exam Probability: **Medium**

30. *Answer choices:*

(see index for correct answer)

- a. Partnership
- b. Perfection
- c. Doing business as
- d. Unfair preference

Guidance: level 1

:: ::

A __________ is a discussion or informational website published on the World Wide Web consisting of discrete, often informal diary-style text entries . Posts are typically displayed in reverse chronological order, so that the most recent post appears first, at the top of the web page. Until 2009, __________s were usually the work of a single individual, occasionally of a small group, and often covered a single subject or topic. In the 2010s, "multi-author __________s" emerged, featuring the writing of multiple authors and sometimes professionally edited. MABs from newspapers, other media outlets, universities, think tanks, advocacy groups, and similar institutions account for an increasing quantity of __________ traffic. The rise of Twitter and other "micro __________ging" systems helps integrate MABs and single-author __________s into the news media. __________ can also be used as a verb, meaning to maintain or add content to a __________ .

Exam Probability: **Low**

31. *Answer choices:*

(see index for correct answer)

- a. co-culture
- b. corporate values
- c. Blog
- d. similarity-attraction theory

Guidance: level 1

:: ::

In marketing jargon, product lining is offering several related products for sale individually. Unlike product bundling, where several products are combined into one group, which is then offered for sale as a units, product lining involves offering the products for sale separately. A line can comprise related products of various sizes, types, colors, qualities, or prices. Line depth refers to the number of subcategories a category has. Line consistency refers to how closely related the products that make up the line are. Line vulnerability refers to the percentage of sales or profits that are derived from only a few products in the line.

Exam Probability: **High**

32. *Answer choices:*

(see index for correct answer)

- a. similarity-attraction theory
- b. corporate values
- c. Product line
- d. hierarchical perspective

Guidance: level 1

:: Business models ::

A _________ , _________ company or daughter company is a company that is owned or controlled by another company, which is called the parent company, parent, or holding company. The _________ can be a company, corporation, or limited liability company. In some cases it is a government or state-owned enterprise. In some cases, particularly in the music and book publishing industries, subsidiaries are referred to as imprints.

Exam Probability: **High**

33. *Answer choices:*

(see index for correct answer)

- a. Copy to China
- b. Dependent growth business model
- c. Business model pattern
- d. Subsidiary

Guidance: level 1

:: Progressive Era in the United States ::

The Clayton Antitrust Act of 1914 , was a part of United States antitrust law with the goal of adding further substance to the U.S. antitrust law regime; the _________ sought to prevent anticompetitive practices in their incipiency. That regime started with the Sherman Antitrust Act of 1890, the first Federal law outlawing practices considered harmful to consumers . The _________ specified particular prohibited conduct, the three-level enforcement scheme, the exemptions, and the remedial measures.

Exam Probability: **Medium**

34. *Answer choices:*

(see index for correct answer)

- a. Clayton Act
- b. Clayton Antitrust Act
- c. Mann Act

Guidance: level 1

:: Competition (economics) ::

__________ arises whenever at least two parties strive for a goal which cannot be shared: where one`s gain is the other`s loss .

Exam Probability: **High**

35. *Answer choices:*

(see index for correct answer)

- a. Self-competition
- b. Level playing field
- c. Tax competition
- d. Wantrapreneur

Guidance: level 1

:: ::

_________ LLC is an American multinational technology company that specializes in Internet-related services and products, which include online advertising technologies, search engine, cloud computing, software, and hardware. It is considered one of the Big Four technology companies, alongside Amazon, Apple and Facebook.

Exam Probability: **Medium**

36. *Answer choices:*

(see index for correct answer)

- a. levels of analysis
- b. process perspective
- c. interpersonal communication
- d. co-culture

Guidance: level 1

:: Marketing ::

__________ is based on a marketing concept which can be adopted by an organization as a strategy for business expansion. Where implemented, a franchisor licenses its know-how, procedures, intellectual property, use of its business model, brand, and rights to sell its branded products and services to a franchisee. In return the franchisee pays certain fees and agrees to comply with certain obligations, typically set out in a Franchise Agreement.

Exam Probability: **Medium**

37. *Answer choices:*

(see index for correct answer)

- a. Klondike Big Inch Land Promotion
- b. Franchising
- c. Negotiation
- d. Branding national myths and symbols

Guidance: level 1

:: ::

Advertising is a marketing communication that employs an openly sponsored, non-personal message to promote or sell a product, service or idea. Sponsors of advertising are typically businesses wishing to promote their products or services. Advertising is differentiated from public relations in that an advertiser pays for and has control over the message. It differs from personal selling in that the message is non-personal, i.e., not directed to a particular individual.Advertising is communicated through various mass media, including traditional media such as newspapers, magazines, television, radio, outdoor advertising or direct mail; and new media such as search results, blogs, social media, websites or text messages. The actual presentation of the message in a medium is referred to as an _________ , or "ad" or advert for short.

Exam Probability: **Medium**

38. *Answer choices:*

(see index for correct answer)

- a. Advertisement
- b. Character
- c. levels of analysis
- d. similarity-attraction theory

Guidance: level 1

:: ::

In logic and philosophy, an _________ is a series of statements , called the premises or premisses , intended to determine the degree of truth of another statement, the conclusion. The logical form of an _________ in a natural language can be represented in a symbolic formal language, and independently of natural language formally defined " _________ s" can be made in math and computer science.

Exam Probability: **High**

39. *Answer choices:*

(see index for correct answer)

- a. levels of analysis
- b. information systems assessment
- c. functional perspective
- d. Argument

Guidance: level 1

:: Budgets ::

A _________ is a financial plan for a defined period, often one year. It may also include planned sales volumes and revenues, resource quantities, costs and expenses, assets, liabilities and cash flows. Companies, governments, families and other organizations use it to express strategic plans of activities or events in measurable terms.

Exam Probability: **Medium**

40. *Answer choices:*

(see index for correct answer)

- a. Budget
- b. Black budget
- c. Link budget
- d. Programme budgeting

Guidance: level 1

:: Commercial item transport and distribution ::

Wholesaling or distributing is the sale of goods or merchandise to retailers; to industrial, commercial, institutional, or other professional business users; or to other _________ rs and related subordinated services. In general, it is the sale of goods to anyone other than a standard consumer.

Exam Probability: **Low**

41. *Answer choices:*

(see index for correct answer)

- a. Worldscale
- b. Wholesale
- c. Point-to-point transit
- d. Refrigerator truck

Guidance: level 1

:: ::

A _________ is a graphic mark, emblem, or symbol used to aid and promote public identification and recognition. It may be of an abstract or figurative design or include the text of the name it represents as in a wordmark.

Exam Probability: **Medium**

42. *Answer choices:*

(see index for correct answer)

- a. Logo
- b. similarity-attraction theory
- c. information systems assessment
- d. hierarchical

Guidance: level 1

:: Consumer behaviour ::

_________ is an activity in which a customer browses the available goods or services presented by one or more retailers with the potential intent to purchase a suitable selection of them. A typology of shopper types has been developed by scholars which identifies one group of shoppers as recreational shoppers, that is, those who enjoy _________ and view it as a leisure activity.

Exam Probability: **Low**

43. *Answer choices:*

(see index for correct answer)

- a. Internality
- b. Net Promoter
- c. Consumer confidence index
- d. Ernest Dichter

Guidance: level 1

:: Costs ::

In economics, _________ is the total economic cost of production and is made up of variable cost, which varies according to the quantity of a good produced and includes inputs such as labour and raw materials, plus fixed cost, which is independent of the quantity of a good produced and includes inputs that cannot be varied in the short term: fixed costs such as buildings and machinery, including sunk costs if any. Since cost is measured per unit of time, it is a flow variable.

Exam Probability: **High**

44. *Answer choices:*

(see index for correct answer)

- a. Road Logistics Costing in South Africa
- b. Prospective costs
- c. Customer Cost
- d. Flyaway cost

Guidance: level 1

:: Advertising by type ::

_________ or advertising war is an advertisement in which a particular product, or service, specifically mentions a competitor by name for the express purpose of showing why the competitor is inferior to the product naming it. Also referred to as "knocking copy", it is loosely defined as advertising where "the advertised brand is explicitly compared with one or more competing brands and the comparison is obvious to the audience."

Exam Probability: **High**

45. *Answer choices:*

(see index for correct answer)

- a. Parody advertisement
- b. Virtual advertising

- c. Local advertising
- d. Comparative advertising

Guidance: level 1

:: Auctioneering ::

An __________ is a process of buying and selling goods or services by offering them up for bid, taking bids, and then selling the item to the highest bidder. The open ascending price __________ is arguably the most common form of __________ in use today. Participants bid openly against one another, with each subsequent bid required to be higher than the previous bid. An __________eer may announce prices, bidders may call out their bids themselves , or bids may be submitted electronically with the highest current bid publicly displayed. In a Dutch __________ , the __________eer begins with a high asking price for some quantity of like items; the price is lowered until a participant is willing to accept the __________eer`s price for some quantity of the goods in the lot or until the seller`s reserve price is met. While __________s are most associated in the public imagination with the sale of antiques, paintings, rare collectibles and expensive wines, __________s are also used for commodities, livestock, radio spectrum and used cars. In economic theory, an __________ may refer to any mechanism or set of trading rules for exchange.

Exam Probability: **Medium**

46. *Answer choices:*

(see index for correct answer)

- a. Auction
- b. Calcutta auction

- c. Online auction
- d. Auto auction

Guidance: level 1

:: Consumer behaviour ::

_________ refers to the ability of a company or product to retain its customers over some specified period. High _________ means customers of the product or business tend to return to, continue to buy or in some other way not defect to another product or business, or to non-use entirely. Selling organizations generally attempt to reduce customer defections. _________ starts with the first contact an organization has with a customer and continues throughout the entire lifetime of a relationship and successful retention efforts take this entire lifecycle into account. A company`s ability to attract and retain new customers is related not only to its product or services, but also to the way it services its existing customers, the value the customers actually generate as a result of utilizing the solutions, and the reputation it creates within and across the marketplace.

Exam Probability: **High**

47. *Answer choices:*

(see index for correct answer)

- a. Internality
- b. Cocooning
- c. Customer retention
- d. Self-brand

Guidance: level 1

:: ::

In legal terminology, a _________ is any formal legal document that sets out the facts and legal reasons that the filing party or parties believes are sufficient to support a claim against the party or parties against whom the claim is brought that entitles the plaintiff to a remedy . For example, the Federal Rules of Civil Procedure that govern civil litigation in United States courts provide that a civil action is commenced with the filing or service of a pleading called a _________ . Civil court rules in states that have incorporated the Federal Rules of Civil Procedure use the same term for the same pleading.

Exam Probability: **High**

48. *Answer choices:*

(see index for correct answer)

- a. open system
- b. corporate values
- c. Complaint
- d. process perspective

Guidance: level 1

:: Management ::

_________ is the organizational discipline which focuses on the practical application of marketing orientation, techniques and methods inside enterprises and organizations and on the management of a firm`s marketing resources and activities.

Exam Probability: **Medium**

49. *Answer choices:*

(see index for correct answer)

- a. Submission management
- b. Managerial economics
- c. Marketing management
- d. Logistics management

Guidance: level 1

:: ::

Distribution is one of the four elements of the marketing mix. Distribution is the process of making a product or service available for the consumer or business user who needs it. This can be done directly by the producer or service provider, or using indirect channels with distributors or intermediaries. The other three elements of the marketing mix are product, pricing, and promotion.

Exam Probability: **Medium**

50. *Answer choices:*

(see index for correct answer)

- a. deep-level diversity
- b. Distribution channel
- c. cultural
- d. interpersonal communication

Guidance: level 1

:: Advertising ::

A __________ is a document used by creative professionals and agencies to develop creative deliverables: visual design, copy, advertising, web sites, etc. The document is usually developed by the requestor and approved by the creative team of designers, writers, and project managers. In some cases, the project's __________ may need creative director approval before work will commence.

Exam Probability: **Low**

51. *Answer choices:*

(see index for correct answer)

- a. Creative brief
- b. Sponsor
- c. Direct Agency / Rep Electronic Connection
- d. Tradio

Guidance: level 1

:: Brand management ::

Marketing communications uses different marketing channels and tools in combination: Marketing communication channels focus on any way a business communicates a message to its desired market, or the market in general. A marketing communication tool can be anything from: advertising, personal selling, direct marketing, sponsorship, communication, and promotion to public relations.

Exam Probability: **Medium**

52. *Answer choices:*

(see index for correct answer)

- a. Sanrio
- b. Prophet
- c. Integrated marketing
- d. Brand engagement

Guidance: level 1

:: Sales ::

__________ is a business discipline which is focused on the practical application of sales techniques and the management of a firm`s sales operations. It is an important business function as net sales through the sale of products and services and resulting profit drive most commercial business. These are also typically the goals and performance indicators of __________.

Exam Probability: **High**

53. *Answer choices:*

(see index for correct answer)

- a. Sale and rent back
- b. Sales operations
- c. Hit rate
- d. Account-based marketing

Guidance: level 1

:: Survey methodology ::

__________ is often used to assess thoughts, opinions, and feelings. Surveys can be specific and limited, or they can have more global, widespread goals. Psychologists and sociologists often use surveys to analyze behavior, while it is also used to meet the more pragmatic needs of the media, such as, in evaluating political candidates, public health officials, professional organizations, and advertising and marketing directors. A survey consists of a predetermined set of questions that is given to a sample. With a representative sample, that is, one that is representative of the larger population of interest, one can describe the attitudes of the population from which the sample was drawn. Further, one can compare the attitudes of different populations as well as look for changes in attitudes over time. A good sample selection is key as it allows one to generalize the findings from the sample to the population, which is the whole purpose of __________ .

Exam Probability: **High**

54. *Answer choices:*

(see index for correct answer)

- a. Total survey error
- b. National Health Interview Survey
- c. Survey research
- d. Political forecasting

Guidance: level 1

:: Industry ::

__________ describes various measures of the efficiency of production. Often, a __________ measure is expressed as the ratio of an aggregate output to a single input or an aggregate input used in a production process, i.e. output per unit of input. Most common example is the labour __________ measure, e.g., such as GDP per worker. There are many different definitions of __________ and the choice among them depends on the purpose of the __________ measurement and/or data availability. The key source of difference between various __________ measures is also usually related to how the outputs and the inputs are aggregated into scalars to obtain such a ratio-type measure of __________.

Exam Probability: **High**

55. *Answer choices:*

(see index for correct answer)

- a. Metal expansion joint
- b. Sexual division of labour
- c. Productivity
- d. Cartoning machine

Guidance: level 1

:: ::

__________, or auditory perception, is the ability to perceive sounds by detecting vibrations, changes in the pressure of the surrounding medium through time, through an organ such as the ear. The academic field concerned with __________ is auditory science.

Exam Probability: **Medium**

56. *Answer choices:*

(see index for correct answer)

- a. imperative
- b. co-culture
- c. Sarbanes-Oxley act of 2002
- d. levels of analysis

Guidance: level 1

:: Financial economics ::

In management, business value is an informal term that includes all forms of value that determine the health and well-being of the firm in the long run. Business value expands concept of value of the firm beyond economic value to include other forms of value such as employee value, _________ , supplier value, channel partner value, alliance partner value, managerial value, and societal value. Many of these forms of value are not directly measured in monetary terms.

Exam Probability: **Low**

57. *Answer choices:*

(see index for correct answer)

- a. Forward exchange rate

- b. Capital asset
- c. Lookback option
- d. Cyclical asymmetry

Guidance: level 1

:: ::

_________ , in general use, is a devotion and faithfulness to a nation, cause, philosophy, country, group, or person. Philosophers disagree on what can be an object of _________ , as some argue that _________ is strictly interpersonal and only another human being can be the object of _________ . The definition of _________ in law and political science is the fidelity of an individual to a nation, either one`s nation of birth, or one`s declared home nation by oath .

Exam Probability: **Low**

58. *Answer choices:*

(see index for correct answer)

- a. Loyalty
- b. hierarchical
- c. imperative
- d. co-culture

Guidance: level 1

:: Economic globalization ::

_________ is an agreement in which one company hires another company to be responsible for a planned or existing activity that is or could be done internally,and sometimes involves transferring employees and assets from one firm to another.

Exam Probability: **Medium**

59. *Answer choices:*

(see index for correct answer)

- a. Outsourcing
- b. global financial

Guidance: level 1

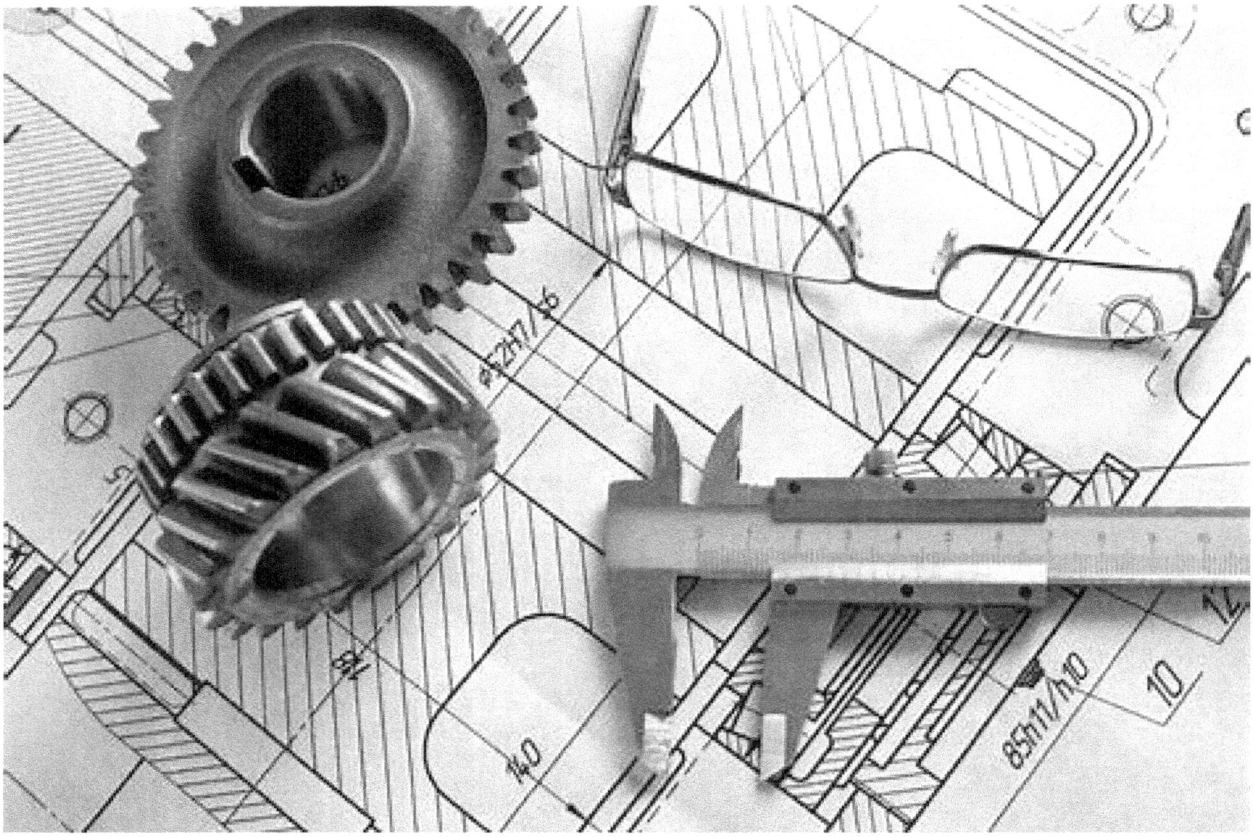

Manufacturing

Manufacturing is the production of merchandise for use or sale using labor and machines, tools, chemical and biological processing, or formulation. The term may refer to a range of human activity, from handicraft to high tech, but is most commonly applied to industrial design , in which raw materials are transformed into finished goods on a large scale. Such finished goods may be sold to other manufacturers for the production of other, more complex products, such as aircraft, household appliances, furniture, sports equipment or automobiles, or sold to wholesalers, who in turn sell them to retailers, who then sell them to end users and consumers.

__________ is an organization`s process of defining its strategy, or direction, and making decisions on allocating its resources to pursue this strategy. It may also extend to control mechanisms for guiding the implementation of the strategy. __________ became prominent in corporations during the 1960s and remains an important aspect of strategic management. It is executed by strategic planners or strategists, who involve many parties and research sources in their analysis of the organization and its relationship to the environment in which it competes.

Exam Probability: **Low**

1. *Answer choices:*

(see index for correct answer)

- a. Business war games
- b. Strategic planning
- c. Community Futures
- d. Joint decision trap

Guidance: level 1

:: Natural resources ::

__________s are resources that exist without actions of humankind. This includes all valued characteristics such as magnetic, gravitational, electrical properties and forces etc. On Earth it includes sunlight, atmosphere, water, land along with all vegetation, crops and animal life that naturally subsists upon or within the heretofore identified characteristics and substances.

Exam Probability: **Medium**

2. *Answer choices:*

(see index for correct answer)

- a. Natural Resources Forum
- b. QEMSCAN
- c. Asteroid mining
- d. Natural resource

Guidance: level 1

:: ::

A __________ or till is a mechanical or electronic device for registering and calculating transactions at a point of sale. It is usually attached to a drawer for storing cash and other valuables. A modern __________ is usually attached to a printer that can print out receipts for record-keeping purposes.

Exam Probability: **Low**

3. *Answer choices:*

(see index for correct answer)

- a. open system
- b. Cash register
- c. Character

- d. imperative

Guidance: level 1

:: Business process ::

_________ is the value to an enterprise which is derived from the techniques, procedures, and programs that implement and enhance the delivery of goods and services. _________ is one of the three components of structural capital, itself a component of intellectual capital. _________ can be seen as the value of processes to any entity, whether for profit or not-for profit, but is most commonly used in reference to for-profit entities.

Exam Probability: **Medium**

4. *Answer choices:*

(see index for correct answer)

- a. Business process outsourcing
- b. Communication-enabled business process
- c. Bonita BPM
- d. Process capital

Guidance: level 1

:: Project management ::

In economics and business decision-making, a sunk cost is a cost that has already been incurred and cannot be recovered.

Exam Probability: **High**

5. *Answer choices:*

(see index for correct answer)

- a. Sunk costs
- b. Effective Development Group
- c. A Guide to the Project Management Body of Knowledge
- d. Starmad

Guidance: level 1

:: Industrial processes ::

A _________ is a device used for high-temperature heating. The name derives from Latin word fornax, which means oven. The heat energy to fuel a _________ may be supplied directly by fuel combustion, by electricity such as the electric arc _________ , or through induction heating in induction _________ s.

Exam Probability: **Medium**

6. *Answer choices:*

(see index for correct answer)

- a. Shell-Paques process
- b. Chemical vapor infiltration
- c. Furnace
- d. Sinter Plant

Guidance: level 1

:: Manufacturing ::

A _________ is an object used to extend the ability of an individual to modify features of the surrounding environment. Although many animals use simple _________ s, only human beings, whose use of stone _________ s dates back hundreds of millennia, use _________ s to make other _________ s. The set of _________ s needed to perform different tasks that are part of the same activity is called gear or equipment.

Exam Probability: **Medium**

7. *Answer choices:*

(see index for correct answer)

- a. Tool
- b. Build to stock
- c. Initial Reject
- d. Part number

Guidance: level 1

:: Fault-tolerant computer systems ::

__________ decision-making is a group decision-making process in which group members develop, and agree to support a decision in the best interest of the whole group or common goal. __________ may be defined professionally as an acceptable resolution, one that can be supported, even if not the "favourite" of each individual. It has its origin in the Latin word consensus , which is from consentio meaning literally feel together. It is used to describe both the decision and the process of reaching a decision. __________ decision-making is thus concerned with the process of deliberating and finalizing a decision, and the social, economic, legal, environmental and political effects of applying this process.

Exam Probability: **Low**

8. *Answer choices:*

(see index for correct answer)

- a. RAID
- b. Single point of failure
- c. Consensus
- d. Failure detector

Guidance: level 1

:: ::

In sales, commerce and economics, a _________ is the recipient of a good, service, product or an idea - obtained from a seller, vendor, or supplier via a financial transaction or exchange for money or some other valuable consideration.

Exam Probability: **Low**

9. *Answer choices:*

(see index for correct answer)

- a. personal values
- b. Customer
- c. information systems assessment
- d. open system

Guidance: level 1

:: ::

An _________ is, most an organized examination or formal evaluation exercise. In engineering activities _________ involves the measurements, tests, and gauges applied to certain characteristics in regard to an object or activity. The results are usually compared to specified requirements and standards for determining whether the item or activity is in line with these targets, often with a Standard _________ Procedure in place to ensure consistent checking. _________ s are usually non-destructive.

Exam Probability: **High**

10. *Answer choices:*

(see index for correct answer)

- a. empathy
- b. deep-level diversity
- c. personal values
- d. Inspection

Guidance: level 1

:: Retailing ::

_________ is the process of selling consumer goods or services to customers through multiple channels of distribution to earn a profit. _________ ers satisfy demand identified through a supply chain. The term " _________ er" is typically applied where a service provider fills the small orders of a large number of individuals, who are end-users, rather than large orders of a small number of wholesale, corporate or government clientele. Shopping generally refers to the act of buying products. Sometimes this is done to obtain final goods, including necessities such as food and clothing; sometimes it takes place as a recreational activity. Recreational shopping often involves window shopping and browsing: it does not always result in a purchase.

Exam Probability: **Medium**

11. *Answer choices:*

(see index for correct answer)

- a. Personal shopper

- b. Convenience store
- c. Home shopping
- d. Retail

Guidance: level 1

:: Project management ::

Some scenarios associate "this kind of planning" with learning "life skills". _________ s are necessary, or at least useful, in situations where individuals need to know what time they must be at a specific location to receive a specific service, and where people need to accomplish a set of goals within a set time period.

Exam Probability: **High**

12. *Answer choices:*

(see index for correct answer)

- a. Time to completion
- b. Time horizon
- c. Concurrent engineering
- d. Research program

Guidance: level 1

:: Production and manufacturing ::

_________ consists of organization-wide efforts to "install and make permanent climate where employees continuously improve their ability to provide on demand products and services that customers will find of particular value." "Total" emphasizes that departments in addition to production are obligated to improve their operations; "management" emphasizes that executives are obligated to actively manage quality through funding, training, staffing, and goal setting. While there is no widely agreed-upon approach, TQM efforts typically draw heavily on the previously developed tools and techniques of quality control. TQM enjoyed widespread attention during the late 1980s and early 1990s before being overshadowed by ISO 9000, Lean manufacturing, and Six Sigma.

Exam Probability: **High**

13. *Answer choices:*

(see index for correct answer)

- a. Total quality management
- b. Profibus
- c. Total productive maintenance
- d. Advanced product quality planning

Guidance: level 1

:: ::

_________ is the quantity of three-dimensional space enclosed by a closed surface, for example, the space that a substance or shape occupies or contains. _________ is often quantified numerically using the SI derived unit, the cubic metre. The _________ of a container is generally understood to be the capacity of the container; i. e., the amount of fluid that the container could hold, rather than the amount of space the container itself displaces.Three dimensional mathematical shapes are also assigned _________ s. _________ s of some simple shapes, such as regular, straight-edged, and circular shapes can be easily calculated using arithmetic formulas. _________ s of complicated shapes can be calculated with integral calculus if a formula exists for the shape`s boundary. One-dimensional figures and two-dimensional shapes are assigned zero _________ in the three-dimensional space.

Exam Probability: **High**

14. *Answer choices:*

(see index for correct answer)

- a. information systems assessment
- b. Character
- c. process perspective
- d. Volume

Guidance: level 1

:: Data management ::

_________ is an object-oriented program and library developed by CERN. It was originally designed for particle physics data analysis and contains several features specific to this field, but it is also used in other applications such as astronomy and data mining. The latest release is 6.16.00, as of 2018-11-14.

Exam Probability: **Low**

15. *Answer choices:*

(see index for correct answer)

- a. PureXML
- b. Data security
- c. ROOT
- d. Performance intelligence

Guidance: level 1

:: Management accounting ::

" _________ s are the structural determinants of the cost of an activity, reflecting any linkages or interrelationships that affect it". Therefore we could assume that the _________ s determine the cost behavior within the activities, reflecting the links that these have with other activities and relationships that affect them.

Exam Probability: **High**

16. *Answer choices:*

(see index for correct answer)

- a. Direct material usage variance
- b. Factory overhead
- c. Management accounting
- d. Total benefits of ownership

Guidance: level 1

:: Unit operations ::

_________ is a discipline of thermal engineering that concerns the generation, use, conversion, and exchange of thermal energy between physical systems. _________ is classified into various mechanisms, such as thermal conduction, thermal convection, thermal radiation, and transfer of energy by phase changes. Engineers also consider the transfer of mass of differing chemical species, either cold or hot, to achieve _________. While these mechanisms have distinct characteristics, they often occur simultaneously in the same system.

Exam Probability: **High**

17. *Answer choices:*

(see index for correct answer)

- a. Heat transfer
- b. Unit Operations of Chemical Engineering

- c. Distillation
- d. Solvent impregnated resin

Guidance: level 1

:: Marketing techniques ::

A __________ is an award to be given to a person, a group of people like a sports team, or organization to recognise and reward actions or achievements. Official __________ s often involve monetary rewards as well as the fame that comes with them. Some __________ s are also associated with extravagant awarding ceremonies, such as the Academy Awards.

Exam Probability: **High**

18. *Answer choices:*

(see index for correct answer)

- a. Premium
- b. Prize
- c. Locals casino
- d. Aaker Model

Guidance: level 1

:: Management ::

An _________ is a loosely coupled, self-organizing network of firms that combine their economic output to provide products and services offerings to the market. Firms in the _________ may operate independently, for example, through market mechanisms, or cooperatively through agreements and contracts. They provide value added service or product to the OEM .

Exam Probability: **High**

19. *Answer choices:*

(see index for correct answer)

- a. Duality
- b. Extended enterprise
- c. Technology scouting
- d. Behavioral risk management

Guidance: level 1

:: Quality assurance ::

The _________ is a United States-based nonprofit tax-exempt 501 organization that accredits more than 21,000 US health care organizations and programs. The international branch accredits medical services from around the world. A majority of US state governments recognize _________ accreditation as a condition of licensure for the receipt of Medicaid and Medicare reimbursements.

Exam Probability: **High**

20. *Answer choices:*

(see index for correct answer)

- a. European Association for Quality Assurance in Higher Education
- b. Arab Network for Quality Assurance in Higher Education
- c. National Certification Corporation
- d. TestLink

Guidance: level 1

:: Knowledge representation ::

__________ s are causal diagrams created by Kaoru Ishikawa that show the causes of a specific event.

Exam Probability: **Medium**

21. *Answer choices:*

(see index for correct answer)

- a. IDAMS
- b. Universal Decimal Classification
- c. Nippon Decimal Classification
- d. Attribute-value system

Guidance: level 1

:: Management ::

_________ is the process of thinking about the activities required to achieve a desired goal. It is the first and foremost activity to achieve desired results. It involves the creation and maintenance of a plan, such as psychological aspects that require conceptual skills. There are even a couple of tests to measure someone's capability of _________ well. As such, _________ is a fundamental property of intelligent behavior. An important further meaning, often just called " _________ " is the legal context of permitted building developments.

Exam Probability: **High**

22. *Answer choices:*

(see index for correct answer)

- a. Target operating model
- b. Intopia
- c. Certified Energy Manager
- d. Planning

Guidance: level 1

:: Supply chain management ::

_________ is a core supply chain function and includes supply chain planning and supply chain execution capabilities. Specifically, _________ is the capability firms use to plan total material requirements. The material requirements are communicated to procurement and other functions for sourcing. _________ is also responsible for determining the amount of material to be deployed at each stocking location across the supply chain, establishing material replenishment plans, determining inventory levels to hold for each type of inventory , and communicating information regarding material needs throughout the extended supply chain.

Exam Probability: **Medium**

23. *Answer choices:*

(see index for correct answer)

- a. Wave picking
- b. Customs-Trade Partnership Against Terrorism
- c. National Centre for Cold-chain Development
- d. Materials management

Guidance: level 1

:: Information technology management ::

_________ is the discipline of engineering concerned with the principles and practice of product and service quality assurance and control. In the software development, it is the management, development, operation and maintenance of IT systems and enterprise architectures with a high quality standard.

Exam Probability: **High**

24. *Answer choices:*

(see index for correct answer)

- a. Virtual chargeback
- b. Business performance management
- c. Quality Engineering
- d. OPIDIS

Guidance: level 1

:: Production and manufacturing ::

Automatic _________ in continuous production processes is a combination of control engineering and chemical engineering disciplines that uses industrial control systems to achieve a production level of consistency, economy and safety which could not be achieved purely by human manual control. It is implemented widely in industries such as oil refining, pulp and paper manufacturing, chemical processing and power generating plants.

Exam Probability: **High**

25. *Answer choices:*

(see index for correct answer)

- a. Process control
- b. Production equipment control

- c. Corrective and preventive action
- d. Earned value

Guidance: level 1

:: Metal forming ::

_________ is a type of motion that combines rotation and translation of that object with respect to a surface , such that, if ideal conditions exist, the two are in contact with each other without sliding.

Exam Probability: **High**

26. *Answer choices:*

(see index for correct answer)

- a. Hubbing
- b. Temper mill
- c. Roll bender
- d. Rolling

Guidance: level 1

:: Insulators ::

A _________ is a piece of soft cloth large enough either to cover or to enfold a great portion of the user`s body, usually when sleeping or otherwise at rest, thereby trapping radiant bodily heat that otherwise would be lost through convection, and so keeping the body warm.

Exam Probability: **Medium**

27. *Answer choices:*

(see index for correct answer)

- a. Nansulate
- b. Blanket
- c. Thermal pad
- d. Vacuum insulated panel

Guidance: level 1

:: Distribution, retailing, and wholesaling ::

The __________ is a distribution channel phenomenon in which forecasts yield supply chain inefficiencies. It refers to increasing swings in inventory in response to shifts in customer demand as one moves further up the supply chain. The concept first appeared in Jay Forrester`s Industrial Dynamics and thus it is also known as the Forrester effect. The __________ was named for the way the amplitude of a whip increases down its length. The further from the originating signal, the greater the distortion of the wave pattern. In a similar manner, forecast accuracy decreases as one moves upstream along the supply chain. For example, many consumer goods have fairly consistent consumption at retail but this signal becomes more chaotic and unpredictable as the focus moves away from consumer purchasing behavior.

Exam Probability: **Low**

28. *Answer choices:*

(see index for correct answer)

- a. Bullwhip effect
- b. Filling station
- c. Chicago Review Press
- d. Open Payment Initiative

Guidance: level 1

:: Management ::

A supply-chain network is an evolution of the basic supply chain. Due to rapid technological advancement, organisations with a basic supply chain can develop this chain into a more complex structure involving a higher level of interdependence and connectivity between more organisations, this constitutes a supply-chain network.

Exam Probability: **Medium**

29. *Answer choices:*

(see index for correct answer)

- a. Best current practice
- b. Business workflow analysis
- c. Supply chain network
- d. Lead scoring

Guidance: level 1

:: Information technology management ::

_________ concerns a cycle of organizational activity: the acquisition of information from one or more sources, the custodianship and the distribution of that information to those who need it, and its ultimate disposition through archiving or deletion.

Exam Probability: **Low**

30. *Answer choices:*

(see index for correct answer)

- a. Configuration Management
- b. Information Technology Infrastructure Library
- c. Soluto
- d. Automic

Guidance: level 1

:: Project management ::

A _________ is one of a series of numbered markers placed along a road or boundary at intervals of one mile or occasionally, parts of a mile. They are typically located at the side of the road or in a median or central reservation. They are alternatively known as mile markers, mileposts or mile posts . Mileage is the distance along the road from a fixed commencement point. Commonly the term " _________ " may also refer to markers placed at other distances, such as every kilometre.

Exam Probability: **Medium**

31. *Answer choices:*

(see index for correct answer)

- a. Product-based planning
- b. Product description
- c. Task management

- d. Milestone

Guidance: level 1

:: Materials ::

A _________ , also known as a feedstock, unprocessed material, or primary commodity, is a basic material that is used to produce goods, finished products, energy, or intermediate materials which are feedstock for future finished products. As feedstock, the term connotes these materials are bottleneck assets and are highly important with regard to producing other products. An example of this is crude oil, which is a _________ and a feedstock used in the production of industrial chemicals, fuels, plastics, and pharmaceutical goods; lumber is a _________ used to produce a variety of products including all types of furniture. The term " _________ " denotes materials in minimally processed or unprocessed in states; e.g., raw latex, crude oil, cotton, coal, raw biomass, iron ore, air, logs, or water i.e. "...any product of agriculture, forestry, fishing and any other mineral that is in its natural form or which has undergone the transformation required to prepare it for internationally marketing in substantial volumes."

Exam Probability: **Low**

32. *Answer choices:*

(see index for correct answer)

- a. Putty
- b. Noil
- c. Ion Gel
- d. Raw material

Guidance: level 1

:: Goods ::

In most contexts, the concept of _________ denotes the conduct that should be preferred when posed with a choice between possible actions. _________ is generally considered to be the opposite of evil, and is of interest in the study of morality, ethics, religion and philosophy. The specific meaning and etymology of the term and its associated translations among ancient and contemporary languages show substantial variation in its inflection and meaning depending on circumstances of place, history, religious, or philosophical context.

Exam Probability: **Medium**

33. *Answer choices:*

(see index for correct answer)

- a. Ordinary good
- b. Case
- c. Anti-rival good
- d. Normal good

Guidance: level 1

:: Outsourcing ::

__________ is an institutional procurement process that continuously improves and re-evaluates the purchasing activities of a company. In the services industry, __________ refers to a service solution, sometimes called a strategic partnership, which is specifically customized to meet the client`s individual needs. In a production environment, it is often considered one component of supply chain management. Modern supply chain management professionals have placed emphasis on defining the distinct differences between __________ and procurement. Procurement operations support tactical day-to-day transactions such as issuing Purchase Orders to suppliers, whereas __________ represents to strategic planning, supplier development, contract negotiation, supply chain infrastructure, and outsourcing models.

Exam Probability: **High**

34. *Answer choices:*

(see index for correct answer)

- a. Divestment
- b. LEO
- c. Chris Ducker
- d. Strategic sourcing

Guidance: level 1

:: Manufacturing ::

_________ or lean production, often simply "lean", is a systematic method for the minimization of waste within a manufacturing system without sacrificing productivity, which can cause problems. Lean also takes into account waste created through overburden and waste created through unevenness in work loads . Working from the perspective of the client who consumes a product or service, "value" is any action or process that a customer would be willing to pay for.

Exam Probability: **Medium**

35. *Answer choices:*

(see index for correct answer)

- a. EMO
- b. Warehouse
- c. Factory Physics
- d. Lean manufacturing

Guidance: level 1

:: Management ::

_________ is an iterative four-step management method used in business for the control and continuous improvement of processes and products. It is also known as the Deming circle/cycle/wheel, the Shewhart cycle, the control circle/cycle, or plan–do–study–act . Another version of this _________ cycle is O _________ . The added "O" stands for observation or as some versions say: "Observe the current condition." This emphasis on observation and current condition has currency with the literature on lean manufacturing and the Toyota Production System. The _________ cycle, with Ishikawa's changes, can be traced back to S. Mizuno of the Tokyo Institute of Technology in 1959.

Exam Probability: **Medium**

36. *Answer choices:*

(see index for correct answer)

- a. Power structure
- b. PDCA
- c. Innovation management
- d. Context analysis

Guidance: level 1

:: Project management ::

_________ s can take many forms depending on the type of project being implemented and the nature of the organization. The _________ details the project deliverables and describes the major objectives. The objectives should include measurable success criteria for the project.

Exam Probability: **Medium**

37. *Answer choices:*

(see index for correct answer)

- a. Grandfather principle
- b. Scope statement
- c. Risk management plan
- d. Decision table

Guidance: level 1

:: Production and manufacturing ::

In industry, _________ is a system of maintaining and improving the integrity of production and quality systems through the machines, equipment, processes, and employees that add business value to an organization.

Exam Probability: **High**

38. *Answer choices:*

(see index for correct answer)

- a. SERCOS III
- b. Division of labour
- c. Total productive maintenance
- d. Equipment service management and rental

Guidance: level 1

:: Production and manufacturing ::

_________ is a comprehensive and rigorous industrial process by which a previously sold, leased, used, worn or non-functional product or part is returned to a 'like-new' or 'better-than-new' condition, from both a quality and performance perspective, through a controlled, reproducible and sustainable process.

Exam Probability: **Medium**

39. *Answer choices:*

(see index for correct answer)

- a. PA512
- b. Remanufacturing
- c. Object Process Methodology
- d. Fiberglass molding

Guidance: level 1

:: Packaging materials ::

_________ is a thin material produced by pressing together moist fibres of cellulose pulp derived from wood, rags or grasses, and drying them into flexible sheets.It is a versatile material with many uses, including writing, printing, packaging, cleaning, decorating, and a number of industrial and construction processes. _________ s are essential in legal or non-legal documentation.

Exam Probability: **Low**

40. *Answer choices:*

(see index for correct answer)

- a. Filament tape
- b. Plastic film
- c. Foam peanut
- d. Velostat

Guidance: level 1

:: Quality ::

A _________ is an initiating cause of either a condition or a causal chain that leads to an outcome or effect of interest. The term denotes the earliest, most basic, `deepest`, cause for a given behavior; most often a fault. The idea is that you can only see an error by its manifest signs. Those signs can be widespread, multitudinous, and convoluted, whereas the _________ leading to them often is a lot simpler.

Exam Probability: **Low**

41. *Answer choices:*

(see index for correct answer)

- a. Independent test organization
- b. Shigeo Shingo
- c. Customer Service Excellence
- d. OptiY

Guidance: level 1

:: Production and manufacturing ::

_________ is the production under license of technology developed elsewhere. It is an especially prominent commercial practice in developing nations, which often approach _________ as a starting point for indigenous industrial development.

Exam Probability: **Medium**

42. *Answer choices:*

(see index for correct answer)

- a. MAPICS
- b. Product layout
- c. Direct Clustering Algorithm

- d. Workmanship

Guidance: level 1

:: Quality management ::

In quality management system, a _________ is a document developed by management to express the directive of the top management with respect to quality. _________ management is a strategic item.

Exam Probability: **High**

43. *Answer choices:*

(see index for correct answer)

- a. Test bay
- b. EFQM
- c. Institute of Standards and Industrial Research of Iran
- d. Quality policy

Guidance: level 1

:: ::

Catalysis is the process of increasing the rate of a chemical reaction by adding a substance known as a _________ , which is not consumed in the catalyzed reaction and can continue to act repeatedly. Because of this, only very small amounts of _________ are required to alter the reaction rate in principle.

Exam Probability: **Low**

44. *Answer choices:*

(see index for correct answer)

- a. cultural
- b. Catalyst
- c. levels of analysis
- d. information systems assessment

Guidance: level 1

:: Information technology management ::

The term _________ is used to refer to periods when a system is unavailable. _________ or outage duration refers to a period of time that a system fails to provide or perform its primary function. Reliability, availability, recovery, and unavailability are related concepts.The unavailability is the proportion of a time-span that a system is unavailable or offline.This is usually a result of the system failing to function because of an unplanned event, or because of routine maintenance .

Exam Probability: **Low**

45. *Answer choices:*

(see index for correct answer)

- a. The International Records Management Trust
- b. Operational-level agreement
- c. Downtime
- d. Mung

Guidance: level 1

:: Metals ::

A _________ is a material that, when freshly prepared, polished, or fractured, shows a lustrous appearance, and conducts electricity and heat relatively well. _________ s are typically malleable or ductile . A _________ may be a chemical element such as iron, or an alloy such as stainless steel.

Exam Probability: **High**

46. *Answer choices:*

(see index for correct answer)

- a. Metal
- b. Tamahagane

- c. Half-metal
- d. Refractory metals

Guidance: level 1

:: Production and manufacturing ::

__________ is a systematic method to improve the "value" of goods or products and services by using an examination of function. Value, as defined, is the ratio of function to cost. Value can therefore be manipulated by either improving the function or reducing the cost. It is a primary tenet of __________ that basic functions be preserved and not be reduced as a consequence of pursuing value improvements.

Exam Probability: **Low**

47. *Answer choices:*

(see index for correct answer)

- a. Equipment service management and rental
- b. Process control
- c. Capacity planning
- d. SafetyBUS p

Guidance: level 1

:: E-commerce ::

_________ is the business-to-business or business-to-consumer or business-to-government purchase and sale of supplies, work, and services through the Internet as well as other information and networking systems, such as electronic data interchange and enterprise resource planning.

Exam Probability: **High**

48. *Answer choices:*

(see index for correct answer)

- a. Marketplace Fairness Act
- b. E-procurement
- c. Want Button
- d. Impulse economy

Guidance: level 1

:: Management ::

_________, also known as natural process limits, are horizontal lines drawn on a statistical process control chart, usually at a distance of ±3 standard deviations of the plotted statistic from the statistic's mean.

Exam Probability: **Low**

49. *Answer choices:*

(see index for correct answer)

- a. Supplier performance management
- b. Action item
- c. Manager Tools Podcast
- d. Control limits

Guidance: level 1

:: Project management ::

__________ is a work methodology emphasizing the parallelisation of tasks , which is sometimes called simultaneous engineering or integrated product development using an integrated product team approach. It refers to an approach used in product development in which functions of design engineering, manufacturing engineering, and other functions are integrated to reduce the time required to bring a new product to market.

Exam Probability: **Low**

50. *Answer choices:*

(see index for correct answer)

- a. Concurrent engineering
- b. Technology roadmap
- c. Point of total assumption
- d. Aggregate planning

Guidance: level 1

:: Production and manufacturing ::

A BOM can define products as they are designed , as they are ordered , as they are built , or as they are maintained . The different types of BOMs depend on the business need and use for which they are intended. In process industries, the BOM is also known as the formula, recipe, or ingredients list. The phrase "bill of material" is frequently used by engineers as an adjective to refer not to the literal bill, but to the current production configuration of a product, to distinguish it from modified or improved versions under study or in test.

Exam Probability: **High**

51. *Answer choices:*

(see index for correct answer)

- a. Nesting
- b. Product layout
- c. Bill of materials
- d. Process layout

Guidance: level 1

:: Management ::

In inventory management, _________ is the order quantity that minimizes the total holding costs and ordering costs. It is one of the oldest classical production scheduling models. The model was developed by Ford W. Harris in 1913, but R. H. Wilson, a consultant who applied it extensively, and K. Andler are given credit for their in-depth analysis.

Exam Probability: **Medium**

52. *Answer choices:*

(see index for correct answer)

- a. Marketing science
- b. Integrated master plan
- c. Core competency
- d. Economic order quantity

Guidance: level 1

:: Lean manufacturing ::

_________ is a scheduling system for lean manufacturing and just-in-time manufacturing . Taiichi Ohno, an industrial engineer at Toyota, developed _________ to improve manufacturing efficiency. _________ is one method to achieve JIT. The system takes its name from the cards that track production within a factory. For many in the automotive sector, _________ is known as the "Toyota nameplate system" and as such the term is not used by some other automakers.

Exam Probability: **Medium**

53. *Answer choices:*

(see index for correct answer)

- a. Lean product development
- b. Computer-aided lean management
- c. Kanban
- d. JobShopLean

Guidance: level 1

:: Data management ::

_________ is the ability of a physical product to remain functional, without requiring excessive maintenance or repair, when faced with the challenges of normal operation over its design lifetime. There are several measures of _________ in use, including years of life, hours of use, and number of operational cycles. In economics, goods with a long usable life are referred to as durable goods.

Exam Probability: **Medium**

54. *Answer choices:*

(see index for correct answer)

- a. Cloud Data Management Interface
- b. Electronic lab notebook

- c. Durability
- d. Data aggregator

Guidance: level 1

:: Management ::

Business __________ is a discipline in operations management in which people use various methods to discover, model, analyze, measure, improve, optimize, and automate business processes. BPM focuses on improving corporate performance by managing business processes. Any combination of methods used to manage a company's business processes is BPM. Processes can be structured and repeatable or unstructured and variable. Though not required, enabling technologies are often used with BPM.

Exam Probability: **High**

55. *Answer choices:*

(see index for correct answer)

- a. Business process improvement
- b. Supply chain optimization
- c. Cross ownership
- d. Quick response manufacturing

Guidance: level 1

:: Elementary mathematics ::

In mathematics, a _________ is an enumerated collection of objects in which repetitions are allowed. Like a set, it contains members . The number of elements is called the length of the _________ . Unlike a set, the same elements can appear multiple times at different positions in a _________ , and order matters. Formally, a _________ can be defined as a function whose domain is either the set of the natural numbers or the set of the first n natural numbers . The position of an element in a _________ is its rank or index; it is the natural number from which the element is the image. It depends on the context or a specific convention, if the first element has index 0 or 1. When a symbol has been chosen for denoting a _________ , the nth element of the _________ is denoted by this symbol with n as subscript; for example, the nth element of the Fibonacci _________ is generally denoted Fn.

Exam Probability: **High**

56. *Answer choices:*

(see index for correct answer)

- a. Radix
- b. Ordinate
- c. Constant
- d. Sequence

Guidance: level 1

:: Metal heat treatments ::

__________ is a group of industrial and metalworking processes used to alter the physical, and sometimes chemical, properties of a material. The most common application is metallurgical. Heat treatments are also used in the manufacture of many other materials, such as glass. Heat treatment involves the use of heating or chilling, normally to extreme temperatures, to achieve a desired result such as hardening or softening of a material. Heat treatment techniques include annealing, case hardening, precipitation strengthening, tempering, carburizing, normalizing and quenching. It is noteworthy that while the term heat treatment applies only to processes where the heating and cooling are done for the specific purpose of altering properties intentionally, heating and cooling often occur incidentally during other manufacturing processes such as hot forming or welding.

Exam Probability: **Medium**

57. *Answer choices:*

(see index for correct answer)

- a. Quench polish quench
- b. Tempering
- c. Heat treating
- d. Case hardening

Guidance: level 1

:: Semiconductor companies ::

_________ Corporation is a Japanese multinational conglomerate corporation headquartered in Konan, Minato, Tokyo. Its diversified business includes consumer and professional electronics, gaming, entertainment and financial services. The company owns the largest music entertainment business in the world, the largest video game console business and one of the largest video game publishing businesses, and is one of the leading manufacturers of electronic products for the consumer and professional markets, and a leading player in the film and television entertainment industry. _________ was ranked 97th on the 2018 Fortune Global 500 list.

Exam Probability: **Low**

58. *Answer choices:*

(see index for correct answer)

- a. Sony
- b. Renesas Electronics
- c. ON Semiconductor
- d. Hana Micron

Guidance: level 1

:: Procurement ::

A _________ is a standard business process whose purpose is to invite suppliers into a bidding process to bid on specific products or services. RfQ generally means the same thing as Call for bids and Invitation for bid .

Exam Probability: **High**

59. *Answer choices:*

(see index for correct answer)

- a. Best value procurement
- b. Request price quotation
- c. Request for quotation
- d. Second-tier sourcing

Guidance: level 1

Commerce

Commerce relates to "the exchange of goods and services, especially on a large scale." It includes legal, economic, political, social, cultural and technological systems that operate in any country or internationally.

:: ::

_________ is the amount of time someone works beyond normal working hours. The term is also used for the pay received for this time. Normal hours may be determined in several ways.

Exam Probability: **High**

1. *Answer choices:*

(see index for correct answer)

- a. process perspective
- b. Overtime
- c. hierarchical
- d. cultural

Guidance: level 1

:: Securities (finance) ::

A __________ is a container that is traditionally constructed from stiff fibers, and can be made from a range of materials, including wood splints, runners, and cane. While most __________ s are made from plant materials, other materials such as horsehair, baleen, or metal wire can be used. __________ s are generally woven by hand. Some __________ s are fitted with a lid, while others are left open on top.

Exam Probability: **Low**

2. *Answer choices:*

(see index for correct answer)

- a. Basket
- b. Medallion signature guarantee
- c. Convertible security
- d. CCASS

Guidance: level 1

:: Marketing ::

_________ or stock control can be broadly defined as "the activity of checking a shop's stock." However, a more focused definition takes into account the more science-based, methodical practice of not only verifying a business` inventory but also focusing on the many related facets of inventory management "within an organisation to meet the demand placed upon that business economically." Other facets of _________ include supply chain management, production control, financial flexibility, and customer satisfaction. At the root of _________ , however, is the _________ problem, which involves determining when to order, how much to order, and the logistics of those decisions.

Exam Probability: **Medium**

3. *Answer choices:*

(see index for correct answer)

- a. European Information Technology Observatory
- b. Marketing channel
- c. Discounting
- d. History of marketing

Guidance: level 1

:: Consumer theory ::

A __________ is a technical term in psychology, economics and philosophy usually used in relation to choosing between alternatives. For example, someone prefers A over B if they would rather choose A than B.

Exam Probability: **Medium**

4. *Answer choices:*

(see index for correct answer)

- a. Preference
- b. Induced consumption
- c. Consumer sovereignty
- d. Marshallian demand function

Guidance: level 1

:: Marketing ::

__________ is the percentage of a market accounted for by a specific entity. In a survey of nearly 200 senior marketing managers, 67% responded that they found the revenue- "dollar __________ " metric very useful, while 61% found "unit __________ " very useful.

Exam Probability: **High**

5. *Answer choices:*

(see index for correct answer)

- a. Multicultural marketing
- b. City marketing
- c. Market share
- d. Generic trademark

Guidance: level 1

:: Customs duties ::

A _________ is a tax on imports or exports between sovereign states. It is a form of regulation of foreign trade and a policy that taxes foreign products to encourage or safeguard domestic industry. _________ s are the simplest and oldest instrument of trade policy. Traditionally, states have used them as a source of income. Now, they are among the most widely used instruments of protection, along with import and export quotas.

Exam Probability: **Low**

6. *Answer choices:*

(see index for correct answer)

- a. World Customs Organization
- b. Tariff
- c. Tariffication
- d. Import Surtaxes

Guidance: level 1

:: Land value taxation ::

_________ , sometimes referred to as dry _________ , is the solid surface of Earth that is not permanently covered by water. The vast majority of human activity throughout history has occurred in _________ areas that support agriculture, habitat, and various natural resources. Some life forms have developed from predecessor species that lived in bodies of water.

Exam Probability: **Medium**

7. *Answer choices:*

(see index for correct answer)

- a. Lands Valuation Appeal Court
- b. Land value tax
- c. Henry George
- d. Harry Gunnison Brown

Guidance: level 1

:: Stock market ::

_________ is freedom from, or resilience against, potential harm caused by others. Beneficiaries of _________ may be of persons and social groups, objects and institutions, ecosystems or any other entity or phenomenon vulnerable to unwanted change by its environment.

Exam Probability: **High**

8. *Answer choices:*

(see index for correct answer)

- a. Concentrated stock
- b. Next: The Future Just Happened
- c. Indian Depository Receipt
- d. Security

Guidance: level 1

:: E-commerce ::

A __________ is a financial transaction involving a very small sum of money and usually one that occurs online. A number of __________ systems were proposed and developed in the mid-to-late 1990s, all of which were ultimately unsuccessful. A second generation of __________ systems emerged in the 2010s.

Exam Probability: **Low**

9. *Answer choices:*

(see index for correct answer)

- a. Micropayment
- b. E-commerce in Southeast Asia
- c. United Nations Convention on the Use of Electronic Communications

in International Contracts
- d. SwapSimple

Guidance: level 1

:: Fraud ::

In law, _________ is intentional deception to secure unfair or unlawful gain, or to deprive a victim of a legal right. _________ can violate civil law , a criminal law , or it may cause no loss of money, property or legal right but still be an element of another civil or criminal wrong. The purpose of _________ may be monetary gain or other benefits, for example by obtaining a passport, travel document, or driver`s license, or mortgage _________ , where the perpetrator may attempt to qualify for a mortgage by way of false statements.

Exam Probability: **High**

10. *Answer choices:*

(see index for correct answer)

- a. Romance scam
- b. Credit card kiting
- c. Fraud
- d. Fraud Squad

Guidance: level 1

:: ::

_________ is the social science that studies the production, distribution, and consumption of goods and services.

Exam Probability: **Low**

11. *Answer choices:*

(see index for correct answer)

- a. interpersonal communication
- b. process perspective
- c. Economics
- d. imperative

Guidance: level 1

:: Business terms ::

_________ ning is an organization`s process of defining its strategy, or direction, and making decisions on allocating its resources to pursue this strategy. It may also extend to control mechanisms for guiding the implementation of the strategy. _________ ning became prominent in corporations during the 1960s and remains an important aspect of strategic management. It is executed by _________ ners or strategists, who involve many parties and research sources in their analysis of the organization and its relationship to the environment in which it competes.

Exam Probability: **Medium**

12. *Answer choices:*

(see index for correct answer)

- a. Strategic plan
- b. churn rate
- c. back office
- d. Personal selling

Guidance: level 1

:: ::

In the broadest sense, _________ is any practice which contributes to the sale of products to a retail consumer. At a retail in-store level, _________ refers to the variety of products available for sale and the display of those products in such a way that it stimulates interest and entices customers to make a purchase.

Exam Probability: **High**

13. *Answer choices:*

(see index for correct answer)

- a. Merchandising
- b. Sarbanes-Oxley act of 2002

- c. deep-level diversity
- d. functional perspective

Guidance: level 1

:: Commercial item transport and distribution ::

A _________ , forwarder, or forwarding agent, also known as a non-vessel operating common carrier , is a person or company that organizes shipments for individuals or corporations to get goods from the manufacturer or producer to a market, customer or final point of distribution. Forwarders contract with a carrier or often multiple carriers to move the goods. A forwarder does not move the goods but acts as an expert in the logistics network. These carriers can use a variety of shipping modes, including ships, airplanes, trucks, and railroads, and often do utilize multiple modes for a single shipment. For example, the _________ may arrange to have cargo moved from a plant to an airport by truck, flown to the destination city, then moved from the airport to a customer`s building by another truck.

Exam Probability: **Low**

14. *Answer choices:*

(see index for correct answer)

- a. Freight interline system
- b. Surface Freight Forwarder Deregulation Act of 1986
- c. Freight forwarder
- d. Voice-directed warehousing

Guidance: level 1

:: Industry ::

_________ , also known as flow production or continuous production, is the production of large amounts of standardized products, including and especially on assembly lines. Together with job production and batch production, it is one of the three main production methods.

Exam Probability: **Low**

15. *Answer choices:*

(see index for correct answer)

- a. Fordism
- b. Standard Industrial Classification
- c. Mass production
- d. Nostalgia industry

Guidance: level 1

:: ::

_________ refers to the overall process of attracting, shortlisting, selecting and appointing suitable candidates for jobs within an organization. _________ can also refer to processes involved in choosing individuals for unpaid roles. Managers, human resource generalists and _________ specialists may be tasked with carrying out _________, but in some cases public-sector employment agencies, commercial _________ agencies, or specialist search consultancies are used to undertake parts of the process. Internet-based technologies which support all aspects of _________ have become widespread.

Exam Probability: **Medium**

16. *Answer choices:*

(see index for correct answer)

- a. Recruitment
- b. information systems assessment
- c. functional perspective
- d. hierarchical

Guidance: level 1

:: Management ::

Logistics is generally the detailed organization and implementation of a complex operation. In a general business sense, logistics is the management of the flow of things between the point of origin and the point of consumption in order to meet requirements of customers or corporations. The resources managed in logistics may include tangible goods such as materials, equipment, and supplies, as well as food and other consumable items. The logistics of physical items usually involves the integration of information flow, materials handling, production, packaging, inventory, transportation, warehousing, and often security.

Exam Probability: **Medium**

17. *Answer choices:*

(see index for correct answer)

- a. Power structure
- b. Failure demand
- c. Authoritarian leadership style
- d. Public sector consulting

Guidance: level 1

:: Asset ::

In financial accounting, an _________ is any resource owned by the business. Anything tangible or intangible that can be owned or controlled to produce value and that is held by a company to produce positive economic value is an _________ . Simply stated, _________ s represent value of ownership that can be converted into cash . The balance sheet of a firm records the monetary value of the _________ s owned by that firm. It covers money and other valuables belonging to an individual or to a business.

Exam Probability: **Low**

18. *Answer choices:*

(see index for correct answer)

- a. Asset
- b. Fixed asset

Guidance: level 1

:: Information technology ::

_________ is the use of computers to store, retrieve, transmit, and manipulate data, or information, often in the context of a business or other enterprise. IT is considered to be a subset of information and communications technology . An _________ system is generally an information system, a communications system or, more specifically speaking, a computer system – including all hardware, software and peripheral equipment – operated by a limited group of users.

Exam Probability: **Low**

19. *Answer choices:*

(see index for correct answer)

- a. Normalized Systems
- b. Local Government ICT Network
- c. Information technology
- d. Omniview technology

Guidance: level 1

:: ::

__________ , also referred to as orthostasis, is a human position in which the body is held in an upright position and supported only by the feet.

Exam Probability: **Low**

20. *Answer choices:*

(see index for correct answer)

- a. similarity-attraction theory
- b. cultural
- c. imperative
- d. personal values

Guidance: level 1

:: ::

_________ is a term frequently used in marketing. It is a measure of how products and services supplied by a company meet or surpass customer expectation. _________ is defined as "the number of customers, or percentage of total customers, whose reported experience with a firm, its products, or its services exceeds specified satisfaction goals."

Exam Probability: **Low**

21. *Answer choices:*

(see index for correct answer)

- a. corporate values
- b. imperative
- c. interpersonal communication
- d. Customer satisfaction

Guidance: level 1

:: E-commerce ::

A _________ is a hosted service offering that acts as an intermediary between business partners sharing standards based or proprietary data via shared business processes. The offered service is referred to as " _________ services".

Exam Probability: **Medium**

22. *Answer choices:*

(see index for correct answer)

- a. Electronic bill payment
- b. E-procurement
- c. MusicPass
- d. Value-added network

Guidance: level 1

:: Insolvency ::

__________ is a legal process through which people or other entities who cannot repay debts to creditors may seek relief from some or all of their debts. In most jurisdictions, __________ is imposed by a court order, often initiated by the debtor.

Exam Probability: **Low**

23. *Answer choices:*

(see index for correct answer)

- a. Bankruptcy
- b. Insolvency
- c. Conservatorship

- d. Financial distress

Guidance: level 1

:: E-commerce ::

_________ is a type of performance-based marketing in which a business rewards one or more affiliates for each visitor or customer brought by the affiliate`s own marketing efforts.

Exam Probability: **High**

24. *Answer choices:*

(see index for correct answer)

- a. Soldsie
- b. Entrust
- c. Affiliate marketing
- d. Demandware

Guidance: level 1

:: Supply chain management terms ::

In business and finance, _________ is a system of organizations, people, activities, information, and resources involved inmoving a product or service from supplier to customer. _________ activities involve the transformation of natural resources, raw materials, and components into a finished product that is delivered to the end customer. In sophisticated _________ systems, used products may re-enter the _________ at any point where residual value is recyclable. _________ s link value chains.

Exam Probability: **Low**

25. *Answer choices:*

(see index for correct answer)

- a. Consumables
- b. Stockout
- c. Will call
- d. Supply chain

Guidance: level 1

:: Management ::

A _________ is an idea of the future or desired result that a person or a group of people envisions, plans and commits to achieve. People endeavor to reach _________ s within a finite time by setting deadlines.

Exam Probability: **Medium**

26. *Answer choices:*

(see index for correct answer)

- a. Community of practice
- b. Defensive expenditures
- c. Virtual customer environment
- d. Managerial hubris

Guidance: level 1

:: ::

__________ is both a research area and a practical skill encompassing the ability of an individual or organization to "lead" or guide other individuals, teams, or entire organizations. Specialist literature debates various viewpoints, contrasting Eastern and Western approaches to __________ , and also United States versus European approaches. U.S. academic environments define __________ as "a process of social influence in which a person can enlist the aid and support of others in the accomplishment of a common task".

Exam Probability: **Medium**

27. *Answer choices:*

(see index for correct answer)

- a. corporate values
- b. Leadership
- c. co-culture

- d. similarity-attraction theory

Guidance: level 1

:: International trade ::

In finance, an _________ is the rate at which one currency will be exchanged for another. It is also regarded as the value of one country's currency in relation to another currency. For example, an interbank _________ of 114 Japanese yen to the United States dollar means that ¥114 will be exchanged for each US$1 or that US$1 will be exchanged for each ¥114. In this case it is said that the price of a dollar in relation to yen is ¥114, or equivalently that the price of a yen in relation to dollars is $1/114.

Exam Probability: **High**

28. *Answer choices:*

(see index for correct answer)

- a. Exchange rate
- b. Trade barrier
- c. Authorized economic operator
- d. Bilateral trade

Guidance: level 1

:: ::

_________ is a type of government support for the citizens of that society. _________ may be provided to people of any income level, as with social security , but it is usually intended to ensure that the poor can meet their basic human needs such as food and shelter. _________ attempts to provide poor people with a minimal level of well-being, usually either a free- or a subsidized-supply of certain goods and social services, such as healthcare, education, and vocational training.

Exam Probability: **Low**

29. *Answer choices:*

(see index for correct answer)

- a. imperative
- b. deep-level diversity
- c. Character
- d. Welfare

Guidance: level 1

:: ::

In marketing jargon, product lining is offering several related products for sale individually. Unlike product bundling, where several products are combined into one group, which is then offered for sale as a units, product lining involves offering the products for sale separately. A line can comprise related products of various sizes, types, colors, qualities, or prices. Line depth refers to the number of subcategories a category has. Line consistency refers to how closely related the products that make up the line are. Line vulnerability refers to the percentage of sales or profits that are derived from only a few products in the line.

Exam Probability: **Medium**

30. *Answer choices:*

(see index for correct answer)

- a. co-culture
- b. deep-level diversity
- c. surface-level diversity
- d. Product mix

Guidance: level 1

:: Auctioneering ::

Unlike sealed-bid auctions , an _________ is "open" or fully transparent, as the identity of all bidders is disclosed to each other during the auction. More generally, an auction mechanism is considered "English" if it involves an iterative process of adjusting the price in a direction that is unfavorable to the bidders . In contrast, a Dutch auction would adjust the price in a direction that favored the bidders .

Exam Probability: **Low**

31. *Answer choices:*

(see index for correct answer)

- a. Reppert School of Auctioneering
- b. World Livestock Auctioneer Championship
- c. Pie supper
- d. English auction

Guidance: level 1

:: ::

In legal terminology, a _________ is any formal legal document that sets out the facts and legal reasons that the filing party or parties believes are sufficient to support a claim against the party or parties against whom the claim is brought that entitles the plaintiff to a remedy . For example, the Federal Rules of Civil Procedure that govern civil litigation in United States courts provide that a civil action is commenced with the filing or service of a pleading called a _________ . Civil court rules in states that have incorporated the Federal Rules of Civil Procedure use the same term for the same pleading.

Exam Probability: **Low**

32. *Answer choices:*

(see index for correct answer)

- a. interpersonal communication
- b. corporate values
- c. co-culture
- d. Complaint

Guidance: level 1

:: Management ::

_________ is a process by which entities review the quality of all factors involved in production. ISO 9000 defines _________ as "A part of quality management focused on fulfilling quality requirements".

Exam Probability: **Medium**

33. *Answer choices:*

(see index for correct answer)

- a. Operations management
- b. Work breakdown structure
- c. Management Week
- d. Crisis plan

Guidance: level 1

:: Industry ::

A __________ is a set of sequential operations established in a factory where materials are put through a refining process to produce an end-product that is suitable for onward consumption; or components are assembled to make a finished article.

Exam Probability: **Low**

34. *Answer choices:*

(see index for correct answer)

- a. The Year in Industry
- b. Private sector
- c. Production line

- d. PROFINET

Guidance: level 1

:: ::

In logic and philosophy, an _______ is a series of statements , called the premises or premisses , intended to determine the degree of truth of another statement, the conclusion. The logical form of an _______ in a natural language can be represented in a symbolic formal language, and independently of natural language formally defined " _______ s" can be made in math and computer science.

Exam Probability: **Low**

35. *Answer choices:*

(see index for correct answer)

- a. levels of analysis
- b. hierarchical
- c. corporate values
- d. Argument

Guidance: level 1

:: Project management ::

Contemporary business and science treat as a _________ any undertaking, carried out individually or collaboratively and possibly involving research or design, that is carefully planned to achieve a particular aim.

Exam Probability: **High**

36. *Answer choices:*

(see index for correct answer)

- a. Project
- b. Advanced Integrated Practice
- c. Kickoff meeting
- d. Australian Institute of Project Management

Guidance: level 1

:: E-commerce ::

The phrase _________ was originally coined in 1997 by Kevin Duffey at the launch of the Global _________ Forum, to mean "the delivery of electronic commerce capabilities directly into the consumer's hand, anywhere, via wireless technology." Many choose to think of _________ as meaning "a retail outlet in your customer's pocket."

Exam Probability: **High**

37. *Answer choices:*

(see index for correct answer)

- a. ChamberSign
- b. Mobile commerce
- c. Electronic billing
- d. SAScon

Guidance: level 1

:: Management accounting ::

_________ , or dollar contribution per unit, is the selling price per unit minus the variable cost per unit. "Contribution" represents the portion of sales revenue that is not consumed by variable costs and so contributes to the coverage of fixed costs. This concept is one of the key building blocks of break-even analysis.

Exam Probability: **Low**

38. *Answer choices:*

(see index for correct answer)

- a. Contribution margin
- b. Direct material total variance
- c. Inventory valuation
- d. Managerial risk accounting

Guidance: level 1

:: ::

Competition arises whenever at least two parties strive for a goal which cannot be shared: where one`s gain is the other`s loss .

Exam Probability: **Medium**

39. *Answer choices:*

(see index for correct answer)

- a. interpersonal communication
- b. Competitor
- c. imperative
- d. surface-level diversity

Guidance: level 1

:: ::

__________ is a means of protection from financial loss. It is a form of risk management, primarily used to hedge against the risk of a contingent or uncertain loss

Exam Probability: **High**

40. *Answer choices:*

(see index for correct answer)

- a. levels of analysis
- b. corporate values
- c. Insurance
- d. information systems assessment

Guidance: level 1

:: Public relations ::

__________ is the public visibility or awareness for any product, service or company. It may also refer to the movement of information from its source to the general public, often but not always via the media. The subjects of __________ include people , goods and services, organizations, and works of art or entertainment.

Exam Probability: **Medium**

41. *Answer choices:*

(see index for correct answer)

- a. Hearts and minds
- b. Media relations

- c. Publicity
- d. International

Guidance: level 1

:: Game theory ::

To _________ is to make a deal between different parties where each party gives up part of their demand. In arguments, _________ is a concept of finding agreement through communication, through a mutual acceptance of terms—often involving variations from an original goal or desires.

Exam Probability: **Medium**

42. *Answer choices:*

(see index for correct answer)

- a. The Intuitive Criterion
- b. Unbeatable strategy
- c. Wait/walk dilemma
- d. Compromise

Guidance: level 1

:: ::

_________ Corporation is an American multinational technology company with headquarters in Redmond, Washington. It develops, manufactures, licenses, supports and sells computer software, consumer electronics, personal computers, and related services. Its best known software products are the _________ Windows line of operating systems, the _________ Office suite, and the Internet Explorer and Edge Web browsers. Its flagship hardware products are the Xbox video game consoles and the _________ Surface lineup of touchscreen personal computers. As of 2016, it is the world`s largest software maker by revenue, and one of the world`s most valuable companies. The word " _________ " is a portmanteau of "microcomputer" and "software". _________ is ranked No. 30 in the 2018 Fortune 500 rankings of the largest United States corporations by total revenue.

Exam Probability: **High**

43. *Answer choices:*

(see index for correct answer)

- a. cultural
- b. co-culture
- c. Microsoft
- d. Sarbanes-Oxley act of 2002

Guidance: level 1

:: Commercial item transport and distribution ::

In commerce, supply-chain management , the management of the flow of goods and services, involves the movement and storage of raw materials, of work-in-process inventory, and of finished goods from point of origin to point of consumption. Interconnected or interlinked networks, channels and node businesses combine in the provision of products and services required by end customers in a supply chain. Supply-chain management has been defined as the "design, planning, execution, control, and monitoring of supply-chain activities with the objective of creating net value, building a competitive infrastructure, leveraging worldwide logistics, synchronizing supply with demand and measuring performance globally."SCM practice draws heavily from the areas of industrial engineering, systems engineering, operations management, logistics, procurement, information technology, and marketing and strives for an integrated approach. Marketing channels play an important role in supply-chain management. Current research in supply-chain management is concerned with topics related to sustainability and risk management, among others. Some suggest that the "people dimension" of SCM, ethical issues, internal integration, transparency/visibility, and human capital/talent management are topics that have, so far, been underrepresented on the research agenda.

Exam Probability: **Low**

44. *Answer choices:*

(see index for correct answer)

- a. Air cargo
- b. Ship transport
- c. Conveyor belt
- d. Supply chain management

Guidance: level 1

:: Quality management ::

_________ ensures that an organization, product or service is consistent. It has four main components: quality planning, quality assurance, quality control and quality improvement. _________ is focused not only on product and service quality, but also on the means to achieve it. _________, therefore, uses quality assurance and control of processes as well as products to achieve more consistent quality. What a customer wants and is willing to pay for it determines quality. It is written or unwritten commitment to a known or unknown consumer in the market . Thus, quality can be defined as fitness for intended use or, in other words, how well the product performs its intended function

Exam Probability: **Low**

45. *Answer choices:*

(see index for correct answer)

- a. External quality assessment
- b. Management by wandering around
- c. Quality Management Maturity Grid
- d. Quality management

Guidance: level 1

:: ::

_________ are electronic transfer of money from one bank account to another, either within a single financial institution or across multiple institutions, via computer-based systems, without the direct intervention of bank staff.

Exam Probability: **Medium**

46. *Answer choices:*

(see index for correct answer)

- a. functional perspective
- b. corporate values
- c. hierarchical
- d. information systems assessment

Guidance: level 1

:: Real property law ::

A _________ is the grant of authority or rights, stating that the granter formally recognizes the prerogative of the recipient to exercise the rights specified. It is implicit that the granter retains superiority , and that the recipient admits a limited status within the relationship, and it is within that sense that _________ s were historically granted, and that sense is retained in modern usage of the term.

Exam Probability: **High**

47. *Answer choices:*

(see index for correct answer)

- a. Qualified intermediary
- b. Charter
- c. Quiet title
- d. Life interest

Guidance: level 1

:: Human resource management ::

An organizational chart is a diagram that shows the structure of an organization and the relationships and relative ranks of its parts and positions/jobs. The term is also used for similar diagrams, for example ones showing the different elements of a field of knowledge or a group of languages.

Exam Probability: **Low**

48. *Answer choices:*

(see index for correct answer)

- a. Organization chart
- b. Job analysis
- c. Behavioral Competencies
- d. Up or out

Guidance: level 1

:: Auctioneering ::

A __________ is one of several similar kinds of auctions. Most commonly, it means an auction in which the auctioneer begins with a high asking price, and lowers it until some participant accepts the price, or it reaches a predetermined reserve price. This has also been called a clock auction or open-outcry descending-price auction. This type of auction is good for auctioning goods quickly, since a sale never requires more than one bid. Strategically, it's similar to a first-price sealed-bid auction.

Exam Probability: **High**

49. *Answer choices:*

(see index for correct answer)

- a. National Auctioneers Association
- b. Unique bid auction
- c. Bidding fee auction
- d. Proxy bid

Guidance: level 1

:: Banking ::

A _________ is a financial institution that accepts deposits from the public and creates credit. Lending activities can be performed either directly or indirectly through capital markets. Due to their importance in the financial stability of a country, _________ s are highly regulated in most countries. Most nations have institutionalized a system known as fractional reserve _________ ing under which _________ s hold liquid assets equal to only a portion of their current liabilities. In addition to other regulations intended to ensure liquidity, _________ s are generally subject to minimum capital requirements based on an international set of capital standards, known as the Basel Accords.

Exam Probability: **Low**

50. *Answer choices:*

(see index for correct answer)

- a. Time deposit
- b. Bank
- c. Bank run
- d. Direct bank

Guidance: level 1

:: ::

_________ is the study and management of exchange relationships. _________ is the business process of creating relationships with and satisfying customers. With its focus on the customer, _________ is one of the premier components of business management.

Exam Probability: **Medium**

51. *Answer choices:*

(see index for correct answer)

- a. hierarchical perspective
- b. Marketing
- c. empathy
- d. co-culture

Guidance: level 1

:: ::

A _________ is an individual or institution that legally owns one or more shares of stock in a public or private corporation. _________ s may be referred to as members of a corporation. Legally, a person is not a _________ in a corporation until their name and other details are entered in the corporation's register of _________ s or members.

Exam Probability: **High**

52. *Answer choices:*

(see index for correct answer)

- a. levels of analysis
- b. Sarbanes-Oxley act of 2002

- c. Shareholder
- d. deep-level diversity

Guidance: level 1

:: Commodities ::

In economics, a _________ is an economic good or service that has full or substantial fungibility: that is, the market treats instances of the good as equivalent or nearly so with no regard to who produced them. Most commodities are raw materials, basic resources, agricultural, or mining products, such as iron ore, sugar, or grains like rice and wheat. Commodities can also be mass-produced unspecialized products such as chemicals and computer memory.

Exam Probability: **High**

53. *Answer choices:*

(see index for correct answer)

- a. Sample grade
- b. Commoditization
- c. Commodity money
- d. IRely

Guidance: level 1

:: Service industries ::

_________ are the economic services provided by the finance industry, which encompasses a broad range of businesses that manage money, including credit unions, banks, credit-card companies, insurance companies, accountancy companies, consumer-finance companies, stock brokerages, investment funds, individual managers and some government-sponsored enterprises. _________ companies are present in all economically developed geographic locations and tend to cluster in local, national, regional and international financial centers such as London, New York City, and Tokyo.

Exam Probability: **High**

54. *Answer choices:*

(see index for correct answer)

- a. Financial services
- b. Allotment
- c. Financial services in China
- d. Pension Administration

Guidance: level 1

:: Marketing by medium ::

_________ , also called online marketing or Internet advertising or web advertising, is a form of marketing and advertising which uses the Internet to deliver promotional marketing messages to consumers. Many consumers find _________ disruptive and have increasingly turned to ad blocking for a variety of reasons. When software is used to do the purchasing, it is known as programmatic advertising.

Exam Probability: **Medium**

55. *Answer choices:*

(see index for correct answer)

- a. New media marketing
- b. Growth hacking
- c. Social video marketing
- d. Online advertising

Guidance: level 1

:: Marketing ::

_________ comes from the Latin neg and otsia referring to businessmen who, unlike the patricians, had no leisure time in their industriousness; it held the meaning of business until the 17th century when it took on the diplomatic connotation as a dialogue between two or more people or parties intended to reach a beneficial outcome over one or more issues where a conflict exists with respect to at least one of these issues. Thus, _________ is a process of combining divergent positions into a joint agreement under a decision rule of unanimity.

Exam Probability: **High**

56. *Answer choices:*

(see index for correct answer)

- a. Behance
- b. Negotiation
- c. Consumer culture theory
- d. Gold party

Guidance: level 1

:: Debt ::

__________ , in finance and economics, is payment from a borrower or deposit-taking financial institution to a lender or depositor of an amount above repayment of the principal sum , at a particular rate. It is distinct from a fee which the borrower may pay the lender or some third party. It is also distinct from dividend which is paid by a company to its shareholders from its profit or reserve, but not at a particular rate decided beforehand, rather on a pro rata basis as a share in the reward gained by risk taking entrepreneurs when the revenue earned exceeds the total costs.

Exam Probability: **High**

57. *Answer choices:*

(see index for correct answer)

- a. Creditor
- b. Perpetual subordinated debt
- c. gearing
- d. Internal debt

Guidance: level 1

:: ::

_________ is the collaborative effort of a team to achieve a common goal or to complete a task in the most effective and efficient way. This concept is seen within the greater framework of a team, which is a group of interdependent individuals who work together towards a common goal. Basic requirements for effective _________ are an adequate team size , available resources for the team to make use of , and clearly defined roles within the team in order for everyone to have a clear purpose. _________ is present in any context where a group of people are working together to achieve a common goal. These contexts include an industrial organization , athletics , a school , and the healthcare system . In each of these settings, the level of _________ and interdependence can vary from low , to intermediate , to high , depending on the amount of communication, interaction, and collaboration present between team members.

Exam Probability: **Medium**

58. *Answer choices:*

(see index for correct answer)

- a. information systems assessment
- b. levels of analysis
- c. Teamwork
- d. cultural

Guidance: level 1

:: Management ::

_________ is the process of thinking about the activities required to achieve a desired goal. It is the first and foremost activity to achieve desired results. It involves the creation and maintenance of a plan, such as psychological aspects that require conceptual skills. There are even a couple of tests to measure someone's capability of _________ well. As such, _________ is a fundamental property of intelligent behavior. An important further meaning, often just called " _________ " is the legal context of permitted building developments.

Exam Probability: **Medium**

59. *Answer choices:*

(see index for correct answer)

- a. Identity formation
- b. Information excellence
- c. Energy monitoring and targeting
- d. Planning

Guidance: level 1

Business ethics

Business ethics (also known as corporate ethics) is a form of applied ethics or professional ethics, that examines ethical principles and moral or ethical problems that can arise in a business environment. It applies to all aspects of business conduct and is relevant to the conduct of individuals and entire organizations. These ethics originate from individuals, organizational statements or from the legal system. These norms, values, ethical, and unethical practices are what is used to guide business. They help those businesses maintain a better connection with their stakeholders.

:: ::

Cannabis, also known as _________ among other names, is a psychoactive drug from the Cannabis plant used for medical or recreational purposes. The main psychoactive part of cannabis is tetrahydrocannabinol , one of 483 known compounds in the plant, including at least 65 other cannabinoids. Cannabis can be used by smoking, vaporizing, within food, or as an extract.

Exam Probability: **High**

1. *Answer choices:*

(see index for correct answer)

- a. cultural
- b. co-culture
- c. empathy
- d. surface-level diversity

Guidance: level 1

:: Writs ::

In common law, a writ of _________ is a writ whereby a private individual who assists a prosecution can receive all or part of any penalty imposed. Its name is an abbreviation of the Latin phrase _________ pro domino rege quam pro se ipso in hac parte sequitur, meaning "[he] who sues in this matter for the king as well as for himself."

Exam Probability: **High**

2. *Answer choices:*

(see index for correct answer)

- a. Qui tam
- b. Writ of assistance

Guidance: level 1

:: Marketing ::

__________ is the marketing of products that are presumed to be environmentally safe. It incorporates a broad range of activities, including product modification, changes to the production process, sustainable packaging, as well as modifying advertising. Yet defining __________ is not a simple task where several meanings intersect and contradict each other; an example of this will be the existence of varying social, environmental and retail definitions attached to this term. Other similar terms used are environmental marketing and ecological marketing.

Exam Probability: **Medium**

3. *Answer choices:*

(see index for correct answer)

- a. Fixed value-added resource
- b. Hype cycle
- c. Keyword research
- d. Green marketing

Guidance: level 1

:: ::

__________ is a private Dominican liberal arts college in Madison, Wisconsin. The college occupies a 55 acres campus overlooking the shores of Lake Wingra.

Exam Probability: **Low**

4. *Answer choices:*

(see index for correct answer)

- a. information systems assessment
- b. Edgewood College
- c. cultural
- d. functional perspective

Guidance: level 1

:: Renewable energy ::

A _________ is a fuel that is produced through contemporary biological processes, such as agriculture and anaerobic digestion, rather than a fuel produced by geological processes such as those involved in the formation of fossil fuels, such as coal and petroleum, from prehistoric biological matter. If the source biomatter can regrow quickly, the resulting fuel is said to be a form of renewable energy.

Exam Probability: **High**

5. *Answer choices:*

(see index for correct answer)

- a. Carbon neutrality
- b. Passive solar building design
- c. Biomass
- d. Biofuel

Guidance: level 1

:: Social enterprise ::

Corporate social responsibility is a type of international private business self-regulation. While once it was possible to describe CSR as an internal organisational policy or a corporate ethic strategy, that time has passed as various international laws have been developed and various organisations have used their authority to push it beyond individual or even industry-wide initiatives. While it has been considered a form of corporate self-regulation for some time, over the last decade or so it has moved considerably from voluntary decisions at the level of individual organisations, to mandatory schemes at regional, national and even transnational levels.

Exam Probability: **Low**

6. *Answer choices:*

(see index for correct answer)

- a. Social venture
- b. Corporate citizenship

Guidance: level 1

:: Hazard analysis ::

Broadly speaking, a _________ is the combined effort of 1. identifying and analyzing potential events that may negatively impact individuals, assets, and/or the environment ; and 2. making judgments "on the tolerability of the risk on the basis of a risk analysis" while considering influencing factors . Put in simpler terms, a _________ analyzes what can go wrong, how likely it is to happen, what the potential consequences are, and how tolerable the identified risk is. As part of this process, the resulting determination of risk may be expressed in a quantitative or qualitative fashion. The _________ is an inherent part of an overall risk management strategy, which attempts to, after a _________, "introduce control measures to eliminate or reduce" any potential risk-related consequences.

Exam Probability: **Medium**

7. *Answer choices:*

(see index for correct answer)

- a. Risk assessment
- b. Hazard identification
- c. Hazardous Materials Identification System

Guidance: level 1

:: ::

MCI, Inc. was an American telecommunication corporation, currently a subsidiary of Verizon Communications, with its main office in Ashburn, Virginia. The corporation was formed originally as a result of the merger of _________ and MCI Communications corporations, and used the name MCI _________, succeeded by _________, before changing its name to the present version on April 12, 2003, as part of the corporation`s ending of its bankruptcy status. The company traded on NASDAQ as WCOM and MCIP. The corporation was purchased by Verizon Communications with the deal finalizing on January 6, 2006, and is now identified as that company`s Verizon Enterprise Solutions division with the local residential divisions being integrated slowly into local Verizon subsidiaries.

Exam Probability: **High**

8. *Answer choices:*

(see index for correct answer)

- a. information systems assessment
- b. cultural
- c. imperative
- d. empathy

Guidance: level 1

:: Corporate governance ::

__________ refers to the practice of members of a corporate board of directors serving on the boards of multiple corporations. A person that sits on multiple boards is known as a multiple director. Two firms have a direct interlock if a director or executive of one firm is also a director of the other, and an indirect interlock if a director of each sits on the board of a third firm. This practice, although widespread and lawful, raises questions about the quality and independence of board decisions.

Exam Probability: **High**

9. *Answer choices:*

(see index for correct answer)

- a. Interlocking directorate
- b. Chief product officer
- c. Control self-assessment
- d. The Samuel and Ronnie Heyman Center on Corporate Governance

Guidance: level 1

:: ::

Sustainability is the process of people maintaining change in a balanced environment, in which the exploitation of resources, the direction of investments, the orientation of technological development and institutional change are all in harmony and enhance both current and future potential to meet human needs and aspirations. For many in the field, sustainability is defined through the following interconnected domains or pillars: environment, economic and social, which according to Fritjof Capra is based on the principles of Systems Thinking. Sub-domains of _________ development have been considered also: cultural, technological and political. While _________ development may be the organizing principle for sustainability for some, for others, the two terms are paradoxical . _________ development is the development that meets the needs of the present without compromising the ability of future generations to meet their own needs. Brundtland Report for the World Commission on Environment and Development introduced the term of _________ development.

Exam Probability: **High**

10. *Answer choices:*

(see index for correct answer)

- a. imperative
- b. empathy
- c. Sustainable
- d. interpersonal communication

Guidance: level 1

:: ::

_________ is the practice of deliberately managing the spread of information between an individual or an organization and the public. _________ may include an organization or individual gaining exposure to their audiences using topics of public interest and news items that do not require direct payment. This differentiates it from advertising as a form of marketing communications. _________ is the idea of creating coverage for clients for free, rather than marketing or advertising. But now, advertising is also a part of greater PR Activities.An example of good _________ would be generating an article featuring a client, rather than paying for the client to be advertised next to the article. The aim of _________ is to inform the public, prospective customers, investors, partners, employees, and other stakeholders and ultimately persuade them to maintain a positive or favorable view about the organization, its leadership, products, or political decisions. _________ professionals typically work for PR and marketing firms, businesses and companies, government, and public officials as PIOs and nongovernmental organizations, and nonprofit organizations. Jobs central to _________ include account coordinator, account executive, account supervisor, and media relations manager.

Exam Probability: **Medium**

11. *Answer choices:*

(see index for correct answer)

- a. Public relations
- b. co-culture
- c. deep-level diversity
- d. personal values

Guidance: level 1

:: Progressive Era in the United States ::

The Clayton Antitrust Act of 1914 , was a part of United States antitrust law with the goal of adding further substance to the U.S. antitrust law regime; the __________ sought to prevent anticompetitive practices in their incipiency. That regime started with the Sherman Antitrust Act of 1890, the first Federal law outlawing practices considered harmful to consumers . The __________ specified particular prohibited conduct, the three-level enforcement scheme, the exemptions, and the remedial measures.

Exam Probability: **High**

12. *Answer choices:*

(see index for correct answer)

- a. pragmatism
- b. Mann Act
- c. Clayton Act

Guidance: level 1

:: ::

_________ is "property consisting of land and the buildings on it, along with its natural resources such as crops, minerals or water; immovable property of this nature; an interest vested in this an item of real property, buildings or housing in general. Also: the business of _________ ; the profession of buying, selling, or renting land, buildings, or housing." It is a legal term used in jurisdictions whose legal system is derived from English common law, such as India, England, Wales, Northern Ireland, United States, Canada, Pakistan, Australia, and New Zealand.

Exam Probability: **High**

13. *Answer choices:*

(see index for correct answer)

- a. open system
- b. functional perspective
- c. hierarchical
- d. Real estate

Guidance: level 1

:: ::

_________ is a cognitive process that elicits emotion and rational associations based on an individual`s moral philosophy or value system. _________ stands in contrast to elicited emotion or thought due to associations based on immediate sensory perceptions and reflexive responses, as in sympathetic central nervous system responses. In common terms, _________ is often described as leading to feelings of remorse when a person commits an act that conflicts with their moral values. An individual`s moral values and their dissonance with familial, social, cultural and historical interpretations of moral philosophy are considered in the examination of cultural relativity in both the practice and study of psychology. The extent to which _________ informs moral judgment before an action and whether such moral judgments are or should be based on reason has occasioned debate through much of modern history between theories of modern western philosophy in juxtaposition to the theories of romanticism and other reactionary movements after the end of the Middle Ages.

Exam Probability: **Low**

14. *Answer choices:*

(see index for correct answer)

- a. surface-level diversity
- b. process perspective
- c. interpersonal communication
- d. Conscience

Guidance: level 1

:: United States federal trade legislation ::

The _________ of 1914 established the Federal Trade Commission. The Act, signed into law by Woodrow Wilson in 1914, outlaws unfair methods of competition and outlaws unfair acts or practices that affect commerce.

Exam Probability: **Low**

15. *Answer choices:*

(see index for correct answer)

- a. Tariff of 1857
- b. Section 22
- c. Force Bill
- d. Federal Trade Commission Act

Guidance: level 1

:: Industry ::

_________ is the manner in which a given entity has decided to address issues of energy development including energy production, distribution and consumption. The attributes of _________ may include legislation, international treaties, incentives to investment, guidelines for energy conservation, taxation and other public policy techniques. Energy is a core component of modern economies. A functioning economy requires not only labor and capital but also energy, for manufacturing processes, transportation, communication, agriculture, and more.

Exam Probability: **High**

16. *Answer choices:*

(see index for correct answer)

- a. Productivity
- b. Sisyphism
- c. International Standard Industrial Classification
- d. Industrial district

Guidance: level 1

:: ::

In ecology, a _________ is the type of natural environment in which a particular species of organism lives. It is characterized by both physical and biological features. A species` _________ is those places where it can find food, shelter, protection and mates for reproduction.

Exam Probability: **Low**

17. *Answer choices:*

(see index for correct answer)

- a. information systems assessment
- b. corporate values
- c. hierarchical
- d. co-culture

Guidance: level 1

:: Corporations law ::

A normal _________ consists of various departments that contribute to the company`s overall mission and goals. Common departments include Marketing, [Finance, [[Operations managementOperations, Human Resource, and IT. These five divisions represent the major departments within a publicly traded company, though there are often smaller departments within autonomous firms. There is typically a CEO, and Board of Directors composed of the directors of each department. There are also company presidents, vice presidents, and CFOs.There is a great diversity in corporate forms as enterprises may range from single company to multi-corporate conglomerate. The four main _________ s are Functional, Divisional, Geographic, and the Matrix.Realistically, most corporations tend to have a "hybrid" structure, which is a combination of different models with one dominant strategy.

Exam Probability: **High**

18. *Answer choices:*

(see index for correct answer)

- a. Legal capital
- b. Corporate structure
- c. Articles of Organization
- d. Unissued stock

Guidance: level 1

:: Anti-competitive behaviour ::

__________ is a secret cooperation or deceitful agreement in order to deceive others, although not necessarily illegal, as a conspiracy. A secret agreement between two or more parties to limit open competition by deceiving, misleading, or defrauding others of their legal rights, or to obtain an objective forbidden by law typically by defrauding or gaining an unfair market advantage is an example of __________. It is an agreement among firms or individuals to divide a market, set prices, limit production or limit opportunities.It can involve "unions, wage fixing, kickbacks, or misrepresenting the independence of the relationship between the colluding parties". In legal terms, all acts effected by __________ are considered void.

Exam Probability: **Low**

19. *Answer choices:*

(see index for correct answer)

- a. Strategic entry deterrence
- b. Suggested retail price
- c. price maintenance
- d. Collusion

Guidance: level 1

:: Supply chain management terms ::

In business and finance, _________ is a system of organizations, people, activities, information, and resources involved inmoving a product or service from supplier to customer. _________ activities involve the transformation of natural resources, raw materials, and components into a finished product that is delivered to the end customer. In sophisticated _________ systems, used products may re-enter the _________ at any point where residual value is recyclable. _________s link value chains.

Exam Probability: **Medium**

20. *Answer choices:*

(see index for correct answer)

- a. Will call
- b. Price look-up code
- c. inventory management
- d. Supply Chain

Guidance: level 1

:: Management ::

_________ or executive pay is composed of the financial compensation and other non-financial awards received by an executive from their firm for their service to the organization. It is typically a mixture of salary, bonuses, shares of or call options on the company stock, benefits, and perquisites, ideally configured to take into account government regulations, tax law, the desires of the organization and the executive, and rewards for performance.

Exam Probability: **High**

21. *Answer choices:*

(see index for correct answer)

- a. Executive compensation
- b. Submission management
- c. Central administration
- d. Narcissistic leadership

Guidance: level 1

:: Leadership ::

__________ is leadership that is directed by respect for ethical beliefs and values and for the dignity and rights of others. It is thus related to concepts such as trust, honesty, consideration, charisma, and fairness.

Exam Probability: **Medium**

22. *Answer choices:*

(see index for correct answer)

- a. servant leader
- b. Ethical leadership
- c. Evolutionary leadership theory
- d. The Leadership Council

Guidance: level 1

:: Timber industry ::

The _________ is an international non-profit, multi-stakeholder organization established in 1993 to promote responsible management of the world's forests. The FSC does this by setting standards on forest products, along with certifying and labeling them as eco-friendly.

Exam Probability: **Low**

23. *Answer choices:*

(see index for correct answer)

- a. Forest Stewardship Council
- b. West Coast lumber trade
- c. Brettstapel
- d. Lumber

Guidance: level 1

:: ::

The __________ is an agency of the United States Department of Labor. Congress established the agency under the Occupational Safety and Health Act , which President Richard M. Nixon signed into law on December 29, 1970. OSHA`s mission is to "assure safe and healthy working conditions for working men and women by setting and enforcing standards and by providing training, outreach, education and assistance". The agency is also charged with enforcing a variety of whistleblower statutes and regulations. OSHA is currently headed by Acting Assistant Secretary of Labor Loren Sweatt. OSHA`s workplace safety inspections have been shown to reduce injury rates and injury costs without adverse effects to employment, sales, credit ratings, or firm survival.

Exam Probability: **Medium**

24. *Answer choices:*

(see index for correct answer)

- a. surface-level diversity
- b. interpersonal communication
- c. Occupational Safety and Health Administration
- d. personal values

Guidance: level 1

:: Agricultural labor ::

The _________ of America, or more commonly just _________ , is a labor union for farmworkers in the United States. It originated from the merger of two workers` rights organizations, the Agricultural Workers Organizing Committee led by organizer Larry Itliong, and the National Farm Workers Association led by César Chávez and Dolores Huerta. They became allied and transformed from workers` rights organizations into a union as a result of a series of strikes in 1965, when the mostly Filipino farmworkers of the AWOC in Delano, California initiated a grape strike, and the NFWA went on strike in support. As a result of the commonality in goals and methods, the NFWA and the AWOC formed the _________ Organizing Committee on August 22, 1966.This organization was accepted into the AFL-CIO in 1972 and changed its name to the _________ Union.

Exam Probability: **High**

25. *Answer choices:*

(see index for correct answer)

- a. Collectivization in the Soviet Union
- b. Bailleur
- c. United Farm Workers
- d. State Agricultural Farm

Guidance: level 1

:: ::

The __________ was a severe worldwide economic depression that took place mostly during the 1930s, beginning in the United States. The timing of the __________ varied across nations; in most countries it started in 1929 and lasted until the late-1930s. It was the longest, deepest, and most widespread depression of the 20th century. In the 21st century, the __________ is commonly used as an example of how intensely the world's economy can decline.

Exam Probability: **Low**

26. *Answer choices:*

(see index for correct answer)

- a. personal values
- b. Great Depression
- c. hierarchical perspective
- d. imperative

Guidance: level 1

:: ::

__________ was a philosopher during the Classical period in Ancient Greece, the founder of the Lyceum and the Peripatetic school of philosophy and Aristotelian tradition. Along with his teacher Plato, he is considered the "Father of Western Philosophy". His writings cover many subjects – including physics, biology, zoology, metaphysics, logic, ethics, aesthetics, poetry, theatre, music, rhetoric, psychology, linguistics, economics, politics and government. __________ provided a complex synthesis of the various philosophies existing prior to him, and it was above all from his teachings that the West inherited its intellectual lexicon, as well as problems and methods of inquiry. As a result, his philosophy has exerted a unique influence on almost every form of knowledge in the West and it continues to be a subject of contemporary philosophical discussion.

Exam Probability: **Medium**

27. *Answer choices:*

(see index for correct answer)

- a. empathy
- b. deep-level diversity
- c. surface-level diversity
- d. Aristotle

Guidance: level 1

:: Real estate ::

_________ s serve several societal needs – primarily as shelter from weather, security, living space, privacy, to store belongings, and to comfortably live and work. A _________ as a shelter represents a physical division of the human habitat and the outside .

Exam Probability: **Medium**

28. *Answer choices:*

(see index for correct answer)

- a. Building
- b. Cul-de-sac
- c. Exclusive buyer agent
- d. International real estate

Guidance: level 1

:: Parental leave ::

_________ , or family leave, is an employee benefit available in almost all countries. The term " _________ " may include maternity, paternity, and adoption leave; or may be used distinctively from "maternity leave" and "paternity leave" to describe separate family leave available to either parent to care for small children. In some countries and jurisdictions, "family leave" also includes leave provided to care for ill family members. Often, the minimum benefits and eligibility requirements are stipulated by law.

Exam Probability: **Low**

29. *Answer choices:*

(see index for correct answer)

- a. Parental leave
- b. Pregnancy discrimination
- c. Equal Opportunities Commission v Secretary of State for Trade and Industry
- d. Pregnant Workers Directive

Guidance: level 1

:: Confidence tricks ::

A _________ is a business model that recruits members via a promise of payments or services for enrolling others into the scheme, rather than supplying investments or sale of products. As recruiting multiplies, recruiting becomes quickly impossible, and most members are unable to profit; as such, _________ s are unsustainable and often illegal.

Exam Probability: **High**

30. *Answer choices:*

(see index for correct answer)

- a. Pyramid scheme
- b. Great Oil Sniffer Hoax
- c. Thai tailor scam

- d. White van speaker scam

Guidance: level 1

:: Workplace ::

In business management, _________ is a management style whereby a manager closely observes and/or controls the work of his/her subordinates or employees.

Exam Probability: **Low**

31. *Answer choices:*

(see index for correct answer)

- a. Micromanagement
- b. Workplace violence
- c. Occupational stress
- d. Workplace revenge

Guidance: level 1

:: Utilitarianism ::

_________ is a family of consequentialist ethical theories that promotes actions that maximize happiness and well-being for the majority of a population. Although different varieties of _________ admit different characterizations, the basic idea behind all of them is to in some sense maximize utility, which is often defined in terms of well-being or related concepts. For instance, Jeremy Bentham, the founder of _________, described utility as

Exam Probability: **Medium**

32. *Answer choices:*

(see index for correct answer)

- a. Average and total utilitarianism
- b. Global Happiness Organization
- c. The Collected Works of Jeremy Bentham
- d. Consequentialism

Guidance: level 1

:: ::

_________ is the study and management of exchange relationships. _________ is the business process of creating relationships with and satisfying customers. With its focus on the customer, _________ is one of the premier components of business management.

Exam Probability: **Medium**

33. *Answer choices:*

(see index for correct answer)

- a. Marketing
- b. information systems assessment
- c. interpersonal communication
- d. deep-level diversity

Guidance: level 1

:: Labor rights ::

The _________ is the concept that people have a human _________, or engage in productive employment, and may not be prevented from doing so. The _________ is enshrined in the Universal Declaration of Human Rights and recognized in international human rights law through its inclusion in the International Covenant on Economic, Social and Cultural Rights, where the _________ emphasizes economic, social and cultural development.

Exam Probability: **Medium**

34. *Answer choices:*

(see index for correct answer)

- a. Kim Bobo
- b. Right to work
- c. China Labor Watch
- d. Kate Mullany House

Guidance: level 1

:: Carbon finance ::

The ________ is an international treaty which extends the 1992 United Nations Framework Convention on Climate Change that commits state parties to reduce greenhouse gas emissions, based on the scientific consensus that global warming is occurring and it is extremely likely that human-made CO2 emissions have predominantly caused it. The ________ was adopted in Kyoto, Japan on 11 December 1997 and entered into force on 16 February 2005. There are currently 192 parties to the Protocol.

Exam Probability: **High**

35. *Answer choices:*

(see index for correct answer)

- a. NGAC
- b. Kyoto Protocol
- c. PopOffsets
- d. The London Accord

Guidance: level 1

:: Reputation management ::

_________ or image of a social entity is an opinion about that entity, typically as a result of social evaluation on a set of criteria.

Exam Probability: **Medium**

36. *Answer choices:*

(see index for correct answer)

- a. ClaimID
- b. Reputation
- c. Distrust
- d. Reputation system

Guidance: level 1

:: ::

_________ refers to a business initiative to increase the access between a company and their current and potential customers through the use of the Internet. The Internet allows the company to market themselves and attract new customers to their website where they can provide product information and better customer service. Customers can place orders electronically, therefore reducing expensive long distant phone calls and postage costs of placing orders, while saving time on behalf of the customer and company.

Exam Probability: **Medium**

37. *Answer choices:*

(see index for correct answer)

- a. levels of analysis
- b. empathy
- c. corporate values
- d. surface-level diversity

Guidance: level 1

:: United States federal labor legislation ::

The _________ of 1988 is a United States federal law that generally prevents employers from using polygraph tests, either for pre-employment screening or during the course of employment, with certain exemptions.

Exam Probability: **High**

38. *Answer choices:*

(see index for correct answer)

- a. Hiring Incentives to Restore Employment Act
- b. Employee Polygraph Protection Act
- c. Landrum-Griffin Act
- d. Civil Rights Act of 1964

Guidance: level 1

:: ::

Oriental Nicety, formerly _________ , Exxon Mediterranean, SeaRiver Mediterranean, S/R Mediterranean, Mediterranean, and Dong Fang Ocean, was an oil tanker that gained notoriety after running aground in Prince William Sound spilling hundreds of thousands of barrels of crude oil in Alaska. On March 24, 1989, while owned by the former Exxon Shipping Company, and captained by Joseph Hazelwood and First Mate James Kunkel bound for Long Beach, California, the vessel ran aground on the Bligh Reef resulting in the second largest oil spill in United States history. The size of the spill is estimated to have been 40,900 to 120,000 m3 , or 257,000 to 750,000 barrels. In 1989, the _________ oil spill was listed as the 54th largest spill in history.

Exam Probability: **Low**

39. *Answer choices:*

(see index for correct answer)

- a. Character
- b. surface-level diversity
- c. corporate values
- d. Exxon Valdez

Guidance: level 1

:: Auditing ::

_________ , as defined by accounting and auditing, is a process for assuring of an organization`s objectives in operational effectiveness and efficiency, reliable financial reporting, and compliance with laws, regulations and policies. A broad concept, _________ involves everything that controls risks to an organization.

Exam Probability: **Low**

40. *Answer choices:*

(see index for correct answer)

- a. Auditor independence
- b. Internal control
- c. Environmental audit
- d. Clinical audit

Guidance: level 1

:: White-collar criminals ::

_________ refers to financially motivated, nonviolent crime committed by businesses and government professionals. It was first defined by the sociologist Edwin Sutherland in 1939 as "a crime committed by a person of respectability and high social status in the course of their occupation". Typical _________ s could include wage theft, fraud, bribery, Ponzi schemes, insider trading, labor racketeering, embezzlement, cybercrime, copyright infringement, money laundering, identity theft, and forgery. Lawyers can specialize in _________ .

Exam Probability: **Low**

41. *Answer choices:*

(see index for correct answer)

- a. Du Jun
- b. White-collar crime

Guidance: level 1

:: Labour relations ::

_________ is a field of study that can have different meanings depending on the context in which it is used. In an international context, it is a subfield of labor history that studies the human relations with regard to work – in its broadest sense – and how this connects to questions of social inequality. It explicitly encompasses unregulated, historical, and non-Western forms of labor. Here, _________ define "for or with whom one works and under what rules. These rules determine the type of work, type and amount of remuneration, working hours, degrees of physical and psychological strain, as well as the degree of freedom and autonomy associated with the work."

Exam Probability: **Low**

42. *Answer choices:*

(see index for correct answer)

- a. European Trade Union Confederation
- b. Inflatable rat

- c. Labour council
- d. Labor relations

Guidance: level 1

:: Fraud ::

In law, _________ is intentional deception to secure unfair or unlawful gain, or to deprive a victim of a legal right. _________ can violate civil law , a criminal law , or it may cause no loss of money, property or legal right but still be an element of another civil or criminal wrong. The purpose of _________ may be monetary gain or other benefits, for example by obtaining a passport, travel document, or driver`s license, or mortgage _________ , where the perpetrator may attempt to qualify for a mortgage by way of false statements.

Exam Probability: **Medium**

43. *Answer choices:*

(see index for correct answer)

- a. Fraud
- b. Hitler Diaries
- c. Parcel mule scam
- d. Extrinsic fraud

Guidance: level 1

:: Business ethics ::

_________ is an area of applied ethics which deals with the moral principles behind the operation and regulation of marketing. Some areas of _________ overlap with media ethics.

Exam Probability: **Low**

44. *Answer choices:*

(see index for correct answer)

- a. Workplace bullying
- b. Sexual harassment
- c. Marketing ethics
- d. Foreign official

Guidance: level 1

:: Professional ethics ::

In the mental health field, a _________ is a situation where multiple roles exist between a therapist, or other mental health practitioner, and a client. _________ s are also referred to as multiple relationships, and these two terms are used interchangeably in the research literature. The American Psychological Association Ethical Principles of Psychologists and Code of Conduct is a resource that outlines ethical standards and principles to which practitioners are expected to adhere. Standard 3.05 of the APA ethics code outlines the definition of multiple relationships. Dual or multiple relationships occur when.

Exam Probability: **Low**

45. *Answer choices:*

(see index for correct answer)

- a. Dual relationship
- b. Continuous professional development
- c. ethical code

Guidance: level 1

:: United States federal defense and national security legislation ::

The USA _________ is an Act of the U.S. Congress that was signed into law by President George W. Bush on October 26, 2001. The title of the Act is a contrived three letter initialism preceding a seven letter acronym , which in combination stand for Uniting and Strengthening America by Providing Appropriate Tools Required to Intercept and Obstruct Terrorism Act of 2001. The acronym was created by a 23 year old Congressional staffer, Chris Kyle.

Exam Probability: **Medium**

46. *Answer choices:*

(see index for correct answer)

- a. Patriot Act
- b. USA PATRIOT Act

Guidance: level 1

:: ::

The __________ , the Calvinist work ethic or the Puritan work ethic is a work ethic concept in theology, sociology, economics and history that emphasizes that hard work, discipline and frugality are a result of a person`s subscription to the values espoused by the Protestant faith, particularly Calvinism. The phrase was initially coined in 1904–1905 by Max Weber in his book The Protestant Ethic and the Spirit of Capitalism.

Exam Probability: **High**

47. *Answer choices:*

(see index for correct answer)

- a. Protestant work ethic
- b. empathy
- c. levels of analysis
- d. imperative

Guidance: level 1

:: Advertising techniques ::

The _________ is a story from the Trojan War about the subterfuge that the Greeks used to enter the independent city of Troy and win the war. In the canonical version, after a fruitless 10-year siege, the Greeks constructed a huge wooden horse, and hid a select force of men inside including Odysseus. The Greeks pretended to sail away, and the Trojans pulled the horse into their city as a victory trophy. That night the Greek force crept out of the horse and opened the gates for the rest of the Greek army, which had sailed back under cover of night. The Greeks entered and destroyed the city of Troy, ending the war.

Exam Probability: **High**

48. *Answer choices:*

(see index for correct answer)

- a. Two Cunts in a Kitchen
- b. Trojan horse
- c. Hard sell
- d. Transfer

Guidance: level 1

:: Industrial ecology ::

__________ is a strategy for reducing the amount of waste created and released into the environment, particularly by industrial facilities, agriculture, or consumers. Many large corporations view P2 as a method of improving the efficiency and profitability of production processes by technology advancements. Legislative bodies have enacted P2 measures, such as the __________ Act of 1990 and the Clean Air Act Amendments of 1990 by the United States Congress.

Exam Probability: **High**

49. *Answer choices:*

(see index for correct answer)

- a. Avoided burden
- b. Cleaner production
- c. Regenerative design
- d. Pollution Prevention

Guidance: level 1

:: Corporate crime ::

__________ LLP, based in Chicago, was an American holding company. Formerly one of the "Big Five" accounting firms , the firm had provided auditing, tax, and consulting services to large corporations. By 2001, it had become one of the world`s largest multinational companies.

Exam Probability: **Medium**

50. *Answer choices:*

(see index for correct answer)

- a. Corporate Manslaughter and Corporate Homicide Act 2007
- b. Titan Corporation
- c. Langbar International
- d. Equity Funding

Guidance: level 1

:: Criminal law ::

__________ is the body of law that relates to crime. It proscribes conduct perceived as threatening, harmful, or otherwise endangering to the property, health, safety, and moral welfare of people inclusive of one`s self. Most __________ is established by statute, which is to say that the laws are enacted by a legislature. __________ includes the punishment and rehabilitation of people who violate such laws. __________ varies according to jurisdiction, and differs from civil law, where emphasis is more on dispute resolution and victim compensation, rather than on punishment or rehabilitation. Criminal procedure is a formalized official activity that authenticates the fact of commission of a crime and authorizes punitive or rehabilitative treatment of the offender.

Exam Probability: **Low**

51. *Answer choices:*

(see index for correct answer)

- a. Mala in se

- b. complicit
- c. Mala prohibita
- d. Self-incrimination

Guidance: level 1

:: ::

__________ is the collection of mechanisms, processes and relations by which corporations are controlled and operated. Governance structures and principles identify the distribution of rights and responsibilities among different participants in the corporation and include the rules and procedures for making decisions in corporate affairs. __________ is necessary because of the possibility of conflicts of interests between stakeholders, primarily between shareholders and upper management or among shareholders.

Exam Probability: **Medium**

52. *Answer choices:*

(see index for correct answer)

- a. hierarchical perspective
- b. Corporate governance
- c. imperative
- d. functional perspective

Guidance: level 1

:: Anti-Revisionism ::

_________ , officially the German Democratic Republic , was a country that existed from 1949 to 1990, when the eastern portion of Germany was part of the Eastern Bloc during the Cold War. It described itself as a socialist "workers` and peasants` state", and the territory was administered and occupied by Soviet forces at the end of World War II — the Soviet Occupation Zone of the Potsdam Agreement, bounded on the east by the Oder–Neisse line. The Soviet zone surrounded West Berlin but did not include it; as a result, West Berlin remained outside the jurisdiction of the GDR.

Exam Probability: **Medium**

53. *Answer choices:*

(see index for correct answer)

- a. Ho Chi Minh Thought
- b. Anti-Revisionism
- c. East Germany
- d. Hoxhaism

Guidance: level 1

:: Ethically disputed business practices ::

__________ is the trading of a public company`s stock or other securities by individuals with access to nonpublic information about the company. In various countries, some kinds of trading based on insider information is illegal. This is because it is seen as unfair to other investors who do not have access to the information, as the investor with insider information could potentially make larger profits than a typical investor could make. The rules governing __________ are complex and vary significantly from country to country. The extent of enforcement also varies from one country to another. The definition of insider in one jurisdiction can be broad, and may cover not only insiders themselves but also any persons related to them, such as brokers, associates and even family members. A person who becomes aware of non-public information and trades on that basis may be guilty of a crime.

Exam Probability: **Medium**

54. *Answer choices:*

(see index for correct answer)

- a. Suicide bidding
- b. False economy
- c. Sugging
- d. Insider trading

Guidance: level 1

:: Statutory law ::

_________ or statute law is written law set down by a body of legislature or by a singular legislator . This is as opposed to oral or customary law; or regulatory law promulgated by the executive or common law of the judiciary. Statutes may originate with national, state legislatures or local municipalities.

Exam Probability: **High**

55. *Answer choices:*

(see index for correct answer)

- a. incorporation by reference
- b. statute law
- c. Statutory law
- d. Statute of repose

Guidance: level 1

:: ::

The _________ to Fight AIDS, Tuberculosis and Malaria is an international financing organization that aims to "attract, leverage and invest additional resources to end the epidemics of HIV/AIDS, tuberculosis and malaria to support attainment of the Sustainable Development Goals established by the United Nations." A public-private partnership, the organization maintains its secretariat in Geneva, Switzerland. The organization began operations in January 2002. Microsoft founder Bill Gates was one of the first private foundations among many bilateral donors to provide seed money for the partnership.

Exam Probability: **Low**

56. *Answer choices:*

(see index for correct answer)

- a. Sarbanes-Oxley act of 2002
- b. corporate values
- c. interpersonal communication
- d. co-culture

Guidance: level 1

:: ::

A __________ is a proceeding by a party or parties against another in the civil court of law.The archaic term "suit in law" is found in only a small number of laws still in effect today.The term " __________ " is used in reference to a civil action brought in a court of law in which a plaintiff, a party who claims to have incurred loss as a result of a defendant's actions, demands a legal or equitable remedy. The defendant is required to respond to the plaintiff's complaint. If the plaintiff is successful, judgment is in the plaintiff's favor, and a variety of court orders may be issued to enforce a right, award damages, or impose a temporary or permanent injunction to prevent an act or compel an act. A declaratory judgment may be issued to prevent future legal disputes.

Exam Probability: **Medium**

57. *Answer choices:*

(see index for correct answer)

- a. surface-level diversity
- b. functional perspective
- c. similarity-attraction theory
- d. Character

Guidance: level 1

:: Law ::

__________ is a body of law which defines the role, powers, and structure of different entities within a state, namely, the executive, the parliament or legislature, and the judiciary; as well as the basic rights of citizens and, in federal countries such as the United States and Canada, the relationship between the central government and state, provincial, or territorial governments.

Exam Probability: **Low**

58. *Answer choices:*

(see index for correct answer)

- a. Comparative law
- b. Constitutional law

Guidance: level 1

:: Anti-capitalism ::

__________ is a range of economic and social systems characterised by social ownership of the means of production and workers` self-management, as well as the political theories and movements associated with them. Social ownership can be public, collective or cooperative ownership, or citizen ownership of equity. There are many varieties of __________ and there is no single definition encapsulating all of them, with social ownership being the common element shared by its various forms.

Exam Probability: **Medium**

59. *Answer choices:*

(see index for correct answer)

- a. Anticapitalist and Communist List
- b. Lesbian Nation
- c. Anti-capitalist
- d. Collectivist anarchism

Guidance: level 1

Accounting

Accounting or accountancy is the measurement, processing, and communication of financial information about economic entities such as businesses and corporations. The modern field was established by the Italian mathematician Luca Pacioli in 1494. Accounting, which has been called the "language of business", measures the results of an organization's economic activities and conveys this information to a variety of users, including investors, creditors, management, and regulators.

A _________ is the period used by governments for accounting and budget purposes, which varies between countries. It is also used for financial reporting by business and other organizations. Laws in many jurisdictions require company financial reports to be prepared and published on an annual basis, but generally do not require the reporting period to align with the calendar year . Taxation laws generally require accounting records to be maintained and taxes calculated on an annual basis, which usually corresponds to the _________ used for government purposes. The calculation of tax on an annual basis is especially relevant for direct taxation, such as income tax. Many annual government fees—such as Council rates, licence fees, etc.—are also levied on a _________ basis, while others are charged on an anniversary basis.

Exam Probability: **Medium**

1. *Answer choices:*

(see index for correct answer)

- a. Sarbanes-Oxley act of 2002
- b. Fiscal year
- c. co-culture
- d. interpersonal communication

Guidance: level 1

:: Generally Accepted Accounting Principles ::

__________ s is an accounting term that refers to groups of accounts serving to express the cost of goods and service allocatable within a business or manufacturing organization. The principle behind the pool is to correlate direct and indirect costs with a specified cost driver, so to find out the total sum of expenses related to the manufacture of a product.

Exam Probability: **Medium**

2. *Answer choices:*

(see index for correct answer)

- a. Trial balance
- b. Earnings before interest and taxes
- c. Cost pool
- d. Generally Accepted Accounting Practice

Guidance: level 1

:: Production and manufacturing ::

_________ consists of organization-wide efforts to "install and make permanent climate where employees continuously improve their ability to provide on demand products and services that customers will find of particular value." "Total" emphasizes that departments in addition to production are obligated to improve their operations; "management" emphasizes that executives are obligated to actively manage quality through funding, training, staffing, and goal setting. While there is no widely agreed-upon approach, TQM efforts typically draw heavily on the previously developed tools and techniques of quality control. TQM enjoyed widespread attention during the late 1980s and early 1990s before being overshadowed by ISO 9000, Lean manufacturing, and Six Sigma.

Exam Probability: **Medium**

3. *Answer choices:*

(see index for correct answer)

- a. SynqNet
- b. Verband der Automobilindustrie
- c. Nuffield Tools and Gauges
- d. Product data record

Guidance: level 1

:: Management accounting ::

In business, a _________ is a division that gains revenue from product sales or service provided. The manager in _________ is accountable for revenue only.

Exam Probability: **Medium**

4. *Answer choices:*

(see index for correct answer)

- a. Revenue center
- b. Managerial risk accounting
- c. Fixed cost
- d. Throughput accounting

Guidance: level 1

:: Partnerships ::

Articles of partnership is a voluntary contract between/among two or more persons to place their capital, labor, and skills into business, with the understanding that there will be a sharing of the profits and losses between/among partners. Outside of North America, it is normally referred to simply as a _________ .

Exam Probability: **Medium**

5. *Answer choices:*

(see index for correct answer)

- a. Limited partner
- b. Uniform Limited Partnership Act

- c. Revised Uniform Partnership Act
- d. Partnership agreement

Guidance: level 1

:: Accounting systems ::

In bookkeeping, a _________ statement is a process that explains the difference on a specified date between the bank balance shown in an organization`s bank statement, as supplied by the bank and the corresponding amount shown in the organization`s own accounting records.

Exam Probability: **Low**

6. *Answer choices:*

(see index for correct answer)

- a. Open-book accounting
- b. Cookie jar accounting
- c. Bank reconciliation
- d. control account

Guidance: level 1

:: Budgets ::

__________ is a method of budgeting in which all expenses must be justified and approved for each new period. Developed by Peter Pyhrr in the 1970s, __________ starts from a "zero base" at the beginning of every budget period, analyzing needs and costs of every function within an organization and allocating funds accordingly, regardless of how much money has previously been budgeted to any given line item.

Exam Probability: **Medium**

7. *Answer choices:*

(see index for correct answer)

- a. Zero-based budgeting
- b. Zero deficit budget
- c. Link budget
- d. Railway Budget

Guidance: level 1

:: Financial statements ::

A Statement of changes in equity and similarly the statement of changes in owner`s equity for a sole trader, statement of changes in partners` equity for a partnership, statement of changes in Shareholders` equity for a Company or statement of changes in Taxpayers` equity for Government financial statements is one of the four basic financial statements.

Exam Probability: **Low**

8. *Answer choices:*

(see index for correct answer)

- a. Statement on Auditing Standards No. 55
- b. Statement on Auditing Standards No. 70: Service Organizations
- c. Statements on auditing standards
- d. Statement of retained earnings

Guidance: level 1

:: Management accounting ::

A _________ is an organizational unit headed by a manager, who is responsible for its activities and results. In responsibility accounting, revenues and cost information are collected and reported on by _________ s.

Exam Probability: **Low**

9. *Answer choices:*

(see index for correct answer)

- a. Profit center
- b. Variance
- c. Financial statement analysis
- d. Pre-determined overhead rate

Guidance: level 1

:: Insolvency ::

_________ is the process in accounting by which a company is brought to an end in the United Kingdom, Republic of Ireland and United States. The assets and property of the company are redistributed. _________ is also sometimes referred to as winding-up or dissolution, although dissolution technically refers to the last stage of _________. The process of _________ also arises when customs, an authority or agency in a country responsible for collecting and safeguarding customs duties, determines the final computation or ascertainment of the duties or drawback accruing on an entry.

Exam Probability: **Medium**

10. *Answer choices:*

(see index for correct answer)

- a. George Samuel Ford
- b. Conservatorship
- c. Insolvency
- d. Liquidation

Guidance: level 1

:: Management accounting ::

_________ are costs that are not directly accountable to a cost object . _________ may be either fixed or variable. _________ include administration, personnel and security costs. These are those costs which are not directly related to production. Some _________ may be overhead. But some overhead costs can be directly attributed to a project and are direct costs.

Exam Probability: **Medium**

11. *Answer choices:*

(see index for correct answer)

- a. Operating profit margin
- b. Construction accounting
- c. Indirect costs
- d. Net present value

Guidance: level 1

:: Generally Accepted Accounting Principles ::

_________ is the accounting classification of an account. It is part of double-entry book-keeping technique.

Exam Probability: **Medium**

12. *Answer choices:*

(see index for correct answer)

- a. Write-off
- b. Earnings before interest, taxes, depreciation, and amortization
- c. Deferral
- d. Normal balance

Guidance: level 1

:: Budgets ::

An __________ is the annual budget of an activity stated in terms of Budget Classification Code, functional/subfunctional categories and cost accounts. It contains estimates of the total value of resources required for the performance of the operation including reimbursable work or services for others. It also includes estimates of workload in terms of total work units identified by cost accounts.

Exam Probability: **High**

13. *Answer choices:*

(see index for correct answer)

- a. Programme budgeting
- b. Budgeted cost of work scheduled
- c. Zero deficit budget
- d. Zero-based budgeting

Guidance: level 1

:: Stock market ::

_________ is a form of stock which may have any combination of features not possessed by common stock including properties of both an equity and a debt instrument, and is generally considered a hybrid instrument. _________ s are senior to common stock, but subordinate to bonds in terms of claim and may have priority over common stock in the payment of dividends and upon liquidation. Terms of the _________ are described in the issuing company`s articles of association or articles of incorporation.

Exam Probability: **High**

14. *Answer choices:*

(see index for correct answer)

- a. Preferred stock
- b. Super-majority amendment
- c. Seeking Alpha
- d. Tech Buzz

Guidance: level 1

:: Accounting in the United States ::

________ is the title of qualified accountants in numerous countries in the English-speaking world. In the United States, the CPA is a license to provide accounting services to the public. It is awarded by each of the 50 states for practice in that state. Additionally, almost every state has passed mobility laws to allow CPAs from other states to practice in their state. State licensing requirements vary, but the minimum standard requirements include passing the Uniform ________ Examination, 150 semester units of college education, and one year of accounting related experience.

Exam Probability: **Medium**

15. *Answer choices:*

(see index for correct answer)

- a. Positive assurance
- b. Certified Public Accountant
- c. Uniform Certified Public Accountant Examination
- d. Association of Government Accountants

Guidance: level 1

:: Income taxes ::

An ________ is a tax imposed on individuals or entities that varies with respective income or profits . ________ generally is computed as the product of a tax rate times taxable income. Taxation rates may vary by type or characteristics of the taxpayer.

Exam Probability: **Low**

16. *Answer choices:*

(see index for correct answer)

- a. Income and Corporation Taxes Act 1970
- b. Negative income tax
- c. Personal allowance
- d. Income tax

Guidance: level 1

:: Management accounting ::

An _________ allows a company to provide a monetary value for items that make up their inventory. Inventories are usually the largest current asset of a business, and proper measurement of them is necessary to assure accurate financial statements. If inventory is not properly measured, expenses and revenues cannot be properly matched and a company could make poor business decisions.

Exam Probability: **Medium**

17. *Answer choices:*

(see index for correct answer)

- a. Net present value
- b. Bridge life-cycle cost analysis

- c. Extended cost
- d. Notional profit

Guidance: level 1

:: Stock market ::

_________ is a form of corporate equity ownership, a type of security. The terms voting share and ordinary share are also used frequently in other parts of the world; " _________ " being primarily used in the United States. They are known as Equity shares or Ordinary shares in the UK and other Commonwealth realms. This type of share gives the stockholder the right to share in the profits of the company, and to vote on matters of corporate policy and the composition of the members of the board of directors.

Exam Probability: **High**

18. *Answer choices:*

(see index for correct answer)

- a. Delivery versus payment
- b. Stockjobber
- c. stock price
- d. Mark Twain effect

Guidance: level 1

:: Management accounting ::

In __________ or managerial accounting, managers use the provisions of accounting information in order to better inform themselves before they decide matters within their organizations, which aids their management and performance of control functions.

Exam Probability: **High**

19. *Answer choices:*

(see index for correct answer)

- a. Management accounting
- b. Responsibility center
- c. Chartered Cost Accountant
- d. RCA open-source application

Guidance: level 1

:: Inventory ::

It requires a detailed physical count, so that the company knows exactly how many of each goods brought on specific dates remained at year end inventory. When this information is found, the amount of goods are multiplied by their purchase cost at their purchase date, to get a number for the ending inventory cost.

Exam Probability: **Low**

20. *Answer choices:*

(see index for correct answer)

- a. Consignment stock
- b. Specific identification
- c. Stock control
- d. Order fulfillment

Guidance: level 1

:: United States federal income tax ::

Under United States tax law, the _________ is a dollar amount that non-itemizers may subtract from their income before income tax is applied. Taxpayers may choose either itemized deductions or the _________, but usually choose whichever results in the lesser amount of tax payable. The _________ is available to US citizens and aliens who are resident for tax purposes and who are individuals, married persons, and heads of household. The _________ is based on filing status and typically increases each year. It is not available to nonresident aliens residing in the United States . Additional amounts are available for persons who are blind and/or are at least 65 years of age.

Exam Probability: **Medium**

21. *Answer choices:*

(see index for correct answer)

- a. Stepped-up basis
- b. Philippines Charitable Giving Assistance Act
- c. Standard deduction
- d. 988 transaction

Guidance: level 1

:: Debt ::

A _________ is a party that has a claim on the services of a second party. It is a person or institution to whom money is owed. The first party, in general, has provided some property or service to the second party under the assumption that the second party will return an equivalent property and service. The second party is frequently called a debtor or borrower. The first party is called the _________ , which is the lender of property, service, or money.

Exam Probability: **Medium**

22. *Answer choices:*

(see index for correct answer)

- a. Student debt
- b. Debt crisis
- c. Vulture fund
- d. Creditor

Guidance: level 1

:: Organizational theory ::

Decentralisation is the process by which the activities of an organization, particularly those regarding planning and decision making, are distributed or delegated away from a central, authoritative location or group. Concepts of _________ have been applied to group dynamics and management science in private businesses and organizations, political science, law and public administration, economics, money and technology.

Exam Probability: **Medium**

23. *Answer choices:*

(see index for correct answer)

- a. Linking pin model
- b. Employee research
- c. Organizational learning
- d. Staff augmentation

Guidance: level 1

:: Accounting terminology ::

_________ are liabilities that reflect expenses that have not yet been paid or logged under accounts payable during an accounting period; in other words, a company`s obligation to pay for goods and services that have been provided for which invoices have not yet been received. Examples would include accrued wages payable, accrued sales tax payable, and accrued rent payable.

Exam Probability: **High**

24. *Answer choices:*

(see index for correct answer)

- a. Accrued liabilities
- b. outstanding balance
- c. profit and loss statement
- d. Total absorption costing

Guidance: level 1

:: ::

The U.S. _________ is an independent agency of the United States federal government. The SEC holds primary responsibility for enforcing the federal securities laws, proposing securities rules, and regulating the securities industry, the nation`s stock and options exchanges, and other activities and organizations, including the electronic securities markets in the United States.

Exam Probability: **High**

25. *Answer choices:*

(see index for correct answer)

- a. information systems assessment
- b. Character
- c. surface-level diversity
- d. Securities and Exchange Commission

Guidance: level 1

:: Accounting systems ::

In accounting, a business or an organization and its owners are treated as two separately identifiable parties. This is called the _________ . The business stands apart from other organizations as a separate economic unit. It is necessary to record the business`s transactions separately, to distinguish them from the owners` personal transactions. This helps to give a correct determination of the true financial condition of the business. This concept can be extended to accounting separately for the various divisions of a business in order to ascertain the financial results for each division. Under the business _________ , a business holds separate entity and distinct from its owners. "The entity view holds the business `enterprise to be an institution in its own right separate and distinct from the parties who furnish the funds"

Exam Probability: **Low**

26. *Answer choices:*

(see index for correct answer)

- a. Dome Publishing
- b. Cookie jar accounting
- c. Entity concept
- d. Unified ledger accounting

Guidance: level 1

:: Accounting in the United States ::

The _________ was formed by the American Institute of Certified Public Accountants in 1972, and developed the Objective of Financial Statements. The committee`s goal was to create financial statements that helped external users make decisions about the economics of companies. In 1978, the Financial Accounting Standards Board , whose purpose is to develop generally accepted accounting principles, adopted the key objectives established by the _________ .

Exam Probability: **Medium**

27. *Answer choices:*

(see index for correct answer)

- a. Adjusted basis
- b. Accounting Research Bulletins
- c. Plug
- d. Trueblood Committee

Guidance: level 1

:: Accounting source documents ::

A _________ is a commercial document and first official offer issued by a buyer to a seller indicating types, quantities, and agreed prices for products or services. It is used to control the purchasing of products and services from external suppliers. _________ s can be an essential part of enterprise resource planning system orders.

Exam Probability: **Low**

28. *Answer choices:*

(see index for correct answer)

- a. Purchase order
- b. Credit memorandum
- c. Remittance advice
- d. Superbill

Guidance: level 1

:: Accounting terminology ::

Accounts are typically defined by an identifier and a caption or header and are coded by account type. In computerized accounting systems with computable quantity accounting, the accounts can have a quantity measure definition.

Exam Probability: **High**

29. *Answer choices:*

(see index for correct answer)

- a. revenue recognition principle
- b. profit and loss statement
- c. Capital expenditure
- d. Chart of accounts

Guidance: level 1

:: Accounting terminology ::

_________ or capital expense is the money a company spends to buy, maintain, or improve its fixed assets, such as buildings, vehicles, equipment, or land. It is considered a _________ when the asset is newly purchased or when money is used towards extending the useful life of an existing asset, such as repairing the roof.

Exam Probability: **Medium**

30. *Answer choices:*

(see index for correct answer)

- a. Capital expenditure
- b. Adjusting entries

- c. Chart of accounts
- d. Accrual

Guidance: level 1

:: Fundamental analysis ::

_________ is the monetary value of earnings per outstanding share of common stock for a company.

Exam Probability: **High**

31. *Answer choices:*

(see index for correct answer)

- a. Terminal value
- b. Restricted stock
- c. Earnings per share
- d. economic Value Added

Guidance: level 1

:: ::

__________ , also known as internet banking, is an electronic payment system that enables customers of a bank or other financial institution to conduct a range of financial transactions through the financial institution's website. The __________ system will typically connect to or be part of the core banking system operated by a bank and is in contrast to branch banking which was the traditional way customers accessed banking services.

Exam Probability: **Medium**

32. *Answer choices:*

(see index for correct answer)

- a. similarity-attraction theory
- b. cultural
- c. Online banking
- d. surface-level diversity

Guidance: level 1

:: Foreign exchange market ::

A currency , in the most specific sense is money in any form when in use or circulation as a medium of exchange, especially circulating banknotes and coins. A more general definition is that a currency is a system of money in common use, especially for people in a nation. Under this definition, US dollars , pounds sterling , Australian dollars , European euros , Russian rubles and Indian Rupees are examples of currencies. These various currencies are recognized as stores of value and are traded between nations in foreign exchange markets, which determine the relative values of the different currencies. Currencies in this sense are defined by governments, and each type has limited boundaries of acceptance.

Exam Probability: **Low**

33. *Answer choices:*

(see index for correct answer)

- a. Trade-weighted effective exchange rate index
- b. Euro calculator
- c. Monetary unit
- d. Avignon Exchange

Guidance: level 1

:: ::

_________ is the act of compensating someone for an out-of-pocket expense by giving them an amount of money equal to what was spent.

Exam Probability: **Medium**

34. *Answer choices:*

(see index for correct answer)

- a. co-culture
- b. corporate values
- c. Reimbursement
- d. open system

Guidance: level 1

:: Investment ::

In economics, _________ is spending which increases the availability of fixed capital goods or means of production and goods inventories. It is the total spending on newly produced physical capital and on inventories —that is, gross investment—minus replacement investment, which simply replaces depreciated capital goods. It is productive capital formation plus net additions to the stock of housing and the stock of inventories.

Exam Probability: **High**

35. *Answer choices:*

(see index for correct answer)

- a. Net investment
- b. Fund administration

- c. Manager of managers fund
- d. Media Development Investment Fund

Guidance: level 1

:: Expense ::

__________ relates to the cost of borrowing money. It is the price that a lender charges a borrower for the use of the lender`s money. On the income statement, __________ can represent the cost of borrowing money from banks, bond investors, and other sources. __________ is different from operating expense and CAPEX, for it relates to the capital structure of a company, and it is usually tax-deductible.

Exam Probability: **Low**

36. *Answer choices:*

(see index for correct answer)

- a. Interest expense
- b. Tax expense
- c. Stock option expensing
- d. expenditure

Guidance: level 1

:: ::

A _________ is a tax paid to a governing body for the sales of certain goods and services. Usually laws allow the seller to collect funds for the tax from the consumer at the point of purchase. When a tax on goods or services is paid to a governing body directly by a consumer, it is usually called a use tax. Often laws provide for the exemption of certain goods or services from sales and use tax.

Exam Probability: **Medium**

37. *Answer choices:*

(see index for correct answer)

- a. hierarchical perspective
- b. levels of analysis
- c. Character
- d. Sales tax

Guidance: level 1

:: Accounting organizations ::

The _________ promotes accounting education, research and practice. Founded in 1916 as the American Association of University Instructors in Accounting, its present name was adopted in 1936. The Association is a voluntary group of persons interested in accounting education and research.

Exam Probability: **High**

38. *Answer choices:*

(see index for correct answer)

- a. American Accounting Association
- b. Taxand
- c. Ordre des Experts-Comptables
- d. Japanese Association of Management Accounting

Guidance: level 1

:: Corporate crime ::

_________ LLP, based in Chicago, was an American holding company. Formerly one of the "Big Five" accounting firms , the firm had provided auditing, tax, and consulting services to large corporations. By 2001, it had become one of the world's largest multinational companies.

Exam Probability: **Medium**

39. *Answer choices:*

(see index for correct answer)

- a. Corporate manslaughter
- b. KPMG tax shelter fraud
- c. Arthur Andersen
- d. Walter Forbes

Guidance: level 1

:: ::

An _________ is a contingent motivator. Traditional _________ s are extrinsic motivators which reward actions to yield a desired outcome. The effectiveness of traditional _________ s has changed as the needs of Western society have evolved. While the traditional _________ model is effective when there is a defined procedure and goal for a task, Western society started to require a higher volume of critical thinkers, so the traditional model became less effective. Institutions are now following a trend in implementing strategies that rely on intrinsic motivations rather than the extrinsic motivations that the traditional _________ s foster.

Exam Probability: **Low**

40. *Answer choices:*

(see index for correct answer)

- a. process perspective
- b. personal values
- c. levels of analysis
- d. interpersonal communication

Guidance: level 1

:: Taxation ::

_________ refers to instances where a taxpayer can delay paying taxes to some future period. In theory, the net taxes paid should be the same. Taxes can sometimes be deferred indefinitely, or may be taxed at a lower rate in the future, particularly for deferral of income taxes.

Exam Probability: **Low**

41. *Answer choices:*

(see index for correct answer)

- a. Tax deferral
- b. Tax basis
- c. Airport improvement fee
- d. Indirect tax

Guidance: level 1

:: Financial ratios ::

The _________ shows the percentage of how profitable a company`s assets are in generating revenue.

Exam Probability: **High**

42. *Answer choices:*

(see index for correct answer)

- a. Days in inventory
- b. Loan-to-value ratio
- c. Market-to-book
- d. Return on assets

Guidance: level 1

:: Corporate governance ::

The __________ is the officer of a company that has primary responsibility for managing the company`s finances, including financial planning, management of financial risks, record-keeping, and financial reporting. In some sectors, the CFO is also responsible for analysis of data. Some CFOs have the title CFOO for chief financial and operating officer. In the United Kingdom, the typical term for a CFO is finance director . The CFO typically reports to the chief executive officer and the board of directors and may additionally have a seat on the board.The CFO supervises the finance unit and is the chief financial spokesperson for the organization. The CFO directly assists the chief operating officer on all strategic and tactical matters relating to budget management, cost–benefit analysis, forecasting needs, and securing of new funding.

Exam Probability: **High**

43. *Answer choices:*

(see index for correct answer)

- a. Chief financial officer
- b. Chartered Secretaries

- c. Directors and officers liability insurance
- d. Chief process officer

Guidance: level 1

:: ::

From an accounting perspective, _________ is crucial because _________ and _________ taxes considerably affect the net income of most companies and because they are subject to laws and regulations .

Exam Probability: **Medium**

44. *Answer choices:*

(see index for correct answer)

- a. empathy
- b. levels of analysis
- c. co-culture
- d. Payroll

Guidance: level 1

:: Management accounting ::

__________ is an accounting methodology that traces and accumulates direct costs, and allocates indirect costs of a manufacturing process. Costs are assigned to products, usually in a large batch, which might include an entire month`s production. Eventually, costs have to be allocated to individual units of product. It assigns average costs to each unit, and is the opposite extreme of Job costing which attempts to measure individual costs of production of each unit. __________ is usually a significant chapter. It is a method of assigning costs to units of production in companies producing large quantities of homogeneous products..

Exam Probability: **Low**

45. *Answer choices:*

(see index for correct answer)

- a. Direct material total variance
- b. Spend management
- c. Throughput accounting
- d. Job costing

Guidance: level 1

:: Macroeconomics ::

__________ is a change in a price of a good or product, or especially of a currency, in which case it is specifically an official rise of the value of the currency in relation to a foreign currency in a fixed exchange rate system. Under floating exchange rates, by contrast, a rise in a currency`s value is an appreciation. Altering the face value of a currency without changing its purchasing power is a redenomination, not a __________ .

Exam Probability: **Medium**

46. *Answer choices:*

(see index for correct answer)

- a. Endogenous money
- b. Revaluation
- c. Gonzalo Garland
- d. Robertson lag

Guidance: level 1

:: Asset ::

In accounting, a __________ is any asset which can reasonably be expected to be sold, consumed, or exhausted through the normal operations of a business within the current fiscal year or operating cycle . Typical __________ s include cash, cash equivalents, short-term investments , accounts receivable, stock inventory, supplies, and the portion of prepaid liabilities which will be paid within a year.In simple words, assets which are held for a short period are known as __________ s. Such assets are expected to be realised in cash or consumed during the normal operating cycle of the business.

Exam Probability: **Medium**

47. *Answer choices:*

(see index for correct answer)

- a. Asset
- b. Fixed asset

Guidance: level 1

:: Password authentication ::

A __________ , or sometimes redundantly a PIN number, is a numeric or alpha-numeric password used in the process of authenticating a user accessing a system.

Exam Probability: **Low**

48. *Answer choices:*

(see index for correct answer)

- a. Password strength
- b. Personal identification number
- c. Passphrase
- d. Challenge-Handshake Authentication Protocol

Guidance: level 1

:: Business law ::

A __________, also known as the sole trader, individual entrepreneurship or proprietorship, is a type of enterprise that is owned and run by one person and in which there is no legal distinction between the owner and the business entity. A sole trader does not necessarily work `alone`—it is possible for the sole trader to employ other people.

Exam Probability: **Low**

49. *Answer choices:*

(see index for correct answer)

- a. Arbitration award
- b. Single business enterprise
- c. Sole proprietorship
- d. Operating lease

Guidance: level 1

:: Accounting software ::

__________ describes a type of application software that records and processes accounting transactions within functional modules such as accounts payable, accounts receivable, journal, general ledger, payroll, and trial balance. It functions as an accounting information system. It may be developed in-house by the organization using it, may be purchased from a third party, or may be a combination of a third-party application software package with local modifications. __________ may be on-line based, accessed anywhere at any time with any device which is Internet enabled, or may be desktop based. It varies greatly in its complexity and cost.

Exam Probability: **Low**

50. *Answer choices:*

(see index for correct answer)

- a. Personable Inc.
- b. Kashoo
- c. Xero
- d. Accounting software

Guidance: level 1

:: Competition (economics) ::

In taxation and accounting, _________ refers to the rules and methods for pricing transactions within and between enterprises under common ownership or control. Because of the potential for cross-border controlled transactions to distort taxable income, tax authorities in many countries can adjust intragroup transfer prices that differ from what would have been charged by unrelated enterprises dealing at arm's length . The OECD and World Bank recommend intragroup pricing rules based on the arm's-length principle, and 19 of the 20 members of the G20 have adopted similar measures through bilateral treaties and domestic legislation, regulations, or administrative practice. Countries with _________ legislation generally follow the OECD _________ Guidelines for Multinational Enterprises and Tax Administrations in most respects, although their rules can differ on some important details.

Exam Probability: **Medium**

51. *Answer choices:*

(see index for correct answer)

- a. Transfer pricing
- b. School choice
- c. Category killer
- d. Economic forces

Guidance: level 1

:: Financial ratios ::

The _________ or dividend-price ratio of a share is the dividend per share, divided by the price per share. It is also a company`s total annual dividend payments divided by its market capitalization, assuming the number of shares is constant. It is often expressed as a percentage.

Exam Probability: **High**

52. *Answer choices:*

(see index for correct answer)

- a. Implied multiple
- b. Capital adequacy ratio
- c. Dividend yield
- d. Accounting rate of return

Guidance: level 1

:: Accounting in the United States ::

The _________ is the source of generally accepted accounting principles used by state and local governments in the United States. As with most of the entities involved in creating GAAP in the United States, it is a private, non-governmental organization.

Exam Probability: **High**

53. *Answer choices:*

(see index for correct answer)

- a. Positive assurance
- b. Accounting Research Bulletins
- c. Certified Government Financial Manager
- d. Revolving fund

Guidance: level 1

:: International trade ::

In finance, an _________ is the rate at which one currency will be exchanged for another. It is also regarded as the value of one country's currency in relation to another currency. For example, an interbank _________ of 114 Japanese yen to the United States dollar means that ¥114 will be exchanged for each US$1 or that US$1 will be exchanged for each ¥114. In this case it is said that the price of a dollar in relation to yen is ¥114, or equivalently that the price of a yen in relation to dollars is $1/114.

Exam Probability: **Medium**

54. *Answer choices:*

(see index for correct answer)

- a. Foreign Sales Corporation
- b. European Customs Information Portal
- c. Exchange rate
- d. Common Fund for Commodities

Guidance: level 1

:: Banking ::

A _________ is a financial account maintained by a bank for a customer. A _________ can be a deposit account, a credit card account, a current account, or any other type of account offered by a financial institution, and represents the funds that a customer has entrusted to the financial institution and from which the customer can make withdrawals. Alternatively, accounts may be loan accounts in which case the customer owes money to the financial institution.

Exam Probability: **High**

55. *Answer choices:*

(see index for correct answer)

- a. Master transaction agreement
- b. Asset-based lending
- c. Fiscal agent
- d. Variance swap

Guidance: level 1

:: Accounting terminology ::

_________ is a legally enforceable claim for payment held by a business for goods supplied and/or services rendered that customers/clients have ordered but not paid for. These are generally in the form of invoices raised by a business and delivered to the customer for payment within an agreed time frame. _________ is shown in a balance sheet as an asset. It is one of a series of accounting transactions dealing with the billing of a customer for goods and services that the customer has ordered. These may be distinguished from notes receivable, which are debts created through formal legal instruments called promissory notes.

Exam Probability: **High**

56. *Answer choices:*

(see index for correct answer)

- a. Impairment cost
- b. Share premium
- c. Mark-to-market
- d. profit and loss statement

Guidance: level 1

:: United States Generally Accepted Accounting Principles ::

In a companies` financial reporting, _________ "includes all changes in equity during a period except those resulting from investments by owners and distributions to owners". Because that use excludes the effects of changing ownership interest, an economic measure of _________ is necessary for financial analysis from the shareholders` point of view

Exam Probability: **High**

57. *Answer choices:*

(see index for correct answer)

- a. Comprehensive income
- b. Accounting for leases in the United States
- c. Permanent fund
- d. Comprehensive annual financial report

Guidance: level 1

:: ::

An _________ , for United States federal income tax, is a closely held corporation that makes a valid election to be taxed under Subchapter S of Chapter 1 of the Internal Revenue Code. In general, _________ s do not pay any income taxes. Instead, the corporation`s income or losses are divided among and passed through to its shareholders. The shareholders must then report the income or loss on their own individual income tax returns.

Exam Probability: **Low**

58. *Answer choices:*

(see index for correct answer)

- a. S corporation
- b. process perspective

- c. Character
- d. personal values

Guidance: level 1

:: Tax avoidance ::

_________ s are any method of reducing taxable income resulting in a reduction of the payments to tax collecting entities, including state and federal governments. The methodology can vary depending on local and international tax laws.

Exam Probability: **Low**

59. *Answer choices:*

(see index for correct answer)

- a. Lagarde list
- b. Tax shelter
- c. Bottom of the harbour tax avoidance
- d. Blocker corporation

Guidance: level 1

INDEX: Correct Answers

Foundations of Business

1. a: Money

2. d: Performance

3. c: Supply chain

4. a: Creativity

5. c: Corporation

6. a: Management system

7. c: Alliance

8. b: Interview

9. c: Benchmarking

10. c: Demand

11. : Initiative

12. a: Return on investment

13. c: Diagram

14. d: Error

15. c: Financial services

16. d: Planning

17. b: Opportunity cost

18. c: Manufacturing

19. a: Size

20. a: Scheduling

21. d: Perception

22. d: Efficiency

23. a: American Express

24. : Globalization

25. d: Explanation

26. c: Risk management

27. a: Law

28. : Quality management

29. b: Human resources

30. d: Stock exchange

31. a: Pattern

32. : Exchange rate

33. : Price

34. c: Tariff

35. : Common stock

36. b: Gross domestic product

37. a: Availability

38. c: Feedback

39. a: Dimension

40. : Advertising

41. b: Trademark

42. a: Goal

43. d: Document

44. b: Restructuring

45. a: Strategic alliance

46. : Duty

47. b: Information

48. a: Cultural

49. d: Sony

50. : Mission statement

51. d: Organizational structure

52. : Property

53. b: Marketing strategy

54. a: Trade

55. : Project

56. c: Project management

57. c: Life

58. : Preferred stock

59. : Patent

Management

1. a: Argument

2. c: Evaluation

3. : Interaction

4. d: Gantt chart

5. c: Mission statement

6. d: Process control

7. : Learning organization

8. a: Task force

9. d: Distance

10. b: Customs

11. d: Firm

12. a: Employee stock

13. c: Cash flow

14. d: Supply chain

15. b: Accounting

16. : Utility

17. a: Situational leadership

18. b: Compromise

19. : Decentralization

20. : Project management

21. c: Project manager

22. b: Overtime

23. : Strategy

24. c: Collaboration

25. : Career

26. d: Justice

27. a: Stereotype

28. b: Bureaucracy

29. c: Linear programming

30. b: Risk management

31. : Franchising

32. b: Job enlargement

33. b: Autonomy

34. c: Planning

35. d: Bottom line

36. b: Ambiguity

37. d: Supply chain management

38. c: Quality control

39. d: Brand

40. c: Consultant

41. d: Description

42. b: Mass customization

43. d: Labor relations

44. c: Industrial Revolution

45. d: Criticism

46. d: Resource management

47. : Inventory

48. c: Offshoring

49. c: Cost leadership

50. d: Recession

51. d: Six Sigma

52. c: Business model

53. d: Budget

54. c: Small business

55. a: American Express

56. a: Revenue

57. : Job description

58. d: E-commerce

59. : Reinforcement

Business law

1. a: Wire fraud

2. b: Market value

3. b: Injunction

4. : Contract law

5. c: Misrepresentation

6. a: Incentive

7. a: Probate

8. : Risk

9. : Res ipsa

10. a: Void contract

11. a: Personal property

12. b: Eminent domain

13. a: Antitrust

14. : Fee simple

15. a: Certiorari

16. : Misdemeanor

17. a: Wage

18. : Impossibility

19. b: De jure

20. a: Insolvency

21. : Delegation

22. : Revocation

23. b: Criminal procedure

24. a: Regulation

25. d: Adoption

26. c: Presumption

27. a: Internal Revenue Service

28. a: Commerce

29. b: Computer fraud

30. c: Labor relations

31. d: Commercial speech

32. c: Trade

33. d: Trial

34. c: Constitutional law

35. a: Economic Espionage Act

36. : Beneficiary

37. a: Federal Arbitration Act

38. c: Free trade

39. a: Shares

40. d: Jury

41. a: Consumer credit

42. d: Copyright

43. b: Disclaimer

44. a: Appeal

45. : S corporation

46. c: Mens rea

47. b: Limited partnership

48. : Authority

49. : Perfection

50. d: Subsidiary

51. b: Due diligence

52. d: Punitive damages

53. d: Acceleration clause

54. c: Good faith

55. d: Treaty

56. d: Cyberspace

57. a: Interest

58. c: Security

59. c: Marketing

Finance

1. a: Bank statement

2. d: Income tax

3. a: S corporation

4. d: Choice

5. : Trial balance

6. d: Contribution margin

7. a: Ending inventory

8. a: Citigroup

9. : Technology

10. a: Financial analysis

11. c: Operating leverage

12. a: Bank account

13. : Accounting method

14. a: Strategy

15. d: Preferred stock

16. d: Monte Carlo

17. : INDEX

18. a: Stock price

19. b: Interest rate

20. a: Raw material

21. c: Convertible bond

22. c: Audit

23. : Annual report

24. a: Fair value

25. : Market risk

26. c: Investment

27. d: Receipt

28. c: Return on investment

29. d: Conservatism

30. : Going concern

31. d: Fixed cost

32. b: Face

33. : Put option

34. a: Expected return

35. d: Indenture

36. b: Tax rate

37. a: Current asset

38. : Presentation

39. : Internal Revenue Service

40. b: Accelerated depreciation

41. : Net asset

42. : Opportunity cost

43. a: Financial market

44. b: Financial risk

45. c: Cost of goods sold

46. c: Return on assets

47. b: Contract

48. : Worksheet

49. : Need

50. d: Net worth

51. b: Capital gain

52. a: Shares

53. d: Management

54. a: Yield curve

55. a: Current ratio

56. d: Long-term liabilities

57. a: Retained earnings

58. b: Cost allocation

59. a: Manufacturing

Human resource management

1. d: Performance improvement

2. b: Cafeteria plan

3. d: Paid time off

4. : Age Discrimination in Employment Act

5. b: Equal Employment Opportunity Commission

6. d: Picketing

7. b: Price Waterhouse v. Hopkins

8. : Ricci v. DeStefano

9. a: Labor union

10. c: Functional job analysis

11. b: Whistleblower

12. : Layoff

13. a: Reasonable person

14. c: Asset

15. a: Prevailing wage

16. a: Alcoholism

17. d: Control group

18. a: Needs assessment

19. c: Health Reimbursement Account

20. c: Employee stock ownership plan

21. : Social loafing

22. c: UNITE HERE

23. : Part-time

24. d: Action learning

25. : Interview

26. c: Compensation and benefits

27. c: Schedule

28. a: Xerox Corporation

29. c: Behavior modification

30. b: Cost leadership

31. c: Business process outsourcing

32. d: Free Trade

33. a: Professional association

34. c: Socialization

35. b: Culture shock

36. a: Rating scale

37. a: Hazard analysis

38. d: Training and development

39. a: Bargaining unit

40. b: Distance learning

41. b: Severance package

42. a: Restricted stock

43. : Total Reward

44. a: Job design

45. d: Professional employer organization

46. c: Affirmative action

47. : Recruitment

48. b: Adaptive

49. d: Survey research

50. b: Content validity

51. d: Mission statement

52. : Mergers and acquisitions

53. : Balance sheet

54. b: Flexible spending account

55. c: Fair Labor Standards Act

56. c: Aggression

57. : Peter Principle

58. c: Substance abuse

59. b: Organizational chart

Information systems

1. d: Security management

2. b: Netscape

3. a: Database design

4. d: Innovation

5. : QR code

6. : Pop-up ad

7. d: Information overload

8. c: Mobile computing

9. d: Web content

10. c: Total cost

11. : Input device

12. b: Virtual reality

13. c: Business intelligence

14. b: Market share

15. : Output device

16. a: Data analysis

17. : Epicor

18. : M-Pesa

19. b: Enterprise systems

20. c: Encryption

21. a: Wide Area Network

22. c: Data mart

23. a: Database management system

24. d: Positioning system

25. d: Worm

26. d: Information security

27. c: Peer production

28. d: Subscription

29. a: Social network

30. a: Commercial off-the-shelf

31. d: Mobile commerce

32. d: Search engine optimization

33. a: Critical success factor

34. d: Online transaction processing

35. b: Total cost of ownership

36. d: Data integration

37. c: Verisign

38. a: Blog

39. : Database model

40. : Fault tolerance

41. b: Interaction

42. d: Mobile payment

43. b: Content management system

44. b: Netflix

45. a: Virtual team

46. b: Consumerization

47. d: Gmail

48. : Transport Layer Security

49. a: Vertical integration

50. c: Content management

51. : Data link

52. b: Joint application design

53. a: Data file

54. d: Data governance

55. a: Information

56. b: Balanced scorecard

57. c: Data model

58. c: Backup

59. : One Laptop per Child

Marketing

1. : Empowerment

2. : Price war

3. b: Statistic

4. : Exploratory research

5. a: Intangibility

6. d: Disintermediation

7. a: Copyright

8. d: Utility

9. : Customer satisfaction

10. b: Authority

11. c: Insurance

12. a: Competitive intelligence

13. : Supply chain

14. a: Direct mail

15. c: Leadership

16. d: Adoption

17. a: Research and development

18. d: Brand management

19. d: Consumerism

20. : Information technology

21. a: Project

22. d: Interview

23. : Relationship marketing

24. c: Microsoft

25. d: Perception

26. d: Product development

27. d: Demand

28. b: New product development

29. : Cost

30. a: Partnership

31. c: Blog

32. c: Product line

33. d: Subsidiary

34. a: Clayton Act

35. : Competition

36. : Google

37. b: Franchising

38. a: Advertisement

39. d: Argument

40. a: Budget

41. b: Wholesale

42. a: Logo

43. : Shopping

44. : Total cost

45. d: Comparative advertising

46. a: Auction

47. c: Customer retention

48. c: Complaint

49. c: Marketing management

50. b: Distribution channel

51. a: Creative brief

52. c: Integrated marketing

53. : Sales management

54. c: Survey research

55. c: Productivity

56. : Hearing

57. : Customer value

58. a: Loyalty

59. a: Outsourcing

Manufacturing

1. b: Strategic planning

2. d: Natural resource

3. b: Cash register

4. d: Process capital

5. a: Sunk costs

6. c: Furnace

7. a: Tool

8. c: Consensus

9. b: Customer

10. d: Inspection

11. d: Retail

12. : Schedule

13. a: Total quality management

14. d: Volume

15. c: ROOT

16. : Cost driver

17. a: Heat transfer

18. b: Prize

19. b: Extended enterprise

20. : Joint Commission

21. : Ishikawa diagram

22. d: Planning

23. d: Materials management

24. c: Quality Engineering

25. a: Process control

26. d: Rolling

27. b: Blanket

28. a: Bullwhip effect

29. c: Supply chain network

30. : Information management

31. d: Milestone

32. d: Raw material

33. : Good

34. d: Strategic sourcing

35. d: Lean manufacturing

36. b: PDCA

37. b: Scope statement

38. c: Total productive maintenance

39. b: Remanufacturing

40. : Paper

41. : Root cause

42. : Licensed production

43. d: Quality policy

44. b: Catalyst

45. c: Downtime

46. a: Metal

47. : Value engineering

48. b: E-procurement

49. d: Control limits

50. a: Concurrent engineering

51. c: Bill of materials

52. d: Economic order quantity

53. c: Kanban

54. c: Durability

55. : Process management

56. d: Sequence

57. c: Heat treating

58. a: Sony

59. c: Request for quotation

Commerce

1. b: Overtime

2. a: Basket

3. : Inventory control

4. a: Preference

5. c: Market share

6. b: Tariff

7. : Land

8. d: Security

9. a: Micropayment

10. c: Fraud

11. c: Economics

12. a: Strategic plan

13. a: Merchandising

14. c: Freight forwarder

15. c: Mass production

16. a: Recruitment

17. : Logistics Management

18. a: Asset

19. c: Information technology

20. : Standing

21. d: Customer satisfaction

22. d: Value-added network

23. a: Bankruptcy

24. c: Affiliate marketing

25. d: Supply chain

26. : Goal

27. b: Leadership

28. a: Exchange rate

29. d: Welfare

30. d: Product mix

31. d: English auction

32. d: Complaint

33. : Quality control

34. c: Production line

35. d: Argument

36. a: Project

37. b: Mobile commerce

38. a: Contribution margin

39. b: Competitor

40. c: Insurance

41. c: Publicity

42. d: Compromise

43. c: Microsoft

44. d: Supply chain management

45. d: Quality management

46. : Electronic funds transfer

47. b: Charter

48. a: Organization chart

49. : Dutch auction

50. b: Bank

51. b: Marketing

52. c: Shareholder

53. : Commodity

54. a: Financial services

55. d: Online advertising

56. b: Negotiation

57. : Interest

58. c: Teamwork

59. d: Planning

Business ethics

1. : Marijuana

2. a: Qui tam

3. d: Green marketing

4. b: Edgewood College

5. d: Biofuel

6. b: Corporate citizenship

7. a: Risk assessment

8. : WorldCom

9. a: Interlocking directorate

10. c: Sustainable

11. a: Public relations

12. c: Clayton Act

13. d: Real estate

14. d: Conscience

15. d: Federal Trade Commission Act

16. : Energy policy

17. : Habitat

18. b: Corporate structure

19. d: Collusion

20. d: Supply Chain

21. a: Executive compensation

22. b: Ethical leadership

23. a: Forest Stewardship Council

24. c: Occupational Safety and Health Administration

25. c: United Farm Workers

26. b: Great Depression

27. d: Aristotle

28. a: Building

29. a: Parental leave

30. a: Pyramid scheme

31. a: Micromanagement

32. : Utilitarianism

33. a: Marketing

34. b: Right to work

35. b: Kyoto Protocol

36. b: Reputation

37. : Global reach

38. b: Employee Polygraph Protection Act

39. d: Exxon Valdez

40. b: Internal control

41. b: White-collar crime

42. d: Labor relations

43. a: Fraud

44. c: Marketing ethics

45. a: Dual relationship

46. a: Patriot Act

47. a: Protestant work ethic

48. b: Trojan horse

49. d: Pollution Prevention

50. : Arthur Andersen

51. : Criminal law

52. b: Corporate governance

53. c: East Germany

54. d: Insider trading

55. c: Statutory law

56. : Global Fund

57. : Lawsuit

58. b: Constitutional law

59. : Socialism

Accounting

1. b: Fiscal year

2. c: Cost pool

3. : Total quality management

4. a: Revenue center

5. d: Partnership agreement

6. c: Bank reconciliation

7. a: Zero-based budgeting

8. d: Statement of retained earnings

9. : Responsibility center

10. d: Liquidation

11. c: Indirect costs

12. d: Normal balance

13. : Operating budget

14. a: Preferred stock

15. b: Certified Public Accountant

16. d: Income tax

17. : Inventory valuation

18. : Common stock

19. a: Management accounting

20. b: Specific identification

21. c: Standard deduction

22. d: Creditor

23. : Decentralization

24. a: Accrued liabilities

25. d: Securities and Exchange Commission

26. c: Entity concept

27. d: Trueblood Committee

28. a: Purchase order

29. d: Chart of accounts

30. a: Capital expenditure

31. c: Earnings per share

32. c: Online banking

33. c: Monetary unit

34. c: Reimbursement

35. a: Net investment

36. a: Interest expense

37. d: Sales tax

38. a: American Accounting Association

39. c: Arthur Andersen

40. : Incentive

41. a: Tax deferral

42. d: Return on assets

43. a: Chief financial officer

44. d: Payroll

45. : Process costing

46. b: Revaluation

47. c: Current asset

48. b: Personal identification number

49. c: Sole proprietorship

50. d: Accounting software

51. a: Transfer pricing

52. c: Dividend yield

53. : Governmental Accounting Standards Board

54. c: Exchange rate

55. : Bank account

56. : Accounts receivable

57. a: Comprehensive income

58. a: S corporation

59. b: Tax shelter

CPSIA information can be obtained
at www.ICGtesting.com
Printed in the USA
LVHW011541301019
635718LV00004B/444/P

9 781538 858288